BRAVE FACE

BRAVE FACE

WILD TALES OF HOCKEY GOALTENDERS IN THE ERA BEFORE MASKS

ROB VANSTONE

TRIUMPH BOOKS

Library of Congress Cataloging-in-Publication Data available upon request.

This book is available in quantity at special discounts for your group or organization. For further information, contact:

Triumph Books LLC
814 North Franklin Street
Chicago, Illinois 60610
(312) 337-0747
www.triumphbooks.com

Printed in U.S.A.
ISBN: 978-1-63727-216-9
Design by Sue Knopf
Page production by Patricia Frey

Photos courtesy of Getty Images unless otherwise indicated

To Mom. G. Helen Vanstone-Mather (1934–2019) was always the first person to whom I proudly presented a copy of my latest book. She treated it like a newborn. I miss her every day and love her always.

To Chryssoula Filippakopoulos (my wife) and a terrier-ish rescue dog named Candy (our life).

And to all the great goalies who made this dream project a reality—with a special acknowledgment of Dave Dryden (1941–2022), who was an invaluable influence on this book and on goaltending in general.

Contents

Part Three: Unsung and Unmasked

Part Four: Modern Times

Foreword

I never played goal professionally without a mask. However, on February 17, 1974, in Fort Worth, Texas, I was the backup to Ron Marlow—who did play maskless, albeit reluctantly.

Starting the pregame warm-up, Ron adhered to his custom by wearing the popular Lefty Wilson–designed, Terry Sawchuk–style fibreglass mask. But then, as described by Jim Palmer of the *Fort Worth Star-Telegram*, Ron was "hit with a puck along his hairline and retired to the dressing room."

Although I started 55 of the Fort Worth Wings' 72 games during the 1973–74 Central Hockey League season, I did not get the call to replace Ron for the start of the aforementioned game against the Albuquerque Six-Guns. Ron, you see, was a tough competitor.

"Marlow started anyway," Palmer continued, "but when the swelling began, he was forced to play the second and third periods without a mask."

That maneuver put Ronnie in exclusive company: only four goalies in professional hockey—Andy Brown, Joe Daley, Gaye Cooley, and Bob Perreault—played maskless at that time.

Just two weeks before that game against Albuquerque, I had made my NHL goaltending debut for the New York Islanders in a 4–2 loss to the California Golden Seals. Two nights after facing the Seals, I was in net once again as we defeated the Minnesota North Stars 6–2 in Uniondale, New York.

The starting goaltender for Minnesota was the once-maskless Cesare Maniago, who was backed up by Fern Rivard. At that time, the Stars were carrying three goaltenders, so the odd man out that night was Gump Worsley.

The following night in Montreal, Worsley—then 44—would start in goal. The Gumper had only started wearing a mask during that 1973–74 season, his last in the NHL.

Gumper's story is in this book, which also tells the tales of Maniago, Brown, and dozens of other goalies who somehow survived the rigours of maskless netminding.

I cannot fathom how those guys went through all that and put up with all they did.

I played without a mask until I was 12 years old. My first mask was primitive by today's standards, but I never played without one after my early days of minor hockey in Regina, Saskatchewan.

I acquired my first mask by default. During tryouts, Lowell Lanigan decided to switch from goalie to defence, so he sold me his mask. From that point onward, I was literally sold on a mask.

I'm proud to be a member of the goaltenders' union. I played goal for 30 years—from the age of eight until I was 38. My 612th and final NHL game was on April 4, 1987, for the Philadelphia Flyers.

Since then, some things have changed, but goaltending remains a complicated position, mentally and physically. Goalies still need to discern when to be patient and when to be aggressive. They need to anticipate the expected but be alert for the unexpected.

However, since 1974 and the disappearance of resolutely maskless goalies from the NHL, netminders have not had to display the kind of fortitude that was needed to face hockey pucks and high sticks without facial protection.

This book is a salute to the courage of those maskless goalies of yesteryear.

Glenn (Chico) Resch *tended goal in the NHL from 1973 to 1987—never without a mask—winning a Stanley Cup with the New York Islanders in 1979–80 before moving on to a career in broadcasting.*

Prologue

Connor Hellebuyck felt the need to be a whistle-blower after the referees weren't so inclined.

The Winnipeg Jets netminder spoke out one day after he had become the rarest of throwbacks—a maskless goaltender.

Hellebuyck had been rankled by the events of November 25, 2022, when Jason Robertson of the Dallas Stars scored on an accidentally barefaced Jets netminder. The puck entered the net shortly after Stars captain Jamie Benn had been pushed into Hellebuyck by Jets defenceman Josh Morrissey.

"The refs made a mistake," Hellebuyck told reporters after the Jets' 5–3 overtime victory. "But I feel that the rule needs to change so that the war room and the refs have the opportunity to realize that they made a mistake.

"They put me in danger. There's a lot of bad things that could have come from that. Plain and simple, when a goalie's mask gets knocked off, the play needs to get blown dead."

Hellebuyck's words—"they put me in danger"—resonate when you consider that his face was exposed for a mere fraction of one of the 1,312 games that were played in the National Hockey League during the 2022–23 regular schedule.

Imagine the occupational hazards that goaltenders of long ago faced when they were all working without a net, in a sense.

For the longest time, there wasn't the slightest buffer between the goalie's face and a flying, potentially injurious chunk of vulcanized rubber.

Even when blood was spilled, games were delayed, and, the odd time, careers were ended, it was unhesitatingly accepted that netminders would not don any form of facial protection.

What's more, people signed up for this—readily and without lavish compensation.

"It's pretty amazing that goalies played without a mask," reflected Martin Biron, who, between 1998 and 2014, tended goal in 531 National Hockey League regular season and playoff games.

"I really don't think there's any other position in the top four pro sports—baseball, football, hockey, and basketball—where you go back and say, 'They did WHAT?!'"

And yet, a maskless goalie—unthinkable in today's game—appeared as recently as February 17, 1978.

For an entire three minutes, in fact.

That was news to me well into the process of writing the first draft of this bucket-list book.

The conclusion—and, in some circles, the assumption—was that the last maskless goalie was Andy Brown, who played his final game of professional hockey on November 13, 1976.

Among hockey researchers, there was a lengthy and, at times, contentious debate about whether Brown or another classic character, Gaye Cooley, had essentially retired the entire classification of "maskless goalie" (save for the aforementioned blip in time in 1978).

Research conducted for this book resolved that question, essential information having been thoughtfully provided by an unlikely but invaluable source—a librarian in Greensboro, North Carolina.

But the book was not closed on maskless goalies, as it turned out. Some 461 days after Brown's final game, Wayne Rutledge of the Houston Aeros unexpectedly made a cameo appearance in relief of Lynn Zimmerman during the third period of a World Hockey Association game against the Cincinnati Stingers.

Rutledge, who in 1967 became an original member of the Los Angeles Kings, had resolutely worn a mask since the autumn of 1970. However, for those three minutes, he opted to go barefaced for reasons that still aren't entirely clear. When that snippet of his career was brought to my attention by Aubrey Ferguson, secretary of the Society for International Hockey Research, a few follow-up phone calls, Facebook messages, and emails resulted in my introduction to Bob Rennison. Rennison was at that February 17, 1978, game, which he remembered with uncanny and unerring precision.

Hence the unexpected but essential addition of a chapter—numbered 18—and even more intrigue for an author who has been fascinated by this niche topic since 1971.

As a seven-year-old sapling, I was already obsessed with hockey and, in particular, goalies.

In elementary school art class in Regina, Saskatchewan, I was once upbraided by a teacher as a consequence of my galling inability to create any sort of magic while brandishing a crayon. Everyone else in my Grade 2 class had mastered the fine art of drawing a duck. My "duck" looked more like an aardvark. I was not a prodigious child.

Yet, as far back as 1971, I could draw pictures of goaltenders. In fact, many of my hockey-loving classmates would ask me to provide a pencilled portrait of their favourite goalie.

I had all their masks, with the inflexible expressions carved into fibreglass, down pat. Tony Esposito, Ernie Wakely, and Al Smith looked forlorn. Gilles Villemure, Dunc Wilson, and a youthful Bernie Parent looked happy. The Eds, Johnston and Giacomin, looked unflappable. Gump Worsley looked like, well, Gump Worsley.

The grizzled Gumper didn't wear a mask. It was, alas, considerably tougher to draw someone's face than eyeholes, airholes, et cetera.

Mom and Dad, for all their wisdom, could not explain to little Robert Vanstone why Worsley was maskless, except to surmise that he was a little crazy.

Their assessment was in effect validated by future Hockey Hall of Fame inductee Gerry Cheevers, who in 1971 released a book—*Goaltender*—that was written in collaboration with Trent Frayne. Replace "crazy" with "nuts" and you have Cheevers' description.

His diary of the Boston Bruins' 1970–71 season turned out to be my eighth-birthday present. I treasure Mom's inscription:

TO OUR BIG HOCKEY-LOVING,

HOCKEY-PLAYING, EIGHT-YEAR-OLD LAD!

WITH LOVE TO ROBERT

FROM MOM, DAD AND LAURA JANE

MARCH 30, 1972

Turn three more pages and you will find Cheevers' priceless dedication:

TO MY TWENTY-SIX LODGE BROTHERS

BEHIND THE MASKS, AND THE TWO

NUTS WITHOUT THEM.

Make that "three nuts without them." When *Goaltender* was written, Worsley and Joe Daley were the NHL's only maskless marvels. Then Andy Brown made his big-league debut, 39 days before my eighth birthday.

Improbably, the number of maskless goalies in the NHL was increasing—albeit slightly—at a time when it seemed logical for the count to be inexorably trending toward zero.

Cheevers, for his part, had jokingly paid homage to the "nuts" a few years earlier by painting stitches on his mask to simulate the damage that would have resulted had the pucks collided with his face instead of fibreglass.

Oh, how I loved—and still love—that classic Cheevers mask. That explains why he became my first hockey hero.

Fast forward to 2021. Well into the COVID-19 pandemic period, local sports in Regina, Saskatchewan, and in Canada were still on hold. For this veteran *Regina Leader-Post* columnist, the paucity of live sports created a problem and an accompanying, enticing opportunity.

My editors, bless their hearts, implored us in this fashion: "If there's anything that you've always wanted to write, now is the time." After all, we had to fill our sports space with...something.

Accordingly, this sports-starved sportswriter suggested "maskless goalies!"

I quickly volunteered to write a 2,000-word epic. Sold!

The first person I interviewed: Joe Daley.

The second: Cheevers.

Suddenly, giddily, my mind raced as I began to think of the project in a larger dimension. The question: "Is there a book here?"

I promptly made a pitch to Triumph Books, for which I had authored a 2019 release—*100 Things Roughriders Fans Should Know & Do Before They Die*—pertaining to the Saskatchewan Roughriders of the Canadian Football League.

That was my third book about the Roughriders—for whom I have been employed since February 21, 2023, as the resident writer and team historian. Previously, I had written separate volumes on the team's championship teams of 1966 and 1989. After immersing myself in those projects, I always presumed that any books that carried my name would focus on football.

What a pleasure it is to be dead wrong.

It has been an indescribable joy to scratch an itch and satisfy a curiosity that dates back more than a half-century.

There has been the accompanying realization of how much I hadn't known about maskless goalies, even though the topic had been a source of fascination (some would say "obsession") since my childhood.

As someone who was born in 1964, I vividly remember three of professional hockey's last seven maskless goalies—Worsley, Daley, and Brown. In the early 1970s, I was also somewhat familiar with Rutledge, whose name often appeared in weekly statistical summaries provided by *The Hockey News*.

But I had never heard of Russ Gillow, Bob Perreault, or Cooley. Who could have imagined that an entire chapter would be devoted to each one of them? Or that 4,000 words would be used to tell the story of an amazing gentleman named Ian Young?

A prized prospect with the Bruins, Young was once envisioned as the heir apparent to Cheevers and Johnston. Then came January 21, 1967, when Young—then playing junior hockey with the Oshawa Generals—was hit in the left eye by a shot emanating from the stick of future NHL sharpshooter Mickey Redmond.

Despite losing most of the sight in the stricken eye, Young nonetheless proved to be a man of vision. I loved telling his story, as much as I winced when he and Redmond candidly recounted the details.

As rewarding as it was to interview goaltending greats such as Cheevers, Parent, Glenn Hall, and Ken Dryden, in addition to relatives of Terry Sawchuk and Johnny Bower, the process of researching and writing became intoxicating—to the extent that the inhalation of coffee can have such an effect on people—when the opportunity arose to document the lives and careers of lesser-known yet compelling throwbacks such as Young, Perreault, Gillow, Daley, Cooley, Brown, and Rutledge.

Brown, for example, had taught his dog to answer the phone. But when the maskless man himself fielded a call in 2021, he politely declined to be interviewed.

Undeterred, I wrote a chapter about him, anyway, and loved every minute of it.

When that chapter was completed, I thought the same closure had applied to this book's third of four parts. Then, as referenced earlier, I received notification of breaking news from 1978. Not long after that, I was informed that Rutledge's dog, Bear, had once devoured a light meal—an entire string of Christmas lights. The process of writing and researching this book was endlessly illuminating.

There is only one regret. I dearly wish that I could have shared this book with my mother, who died on December 11, 2019.

After interviewing Cheevers, my first impulse was to call Mom and exclaim: "Guess who I just talked to?!" I know exactly what she would have said when I resorted to name-dropping: "You never did...." Well, Mom, I did.

Sports was always my strongest bond with G. Helen Vanstone-Mather. We frequented Roughriders games as far back as I can remember. We attended the CFL's championship game, the Grey Cup, on an annual basis in the late 1970s and early 1980s. It didn't matter to us if the Roughriders weren't in the game. The Grey Cup excursion was our November ritual.

Fortuitously, the 67th Grey Cup game was played in Montreal on November 25, 1979, when the Edmonton Eskimos (now Elks) defeated the host Alouettes 17–9. The game, as the score would suggest, was unexceptional. The real, unexpected treat was served up the night before, when the Bruins played the Canadiens at the Montreal Forum. We were able to secure two tickets (thank you, Dave Ash) and ended up sitting somewhere near the rafters.

I was a nervous wreck as the game approached, for one simple reason: I simply *had* to see Cheevers play for Boston. It was a once-in-a-liftimee opportunity, or so I hoped. Ergo, I sweated it out and fidgeted in my seat.

Would Cheevers, then 39 and in what proved to be his swan-song season as a player, or Gilles Gilbert get the start in goal?

Then…a sighting!

Cheevers was the first Bruin to step on to the ice. He approached the net and put on *the* mask. That was all I needed to see. The night was complete before the game even began.

Montreal won 3–1, but Cheevers was the first star in my appraisal.

Even when Boston had the puck in Montreal territory, I watched the Bruins' No. 30 stand idly in his goal crease—even though it was my first opportunity to see the Canadiens' Guy Lafleur, whom I will always regard as the most exciting of all hockey players, in person.

I must have stood out on that evening. A vast majority of the 18,080 attendees at the Forum were: (a) cheering for the Canadiens; and, (b) actually paying attention to the flow of the game. There I was, resplendent in an unwashed green football jersey—bearing the name and number (17) of Roughriders star receiver Joey Walters—and fixated on a lonely goalie standing in his crease.

Another 15,065 days elapsed before I interviewed Cheevers and found him to be the wonderful guy that I had presumed him to be 50 years earlier.

I felt like a wide-eyed kid—which I am, at heart—while interviewing Cheevers (on February 22, 2021, from 3:11 to 3:30 PM) and another one of my idols, Bernie Parent.

The latter conversation was initiated when the personable Parent said, "I'm a goalie. Shoot."

How could I not love this stuff? I was hooked. I had been reeled into the goalies' net, as it were. The only apprehensions stemmed from the few occasions when, as part of the writing process, I felt compelled to reference an old Eastern Hockey League team known as the (gulp) Long Island Ducks.

Ducks…not again!

With a beak, er, book deal in hand and a deadline in mind, there emerged the imperatives of writing and organizing.

There were more outlines than chapters, honestly, as additional stories came to my attention. In fact, this is the fifth version of the prologue, which was once called the introduction.

Three chapters remained and I was still fiddling with the formatting.

The initial inclination had been to tell the whole story chronologically. By the time I got to Chapter 5, however, I realized that an amended approach was in order, because the timeline would have jumped all over the place as I expanded on the goalies' long and often concurrent careers.

The solution, I hope, was to split the book into four thematic parts, which allowed me to circle back and elaborate on some stories that were introduced earlier on, when the approach was more linear in nature. On the pages that follow, you will find some sad stories, along with tales of some eyebrow-raising (or eyebrow-cutting) episodes and milestones in hockey history. But, more than anything, this book is an affectionate tribute to the colourful and conventionally comedic characters who went to extraordinary lengths to stop the puck—even if the occupational hazards were a few lost teeth, a blood-stained jersey, or even—please read this while sitting down—an eyeball that was stitched up after being temporarily removed from its socket.

The sincere hope here is that you, like the gallant goalies whose lives and careers are celebrated on these pages, will often be left in stitches.

PART ONE:
THE PIONEERS

1

Blasts from the Past

The slow disappearance of the anti-mask movement

Clint Benedict was a well-established NHL goaltender when, in 1930, a fellow future Hockey Hall of Famer unleashed a shot that hit the maskless Montreal Maroons mainstay on the nose and sent him scurrying to the dressing room for repairs.

The accident prompted this prescient passage from a contemporaneous *Montreal Gazette* account: "Someday, the league will authorize masks for netminders as baseball does for catchers, and these accidents will be avoided."

That "someday" was nearly 30 years away from the standpoint of a mask becoming a fixture. Benedict, by contrast, was a mere six weeks shy of his introduction to headgear when he was plunked on the proboscis by Howie Morenz of the Montreal Canadiens.

"Had it been half an inch to the left or right, the veteran Maroon netminder would have lost an eye," a reporter for the *Gazette* observed in a non-bylined description of an intra-city game from January 7, 1930, during the 28 years in which the histories of two distinct Montreal clubs overlapped. "Benny dropped like a log when one of Morenz's burning shots struck him, and he lay on the ice writhing until players of both clubs and the referees picked him up and carried him off the ice. There was a trail of blood from the south goal into the Maroons dressing room, and even the wall along the corridor was spattered by the flow. The accident was the most serious injury any netminder has suffered in the Forum since Lorne Chabot got hit two years ago in a Stanley Cup Final."

Even in a losing effort, the Maroons' Benedict had been more fortunate—OK, that is arguable—nearly two years earlier, when he suited up for Game 2 of the league final against the Lester Patrick-coached/managed New York Rangers. The game was scoreless in the second period when a shot by Montreal's Nels Stewart tested Chabot, who skillfully stopped the puck with his left eye on April 7, 1928.

"Chabot went down like a man who had been sandbagged," Hal Bock wrote in *Save: Hockey's Brave Goalies*. "He was carried off the ice on a stretcher, blood spurting from the wound opened by the shot." (This is the very same Lorne Chabot who made it a habit to shave on game days "because I stitch better when my skin is smooth.")

Suddenly *sans* Chabot, the Rangers were in a predicament.

"Patrick now found himself without a goaltender since, either due to poor planning or in an effort to save a little money, he had decided not to bring along a spare netminder, even though all of the games would be played in Montreal due to the circus taking over Madison Square Garden," George Grimm wrote in *Guardians of the Goal*—a comprehensive history of Rangers goaltenders.

Per the protocol of the day, the Rangers had a scant 10 minutes to scrounge up a goaltender, or even some poor soul who was amenable to being a maskless mannequin. The alternative was to forfeit.

Alec Connell, who had played goal for the first incarnation of the Ottawa Senators, just happened to be in the stands. One problem: When Patrick asked rival manager-coach Eddie Gerard to allow the Rangers to replace Chabot with Connell, "The Montreal boss snickered," Bock recounted, detailing this unsympathetic response from Gerard: "If I let you take Connell, it would cost me. Suckers were born yesterday and you're talking to the wrong man. I can't hear you."

Patrick had also hoped to use a minor league goalie, Hugh McCormick, but was once again rebuffed by Gerard.

Various options, not one of which was particularly palatable, were considered before Patrick appointed himself the goaltender.

Chabot, meanwhile, was being whisked to Montreal's Royal Victoria Hospital with what the *Gazette* later reported to be "a hemorrhage of the anterior and posterior chambers of the eye."

Doctors were soon able to celebrate a save. Chabot's eyesight would be preserved and, better yet, unaffected. However, the immediate priority for the Blueshirts was to somehow scrape through Game 2 after having lost 2–0 in the opener of the best-of-five series.

"It was Patrick or nothing and eventually the Rangers boss realized it," Bock wrote. "So, he climbed into Chabot's blood-stained uniform, trembling as he considered the task that lay ahead."

Improbably, Patrick repelled every Maroons shooter until 1:09 remained in the third period, when Stewart banged in a rebound of a Hooley Smith shot to create a 1–1 tie and ultimately necessitate overtime. "The Silver Fox" could not be outfoxed thereafter, setting the stage for Frank Boucher's game-winner at 7:05 of OT.

The losing goaltender? Clint Benedict.

With Chabot sidelined for the remainder of the series, Patrick again looked for alternatives—without looking in the mirror. As a last resort, he sought permission to use Joe Miller.

Miller was certainly an average Joe while toiling for the last-place New York Americans, so nary an objection was heard from Gerard. The boss for the Maroons may well have been salivating, considering that Patrick's final option had already been red-flagged as "Red Light Miller."

With Miller in goal for Game 3—his first appearance in four weeks—the Rangers were blanked 2–0 by Benedict and associates.

Needing back-to-back victories to cop the Cup, the Rangers accomplished precisely that, winning 1–0 and 2–1.

Early in Game 5, Miller was clipped over the right eye by a shot taken by Montreal's Hooley Smith. The Rangers were suddenly experiencing their second goaltending crisis of the series.

Miller used every precious second of the by-now-familiar 10-minute time limit to apply ice to the wound. To everyone's relief, and that of Patrick in particular, the head coach was not required out of the bullpen.

"It was a game and heroic display," the Associated Press wrote of Miller, who could barely see out of his swollen right eye, after the Rangers won 2–1 and were therefore crowned champions. Miller, the victorious goaltender, had just participated in what would be the only three playoff games of an NHL career that also included 130 regular season appearances.

Benedict had three times as much experience, with the consequent accumulation of scars.

Three days before being beaned by Morenz during the January 7, 1930, game, Benedict had been rendered unconscious by a shot to the head.

The time limit was extended to 35 minutes to accommodate substitute goaltender Flat Walsh, who was not feeling well and consequently Flat on his back in bed at the moment Morenz bonked Benedict between the eyes. An ailing but nonetheless willing Walsh was rushed to the rink and into the game while Benedict, who had been helped off the ice, continued to receive medical attention.

Benedict was soon diagnosed with a broken nose, which required seven stitches, and a fractured cheekbone. The *Gazette* noted that he would likely be sidelined until early February.

Make that late February. Benedict returned to the ice on February 20, 1930, when the Maroons tied the Americans 3–3 in New York. Benedict, according to the *Gazette*, was sporting "a large protector over the upper part of his face, but was not hampered by it, turning in a fine game."

It was, according to a flashback by NHL historian Dave Stubbs, "a crude leather mask" that was more like "a thick nosepiece"—the handiwork of a Boston sporting goods manufacturer.

Benedict's opposite number on the night he was injured was George Hainsworth, who himself had sustained a broken beak the previous year. When Hainsworth again assumed his customary position in front of the Canadiens' cage, he was wearing a thick bandage that some observers interpreted to be marginally mask-like.

"Indeed, there is mild argument that it was, in fact, Hainsworth who was the first to wear a mask in an NHL game, foggy reports from 1929 suggesting that he had worn a heavy plaster bandage into action to partially cover his shattered face," Stubbs wrote on nhl.com in 2017. "As you watch today's modern goalies shuffling, scraping and post-tapping superstitiously, consider that the market in goaltending kookiness had been cornered going on a century ago, and for that the 1930 mask pioneer deserves credit, too. Benedict figured a little luck would hurt him less than a puck in the teeth. So this great innovator and arguably the greatest goaltender of his generation trusted his bare face to something more dependable than a mask. He hung a horseshoe in the back of his net."

It didn't necessarily signal good fortune. Benedict soon discarded the mask, concluding that it partially impeded his vision, and resumed playing barefaced during his 17th—and last—NHL season.

Benedict played his final regular season game on March 4, 1930, when the Maroons played the host Ottawa Senators with the playoffs just over two weeks away.

"Clint Benedict looked as though he was all set for a Halloween party when he skated out with his new mask on," the *Ottawa Journal* reported.

Ottawa ended up winning 6–2 on the strength of four goals from Hec Kilrea.

"Clint started the game for Maroons," the *Gazette* reported, "but shortly after Kilrea's first tally, somebody fell on Benny in a scramble around the Maroon goal-mouth and bent his injured nose, despite the protection of his new mask. Clint had to retire and the game was held up 10 minutes while [Flat] Walsh donned goalie's regalia and replaced the veteran in the Montreal citadel."

The oft-injured Benedict soon decided against playing for the remainder of the season, in adherence to medical advice. When he returned to the nets in the fall of 1930, it was with the International Hockey League's Windsor Bulldogs.

"Clint Benedict goes to Windsor, having come to terms with Maroons on that point," Baz O'Meara wrote in the *Montreal Star*. "Thus passes into the minors the greatest goal tend over a span of years that hockey has seen. He and the immortal [Georges] Vézina were two of the old invincibles.

"When Montreal broke into hockey, they had few players of big-time calibre and it was Benedict who gave them a top-line touch with his masterly work. He was for years a standout with Ottawa and as a 'money player' was in a class by himself.

"Time has put its finger on him, and he departs for another field where he should shine.... He has played since 1913 and that's a long spell. His numerous friends wish him luck and his work will endure in the annals of the game."

Benedict, then 38, played in 40 games for Windsor, fashioning a typically stingy 2.18 goals against average. That much could be quantified.

"I lost count of the number of stitches they put in my head," Benedict is quoted as saying in *Save*. "I remember at least four times being carried into the dressing room to get all stitched up and then going back in to play. There were other times, too, but I don't remember them."

It may have been too painful to recall.

"Why didn't goalies start wearing a mask?" mused Glenn (Chico) Resch, a 14-year NHL netminder and a long-time hockey history buff, repeating the question that had been posed to him.

"When it started out, there was never any fear of getting hit in the face. No. 1, goalies couldn't go down on the ice. No. 2, they didn't even stand in a goalie stance. And No. 3, nobody could shoot the puck high. Around the turn of the century, there wasn't even a crossbar. The two pipes went up. They had a mesh at the back, but the mesh was stretched and there was no crossbar."

You read Resch's first point correctly. Goaltenders were not permitted to flop to the ice.

"Actually," Bock wrote, "the rules were even stricter than that. Not only weren't goalies allowed to sprawl to the ice to save, but referees could impose a fine of two dollars on those netminders who tried to bend that rule."

Two bucks was the cost of bucking authority until 1918, when the rule was revised. The new-found latitude to go down on one's knees, although beneficial to goalies in many respects, did put them in harm's way more frequently. Nonetheless, the risks weren't considered to be substantial.

"If you saw a one-piece hockey stick—and I've got one from 1892—no one was lifting the puck," Resch said. "If you got it three inches off the ice, it was something. If you said 'I'll give you $10 if you can hit that goalie in the face' in 1910, they couldn't shoot it that high. Or, take the straight stick of the '20s. They were just coming out of the one-piece stick, so you didn't really need a mask in the '20s. In the '30s, were there occasions when it would have helped? Yes. But it wasn't like an epidemic where goalies were going down all the time."

There were, of course, exceptions—such as the injuries to Chabot (1928) and Benedict (1930).

"But even in the '30s," Resch pointed out, "if there was a game of 30 shots and you got four or five even close to what you would consider high shots, that was a lot. In the late '50s and in the '60s, there was the [curved] banana blade, and that was the game-changer. But up until that time, it was different."

So was the occasional masked (or semi-masked) goaltender. A 2018 story on puckstruck.com related the story of Franklin Farrell, who played goal for the United States during the 1932 Winter Olympic Games. Farrell, nicknamed Specs, wore a shield that was designed to protect his eyeglasses. The lower part of his face was uncovered.

According to *Saving Face: The Art and History of the Goalie Mask*, the Hockey Hall of Fame's collection includes photos of an unidentified

North American goalie wearing a mask—reminiscent of a baseball catcher's facial protection—in Switzerland in the late 1930s.

In another photo, Japanese goalie Teiji Honma is shown during the 1936 Winter Olympics, wearing something that closely resembled a catcher's mask. Honma reportedly wore the mask to protect his glasses.

"It is more than plausible," Jim Hynes and Gary Smith wrote in *Saving Face*, that amateur goalies would have worn a catcher's mask, conceptualized by Harvard's Fred Thayer in 1877 and patented the following year, once it became a staple of sporting-goods stores. But the adapted catcher's cranial contraption didn't catch on in hockey circles.

Neither did a fencing mask, such as that worn by Elizabeth Graham—of the Queen's University women's hockey team in Kingston, Ontario—during a 3–2 victory over the University of Toronto on February 7, 1927.

Another outlier, documented in *Saving Face*, was Roy Musgrove of the British National Hockey League. There is photographic evidence of Musgrove, a member of the Wembley Lions from 1936 to 1939, wearing something that resembled a field lacrosse mask that covered only the upper half of the face.

The Lions' coach, Hynes and Smith pointed out, just happened to be Clint Benedict. And around it goes…

The mask issue percolated, at least for a fraction of time, during the 1933–34 NHL season.

Midway through the second period of the Detroit Red Wings' 5–2 victory over the visiting New York Americans at the old Olympia, a shot taken by Frank Carson struck Americans goalie Morris Roberts in the face.

"The puck, fired with terrific force, cut him across the upper lip and five stitches were required to close the wound," Jack Carveth wrote in the *Detroit Free Press*.

The game was delayed 15 minutes while Roberts received medical attention and a frantic search for a replacement took place. Abbie Cox saved the day, if not every puck he faced, as the Americans went on to lose 5–2.

Carveth found the situation to be intriguing enough to turn it into a follow-up story, headlined "Goalies Find Masks Obscure Vision."

"Why do not hockey goaltenders wear a mask similar to those used by catchers in baseball," began Carveth's feature in the December 10, 1933, *Free Press*. "It is an old question ever new. One that has been answered by goaltenders since the time of the immortal Georges Vézina, but every so often it bounces back again, especially after one of the noble young men who stand between the gas pipes stops a flying puck with his face."

Young men such as the Americans' Roberts, whose misfortune in the opener against the Red Wings sparked "a new bunch of inquiries," in the words of the Detroit scribe.

Carveth went on to cite Vernon (Jackie) Forbes, formerly of the NHL's Toronto St. Pats, as "one of the first to try the baseball mask."

In 1920, Forbes was replaced as the St. Pats' goaltender John Ross Roach, who likewise experimented with a catcher's mask and was comparably unimpressed.

"Others have tried it since, all with the same result—it was promptly discarded because it interfered with the vision of the wearer," Carveth wrote.

Carveth went on to quote Roach, back in the pre-sound-bite era when athletes' words rarely appeared in sports stories.

"[Pucks] are tough enough to see now without a mask to obscure the vision," Roach told Carveth. "If a goaltender wore a mask in professional hockey, he probably would retire from the game with his features unmarred, but you can bet your last dime that his career would be short."

Roach went on to assert that, in terms of masks and their practicality, baseball–hockey was akin to an apples–oranges comparison.

"He pointed out that the mask is worn by the baseball catcher as a protection against foul tips," Carveth wrote. "There are no foul tips of a hockey puck, but they are fired at the goaltender from much closer range, and of necessity, clear vision is imperative.

"According to Roach, a goalie often will find it impossible to get his eye on a fast-angle shot when wearing the mask. The mask creates shadows under artificial lighting that do not exist in sun-lit ballparks, and Roach wants no shadows impairing his vision when fellows like Charlie Conacher, Billy Cook, Howie Morenz, or dozens of others are winding up for a drive of 10 feet in front of him.

"Perhaps someday in the not-too-distant future, a mask will be made that will eliminate the shadows. Until such a product arrives, Roach and his fellow workmen will keep their averages up at the expense of their faces, having the lacerations sewn up and head bumps reduced by the skilled hands of the club physician.

"And after they create the mask that casts no shadows, there will be other objections. How are they going to keep the contraption on the heads of guys who hop, bob and jump around the goal mouth like Roach and Forbes? Besides, a mask would cramp Roach's gum-chewing and he would never stand for that."

Future Hall of Fame hockey broadcaster and author Dick Irvin Jr. was barely a year old when Carveth's story appeared. At the time, Dick Irvin Sr. was a big-league bench boss.

"My father coached for 26 years and he never had a goalie who wore a mask," the junior Irvin noted, "and he never played against a goalie who wore a mask."

The elder Irvin entered the NHL in 1926, at age 34, and became the Black Hawks' first captain. Upon retiring as a player, Irvin became a coach and served in that capacity for the Black Hawks (1929–31, 1955–56), Toronto Maple Leafs (1931–40), and Montreal Canadiens (1940–55), winning four Stanley Cups and 692 regular season games.

Walter (Turk) Broda was the Leafs' starting goaltender during Irvin's final four seasons in Toronto. The first NHL goaltender to reach 300 victories, Broda was a workhorse for the Leafs from 1936 into the early 1950s.

In addition to backstopping Toronto to five titles, Broda twice received the Vezina Trophy by virtue of being the league's stingiest goaltender.

Early in training camp after his first Vezina-winning season (1940–41), there was a scare. As described by Ed Fitkin in his 1950 biography of the legendary Leafs netminder, "a fast, high shot from Bill Taylor's stick creased Broda's face, leaving a jagged rip in his cheek. Blood streaming from the cut, Turk went off the ice to have trainer Tim Daly patch it up." That being done, Daly advised Broda that he could "bravely face danger again."

Broda was nicked during the kind of session Irvin Jr. routinely attended during his lengthy broadcasting career. His preparation for telecasts conventionally included attending teams' practices and morning skates.

"I'd often stand behind the net at ice level," Irvin Jr. recalled. "Players would be firing puck after puck at the goalie. I'd think to myself, 'Who would want to be a goalie?' It's a really strange position, no doubt about it, but they do it."

They did it without a mask, for the longest time, while accepting the inherent risks.

A classic example of the perils of maskless minding of the net is Chuck Rayner, who spent most of his 10-year NHL career with the New York Rangers.

On November 12, 1947, at Madison Square Garden, a blast by Boston's Jack Crawford knocked Rayner out cold at 10:40 of the third period. Grimm noted that six players were required to carry the groggy goalie to the dressing room. He emerged with a three-inch cut underneath his right eye, which was swollen shut.

Cue the NHL debut—and denouement—of 20-year-old Bob DeCourcy, who was more accustomed to the inglorious role of second-string goaltender with the Eastern Hockey League's New York Rovers. Welcome to the big leagues, kid.

The Rangers were already trailing 2–1 when DeCourcy entered the game, only to lose 8–2. Boston dented the rattled rookie for six goals within a span of 11:07 in the third period.

On another occasion, Rayner—a 1973 Hall of Fame inductee—was able to memorably return to the crease despite taking another shot to the noggin.

"Many long-time Rangers fans remember the night Chuck stopped a point-blank shot with his forehead and had to be carried off the ice, leaving a long stream of blood from the crease to the bench," Grimm wrote. "Remember, this was in the days before teams were required to carry a backup goaltender, so 10 minutes later, a stitched-up Rayner returned to the ice with a white turban of bandages wrapped around his head."

Grimm went on to quote Rayner's recollection of the gruesome episode: "Back when I was playing, they gave you 10 minutes to get stitched. One night I was getting sewn up by the doctor when the referee, King Clancy, opened the door and yelled, 'Time!' I went back out with a towel around my head."

Bock, in his book about goaltenders, related this tale of the brave soul who concluded his big-league career in 1953: "Once, Chuck Rayner stopped a shot with his jaw and the save cost him four teeth. He underwent oral surgery to remove the roots of the broken teeth and was back in his cage the next night. He turned the other cheek, blocking another shot and opening another gash in his already well-sutured profile. As he waited for the doctor to do some more hem-stretching, Rayner had a philosophical observation about his vocation. 'It's a wonder,' he said, 'that somebody doesn't get badly hurt in this job.'"

Terry Sawchuk, for one, suffered an injury that could have ended his hockey-playing days on his 18th birthday (December 28, 1947). At the time, he was playing for the United States Hockey League's Omaha Knights against the host Houston Huskies.

The game was halted, and the crowd mortified, when the stick of teammate George Agar accidentally connected with Sawchuk's right eyeball.

The wounded goalie was rushed to the hospital, where "a doctor told him he might lose the eye," Brian Kendall wrote in *Shutout: The Legend of Terry Sawchuk*. "There was even an outside chance that infection could spread to the other one. As the horrified teenager watched through an arrangement of mirrors, his damaged eyeball was removed from its socket and sewn with three stitches."

"He cried like a baby," Jerry Sawchuk, Terry's son, said in an interview for this book. "He thought he wasn't going to be able to play again. And that was a big operation back then—to pop your eye out, lay it on your cheek, stitch it up, and put it back in."

Fortunately, and rather remarkably, Sawchuk recovered without any setbacks or complications. He missed only eight games.

Baz Bastien wasn't nearly as fortunate.

Joseph Aldège Albert Bastien was 29, and a well-established American Hockey League star with the Pittsburgh Hornets, when training camp began in Welland, Ontario, on September 30, 1949. Early in the Hornets' opening on-ice session, Bastien was hit in the right eye by a screened shot. A laceration to the eyeball and a fractured cheekbone resulted.

Bastien was rushed to hospital, where doctors determined that there wasn't any option but to remove the stricken eye.

"Bastien's injury was one of the few such misfortunes on record in organized hockey," Vince Johnson wrote in the *Pittsburgh Post-Gazette*. "He is believed to be the first goalie ever to suffer loss of an eye."

In 1945, Bastien had turned pro with the Maple Leafs' organization—which quickly rallied around the injured goaltender. The big-league club collaborated with the Hornets to hold an exhibition benefit game in Pittsburgh. A total of $4,512.07 in proceeds—roughly $50,000 in today's currency—went to assist Bastien, who had been fitted with a glass eye.

The Hornets ensured that he would remain in the organization by appointing him an assistant coach and scout. He was soon elevated to a head-coaching role and, leading up to the 1950–51 campaign, added the general manager's duties to his ever-expanding portfolio. Oh, and there was one more role to fill—that of practice goalie.

Jimmy Jordan of the *Post-Gazette* reported on December 5, 1950, that Bastien was back between the pipes, sporting a plastic mask to protect his eyes. In 1952, while employed as the Hornets' business manager, Bastien was still seen moonlighting as a practice goalie.

The 1949 injury to Bastien ignited a debate about goaltenders' protection, such as it was. Witness an October 28, 1949, story by the

Canadian Press, which summarized the opinions of three Eastern Canadian sportswriters.

Bill Westwick of the *Ottawa Journal* subscribed to the view that "it would be tougher for the goalies trying to manage the awkward device. In the end it will be the goalies who will probably decide and, as dangerous as their jobs are, you aren't apt to find many favouring the idea. Those opposed to the idea seem to be of the opinion that serious accidents aren't frequent enough to warrant the added protection."

Al Parsley of the *Montreal Herald* opined that goaltenders would inevitably balk at wearing a mask. He cited the example of former Maple Leafs star Ace Bailey, whose NHL career was abruptly ended in 1933 by a skull fracture that resulted from a vicious check from behind by Boston defenceman Eddie Shore.

"While the Toronto forward hovered near death for weeks there was a cry for all hockey players to wear helmets," Parsley pointed out. "They wore them under compulsion of league authorities for a good part of the season, but as the memory of Bailey's accident wore off the helmets were discarded."

Parsley's *Herald* colleague, Elmer Ferguson, weighed in as follows: "One suggestion is for some sort of fibre or plastic headband to protect the temples and a nose guard to help ward pucks away from the face. But masks like those worn by baseball catchers are generally acknowledged to be useless because of their awkwardness and bulkiness and because they do not give the goaler a chance on low shots. It's a hard life for the goalers, and no help is in sight unless someone devises a mask of shatter-proof glass."

Someone had already embraced that concept, actually. His name: Dr. G. Edward Crane.

In 1949, Crane—then the resident physician for all the sports teams at Providence-based Brown University—designed a clear plastic face mask that was worn by Don Whiston.

Whiston had been hit in the mouth by a puck during a game against Princeton. The impact pushed back his bottom teeth into his tongue.

"Thinking quickly and fashioning some stainless-steel wire from the Princeton infirmary, Dr. Crane wired the teeth back in place," reads a portion of a story that appears on the Rhode Island Hockey Hall of Fame's website.

Whiston was back in goal the following night in a road game against Army. He donned a football helmet, borrowed from West Point, and a face guard. Those accessories sufficed in the short term, but the future All-American goalie and Olympian was hoping for a permanent solution.

Therefore, Crane's expertise proved to be invaluable beyond the process of straightening a goalie's teeth.

"Whiston didn't want to wear anything that would block his vision," Crane, who died in 1981, is quoted as saying on the Rhode Island hockey shrine's website. "But the boy had suffered a serious injury and it was necessary to come up with something that would protect him from having another puck hit him in the same area.

"There was an outfit in Brooklyn that had been experimenting with football face masks made of plastic. I designed a special mask for Whiston, sent it to this firm, and they produced it for me.

"The mask covered Whiston's cheekbones, nose, mouth and chin, but left the eyes free."

It would be another decade, though, before the ranks of professional hockey would include a masked trail blazer.

2

Face Plant(e)

Jacques Plante turns hockey on its head

When a professional hockey goaltender finally did command headlines by donning headgear in a game for the first time since Clint Benedict's abbreviated experiment with primitive protection in 1930, it was not in the form of a mask.

"Jacques Plante used to wear a toque," author/broadcaster Dick Irvin Jr. noted. "He knitted the toques himself.

"I saw him play for the [Quebec senior league's] Montreal Royals and he would skate into the corner or up to the blue line to play the puck, wearing a toque.

"My dad was Plante's first coach in the NHL. When the Canadiens called him up, my dad would not allow him to wear a toque. He felt it was demeaning to the NHL for Plante to wear a toque. A couple of newspaper guys in Montreal lambasted my father and said he was going to ruin Plante's career."

Sportswriter Elmer Ferguson expressed such a sentiment in the *Montreal Herald* of November 1, 1952—the morning of Plante's NHL debut with the Montreal Canadiens, and seven years to the day before he would make NHL history by wearing a goalie mask in a game.

"This is the point at which your agent and Canadiens coach Dick Irvin come to a parting of the ways," Ferguson wrote after Plante was called up from the Royals for a three-game look-see. "We find our views do not coincide.

"Your agent, in rebuttal, takes the stand that Plante by conveying his toque into the big time would add a dash of colour, individuality and personality, qualities that are steadily declining in production line hockey now being purveyed in the major league in which personalities are so vibrant that they can force their way into attention."

Ferguson added: "We believe that the anti-toque ruling holds a hidden danger. Plante, accustomed to his toque, may become disturbed, lose his poise. It's a dangerous practice to suddenly route an athlete into a strange pathway or break a standing habit. It gets on his high-strung nerves. If tonight Plante, with his head bared, should succumb to the Rangers, we shall certainly attribute this in part to his toque-less condition."

The Rangers' offence was virtually toothless as Plante backstopped Montreal to a 4–1 victory, making 19 saves.

"Plante ended up playing really well," the junior Irvin noted, "and he said after the game that he would never wear the toque again."

Plante was distinctive in another context. Unlike most goaltenders of that era, he routinely strayed from the net to handle and pass the puck.

"Plante really did revolutionize goaltending," Irvin Jr. said. "Goalies like Turk Broda and Bill Durnan never left the goal crease to play the puck. If the puck was shot into the corner, they'd probably watch it. Now here's someone who's running all over the ice. He was the innovator."

And someone who wasn't fazed by the risks.

"Even before he introduced the mask to the game, he would venture out of the crease to set and position himself to cut down the shooter's angle to the net," former NHL goalie Ed Staniowski recalled. "Playing the angles thus would be to his advantage. However, it would put Jacques and his unprotected face closer to the shooter, resulting in him having less time to react if the shot was high and hard."

Mastery of the angles, even at an early juncture in what would be an illustrious hockey career, contributed to Plante allowing only four goals over his first three regular season games with the Canadiens—who, sufficiently impressed, signed him to an NHL contract in January 1953 and summarily sent him to the American Hockey League's Buffalo Bisons.

Plante rejoined the big-league club for the playoffs, for the third consecutive spring, as an insurance policy behind starter Gerry McNeil. But it would not be a leisurely time for Plante, who was surprisingly elevated to front-line duty after Montreal fell behind 3–2 to the Chicago Black Hawks in a best-of-seven semifinal.

Todd Denault, author of *Jacques Plante: The Man Who Changed the Face of Hockey*, wrote that McNeil—who was battling an acute case of the nerves—asked Coach Irvin to be replaced by the 24-year-old understudy for Game 6.

"My dad said to Jacques Plante in the hotel lobby, 'You're playing tonight and you're going to get a shutout,'" Irvin Jr. recalled. "Plante was so nervous before the game that he couldn't even tie his skates. The trainer had to do it for him."

The jitters dissipated early in the game, when Plante foiled Chicago's Jimmy McFadden on a breakaway—prompting a robust salute from the Montreal players who were seated on the bench. Quality scoring chances were subsequently scarce as Plante made 23 saves and, as predicted by his head coach, blanked the Black Hawks. A 3–0 victory enabled Montreal to tie the series at 3–3. Plante stopped 32 more shots in Game 7 as Montreal won 4–1 and advanced to the Stanley Cup Final.

With McNeil shelved by a sore ankle—the result of a blast fired by Maurice (Rocket) Richard during practice—Plante also started the first two games of the championship series. A 4–2 Canadiens victory over the Boston Bruins was followed by a 4–1 loss. In the latter game, four of the Bruins' 23 shots eluded Plante. An unimpressed Coach Irvin turned to McNeil for the remainder of the series. Montreal won its final three games, including two by a shutout, to claim NHL supremacy.

Plante, despite a porous performance in Game 2, also felt that he, like his team, was the best. It was a bold statement by a 24-year-old who possessed a mere seven games of big-league experience.

"I was totally and immodestly convinced that I was the best damn goalkeeper in the whole, wide world of hockey," he wrote in *The Jacques Plante Story*, a collaboration with Andy O'Brien.

McNeil made 53 appearances the following season before suffering a badly sprained ankle. Plante, who had shuffled off to Buffalo after the Canadiens' 1953 training camp, was again summoned by the big club and played in its final 17 regular season games. He posted five shutouts (only one fewer than McNeil) and a microscopic goals against average of 1.59. McNeil checked in at 2.15.

Despite Plante's staggering statistics, the Canadiens' initial blueprint nonetheless called for him to return to Buffalo for the AHL playoffs.

"But then, in a St. Patrick's Day practice, a puck struck McNeil on the forehead," Denault wrote in his brilliant biography of Plante. "He retired to the dressing room, where he was stitched up before returning to the ice. Finally, a conflicted Dick Irvin was forced to choose between his two goaltenders. Because of his stellar play in the season's later games, he chose Plante."

Good plan. Montreal proceeded to sweep Boston in a best-of-seven semifinal. Over the four games, Plante permitted only four goals and registered two shutouts. In other words, he blanked the opposition in one-third of his appearances with the Canadiens in 1954.

Plante then started the first four games of the Stanley Cup Final against the Detroit Red Wings, who assumed a 3–1 series lead before Irvin reverted to McNeil. The veteran goaler started the final three games, the last of which culminated in an all-the-marbles overtime session. Detroit's Tony Leswick settled matters 4:29 into sudden-death play, giving the host Red Wings a 2–1 victory and their first of two consecutive titles.

"Boy, it was a long skate back to the other end of the rink, because our dressing room was there," McNeil told Irvin Jr., for *The Habs: An Oral History of the Montreal Canadiens, 1940–1980*. "There's no way you can express how you feel at a time like that when you're a goalie. It's like the end of the world. I'll always remember that long skate to the other end."

That would be the end, period, for McNeil as an NHLer. He decided in the autumn of 1954 to leave the game, clearing the way for Plante to take over full-time. He enjoyed a spectacular start to the 1954–55 season, allowing only 18 goals over the Canadiens' first 11 games, before being felled shortly before a November 11 home date with Chicago.

"A shot by Bert Olmstead in the pregame warmup struck Plante in the face and dropped him to the ice unconscious," Dink Carroll wrote in the *Montreal Gazette*. "He was hustled across the square to the Western Division of the Montreal General Hospital where it was discovered that his right cheekbone was fractured."

With substitute goalie Andre Binette taking over for what would be his only NHL appearance, the Canadiens went on to win 7–4. Plante, for his part, was preparing for surgery that he underwent shortly after the game.

"The fractured bone was snapped back into place and it looks as though wiring will not be necessary," the *Gazette* reported. "This means he may be able to return to the ice in three weeks, give or take a few days."

Claude Evans, called up from the Montreal Royals, started the next four games for the Canadiens before stepping aside for Charlie Hodge, who handled the netminding until Plante returned to the lineup December 16 and celebrated a 5–1 victory over the Rangers.

"Returning to the ice with his face exposed to oncoming pucks must have taken incredible mental fortitude," Denault wrote. "But the papers made scant mention of this, instead focusing on the scores, the league standings, and so on. Nowhere was there any mention of the courage it must have taken to overcome what must have been a frightening experience and ordeal, and to come back and stare down the opposition once again without the aid of protection.

"But this omission simply reflected the thinking of the time. Injuries were part of the game, whether it was a broken cheekbone or a broken leg. Once the injury healed you were expected to resume playing. The pressure to return was immense. Those who didn't were branded cowards or worse and were quickly replaced. Others soldiered on, putting their own safety—their careers, in fact—at risk every time they skated on to the ice."

The occupational hazards were again underlined during a Canadiens practice on December 16, 1955.

"Plante suffered the injury when he was hit by a puck fired by Donnie Marshall and deflected by Butch Bouchard," read a portion of a story in the *Gazette*. "It was reported that both nasal bones and the left orbital bone were fractured."

Plante had posted his sixth shutout of the young season one night before suffering the injury, which forced him to miss six games.

"Resting idly in his hospital bed, Plante came to the realization that both injuries could have been prevented had he been wearing a mask," Denault wrote, referencing the successor to Irvin as the Canadiens' head coach. "Toe Blake agreed with him, and upon Plante's return to the ice he began wearing a protective shield in practice. But he found the mask uncomfortable, and he never even considered wearing it in a game."

That early mask, according to author/historian Tom Adrahtas, was a "primitive plastic shield" that an anonymous manufacturer had given to Plante.

"The mask provided minimal protection and left his forehead exposed, but he tried it for a time in practice and became intrigued with creating something more practical," Adrahtas wrote in *The '60s: Goaltending's Greatest Generation*.

In *The Jacques Plante Story*, a 1972 authorized biography written by Andy O'Brien, the goaltending great had this to say about the early mask: "I wore it for a while, but it obscured my vision. I was just thinking of taking it off when a puck hit the mask right in front of the eyeholes. I kept it on religiously in practices from then on, wondering all the while what kind of mask would be practical for wearing in games."

Plante and contemporaries such as Terry Sawchuk, Glenn Hall, and Johnny Bower had begun to wear face gear during practices into the latter half of the 1950s.

As Adrahtas wrote: "Several goalies of that era were gifted a contraption designed by one Delbert Louch. 'The Louch' was a thick, clear Plexiglas shield that was ill-fitting, fogged up in minutes and was as slippery as all get-out. There are photos of that era with Sawchuk, Bower, and Hall modelling the contraption. None considered using it in a game."

It was more warmly received by youth hockey associations in Canada and the United States, according to *Saving Face* co-authors Jim Hynes and Gary Smith.

But, at the NHL level, resistance reigned. Coaches such as Blake were steadfast in their general opposition to a goalie donning a mask in a game. But even Blake saw merit in the idea of facial protection being worn, albeit selectively. In 1981, for example, he said during an interview that he recommended to Plante that he use a mask while recuperating from the broken cheekbone.

"I had been an umpire in the old provincial baseball league, you know, so I brought down my old mask," Blake told the *Toronto Star*. "Kenny [Reardon, a former Canadiens defenceman who was named the team's vice-president in 1956] and I asked Jacques to wear it in practice."

Meanwhile, the stitch count continued to mount during the 1950s, as did injuries of greater severity.

The accomplished career of Boston's Sugar Jim Henry came to an abrupt halt on March 29, 1955, when his right cheekbone was fractured in three places by a shot. And get this: Henry finished the game!

He was stricken with 3½ minutes remaining in Game 4 of a best-of-five semifinal versus Montreal. The game was delayed as the facial cut received medical attention. With the repairs out of the way, the banged-up Boston goaler returned to the crease.

Marshall ended the game by scoring at 3:05 of sudden-death play. Henry spent the rest of that Tuesday night and a significant portion of Wednesday morning at Massachusetts General Hospital.

"It doesn't look as if he'll be able to play Thursday," Dr. Charles W. Crowley, a dental surgeon, told Tom Fitzgerald of the *Boston Globe*.

Imagine that. With Henry having sustained an injury of that magnitude, there was nonetheless a measure of uncertainty as to his status for the next game. Such were the times.

Any doubt was soon removed when the 34-year-old Henry, having undergone a 90-minute operation to repair the facial fractures, announced his retirement from hockey—although he would later play at the senior level and briefly return to the pro ranks in 1960 for a nine-game stint with the International League's St. Paul Saints.

The benefits of facial protection, insufficient as it was by today's standards, were evident on April 6, 1958, while the Canadiens conducted one final tune-up before facing Boston in the Stanley Cup Final.

"During the workout, goalie Jacques Plante escaped injury when his face mask—which he wears only in practice—was smashed by a shot he didn't see," the Associated Press reported. "The puck hit him flush on the mask where it protects his forehead just above the nose."

No harm was done, at least for the time being. As Denault wrote, Plante was hit in the forehead by a shot and knocked out during the ensuing final against the Bruins. The game was delayed 20 minutes while the groggy goalie shook off the cobwebs, whereupon the proceedings resumed. The blow to the head was, in some ways, a blessing for Plante—and for goaltenders in general.

"Sitting in the crowd that night at the Montreal Forum was a 35-year-old marketing rep from Fibreglass Canada named Bill Burchmore," Denault wrote. "The next day at work, Burchmore couldn't escape thoughts of what he had witnessed at the game."

Burchmore followed up by reaching out to Plante, who had become wary of receiving out-of-the-blue, albeit well-intentioned, suggestions from strangers. However, Burchmore offered an advanced level of expertise and therefore got Plante's attention.

"I found myself staring at a sample fibreglass mannequin on my desk one day and suddenly saw what could be the solution," Burchmore wrote, according to *The Jacques Plante Story*. "Make a mask molded to the face, just like that mannequin's face."

Burchmore had indeed struck on a solution, as future events would establish, but the idea needed some time to marinate.

In the meantime, light bulbs were going off for Gene Long—trainer of the Hamilton College men's hockey team in Ithaca, New York.

Long began tinkering with a form of facial protection in 1958, when Clinton Comets goaltender Gordon (Spider) Brown suffered a broken jaw during an Eastern Hockey League game.

"Long made him a fibreglass shield for the jaw and Brown went on playing," read a portion of a story that was distributed in 1960 by the Associated Press.

"Then Long began to work on a mask for Hamilton players. He exhibited one at a meeting of American hockey coaches in Boston in 1958."

The story added that masks were being used in games and/or practices by other colleges, such as Middlebury College, Brown University, Amherst College, Cornell University, Dartmouth College, Colgate University, Williams College, and Norwich University.

Fred Addis, in an article published by the Society for International Hockey Research in 2005, wrote that Long made masks for three Hamilton College goalies—Don Spencer, John Collins, and Herbie Heintz.

When contacted as part of the research process for this book, Addis noted that Long built a form-fitting fibreglass mask for Spencer in February 1959. As for Heintz, he wore a mask in Hamilton's season opener against Norwich College in November 1959.

Leading up to that eventful month, maskless goalies continued to periodically pay a painful price.

Boston's Harry Lumley, for one, was hit on the left upper lip by a shot from the Toronto Maple Leafs' Dick Duff early in the second period of the seventh and deciding game of a 1959 semifinal series.

Even though Lumley was clearly in distress, play continued until the Bruins' goalie stopped a long shot by George Armstrong and froze the puck for a faceoff. Only then could Lumley scurry to the home team's dressing room.

"The blood from his smashed mouth had spattered the crease when Lumley skated off to have seven stitches taken and a cracked tooth extracted," Francis Rosa wrote in the April 8, 1959, edition of the *Boston Globe*, noting that Lumley had left the ice at 9:06 PM. "He returned at 9:34 amid a burst of applause that grew and grew as he skated to his cage at the east end of the Garden. It was one of the finest ovations ever given a professional athlete at the Garden. And the clutch goalie responded with three brilliant saves in that second period."

But he could not solve the Maple Leafs' Gerry Ehman, whose goal snapped a 2–2 tie with 2:33 remaining in the third period and ultimately concluded the scoring—and the Bruins' season.

"I don't know which hurts most," Lumley lamented, "the mouth or the losing."

Losing would become chronic for the Bruins, who did not reach the playoffs again until 1968. By then, the face of goaltending was drastically different. The catalyst for change was a game that was played slightly more than 200 days after Lumley numbly spoke to reporters through a mangled mouth.

Having disposed of Boston, Toronto proceeded to the championship series and lost in five games to a Montreal side that captured its fourth successive Stanley Cup title.

By then, goalie masks were already mandatory in some regions of the hockey universe.

Consider this excerpt from the January 17, 1959, edition of the *Montreal Star*, which reported on the use of what appeared to be clear plastic masks by goalies:

> The day may not be far off when all goalkeepers in hockey will wear protective face masks in games and when it does occur, the Ponsard Park Hockey Association can boast of starting the innovation among Montreal's minor set.
>
> The progressive Snowdon district has taken the lead in the introduction of the face masks by making it compulsory for all

their young netminders from mosquito to bantam inclusive to wear the guards to curb injuries.

The masks worn by the Snowdon goalers are similar to the one fitted for Jacques Plante, Charlie Hodge, and other puck-stoppers in the Canadiens' organization.

Snowdon president Gerry Snyder says the masks are a revelation for the kids. "I think they tend to give a youngster more confidence when he's out there on the ice. They'll also allow a boy to hold on to his teeth longer and keep his nose from being broken as is so often the case in hockey."

The masks don't fog up on the kids any longer when playing outdoors. This has been the common complaint among pro goalies. Snyder has disclosed they now have a new anti-fog solution that is wiped on the mask to overcome the problem.

"The parents are extremely pleased with their use in our leagues," said Snyder. "It keeps their boys from coming home disfigured after a game."

Change was also coming at the highest level of hockey in Montreal, with Plante at the forefront.

During the summer of 1959, the Canadiens' team physician (Dr. Ian Milne) and physiotherapist (Bill Head) were so intrigued by Burchmore's mask concept that they kept touting its merits to Plante, who eventually gave in.

"A facial plaster cast was taken at the Montreal General Hospital with Dr. Milne supervising because it came under medical regulations," Andy O'Brien wrote in *The Jacques Plante Story*. "Then Burchmore went to work. From fibreglass emerged a mask—woven roping saturated in polyester resin. Only one-eighth of an inch thick, it was tough as steel. Inside there was padding, thin strips of sponge rubber at the forehead, cheekbones and chin to cushion the impact. But it was enough to scare onlookers out of their wits—flesh-coloured with two holes for the eyes, one for the nostrils and another for the mouth."

Ingenious! Now, would it work?

"In testing the mask's durability, Burchmore swung a steel ball from a pendulum and struck the mask with the simulated force of a Bernie Geoffrion slap shot," Denault wrote. "Despite repeated attempts to damage the mask, Burchmore was unsuccessful."

The lack of success, in that context, constituted success.

Plante, despite not initially being amenable to the idea, eventually gave it a shot. In 1959, he began wearing Burchmore's creation in practices and in some exhibition games. Early reviews were positive.

"Jacques Plante has made up his mind that he will use a face mask—a new type he helped to design—in National Hockey League games," a September 25, 1959, *Montreal Gazette* story began. "The all-star goalie of the Montreal Canadiens has been toying with the idea for some time. Two cheekbone fractures from flying pucks helped to convince him."

Author/historian Tom Adrahtas noted that Plante went so far as to visit NHL president Clarence Campbell "to make sure the league would give him its blessing to wear it and Campbell did so enthusiastically."

There was less enthusiasm from the Canadiens' head coach.

"I think the mask is causing Plante to lose sight of the puck when it's at his feet," Toe Blake said.

Shrugging off the skepticism, Plante was inching closer to wearing a mask in regular season play, even though he remained barefaced when meaningful games began in the fall of 1959. Burchmore's brainchild began to make road trips on a just-in-case basis. One of those excursions was to New York, where the Canadiens were to play the Rangers on the first night of November.

3

The Mask-terpiece

The game that changed the face of hockey

Madison Square Garden: November 1, 1959.

The Montreal Canadiens' Jacques Plante was barefaced, as had been the custom for every NHL goaltender since Clint Benedict in 1930, to begin a Sunday night game at Madison Square Garden.

The contest proceeded uneventfully for a mere three minutes six seconds. Then things got ugly.

"Andy Bathgate of the New York Rangers rifled a puck at the Montreal net which Plante stopped beautifully with his nose," Trent Frayne wrote while providing the text for *Hockey*, a 1969 hardcover pictorial tribute to the NHL. "Bleeding profusely, he was led to the infirmary where seven stitches were taken in his swelling bugle."

That was anything but swell for Plante, who a few days earlier had suffered a five-stitch cut under his chin after being accidentally hit by a shot against the Chicago Black Hawks. Initially, it likewise appeared that there had not been any malicious intent on Bathgate's part. The real story became apparent over time.

"I was there," recalled author/historian Stan Fischler, who was then 27 and covering the Rangers versus Canadiens for *The Hockey News*. "It was deliberate. [Bathgate] went for Plante's face because Jacques played dirty and nearly injured Andy earlier in the game."

A scandal—let's call it Bath-gate—was born.

"Andy Bathgate said that he was steamed at Plante because, early in the game, he had come out of the net and given Bathgate a big hip check, which you're not expecting from a goalie," said author/broadcaster Dick Irvin Jr., who interviewed Bathgate for *In the Crease: Goaltenders Look at Life in the NHL*. "He said, 'I just flipped it at his face.' It wasn't the slap shot that you read about."

The shot heard 'round the (goaltending) world hit Plante on the left side of the nose. He was especially vulnerable because he was in a crouch.

"Jacques was knocked cold, his blood darkening the ice," Andy O'Brien wrote in *The Jacques Plante Story*.

Upon regaining consciousness, Plante rushed to the Garden's first-aid room, where he was greeted by head coach Toe Blake. Also on the scene was the ubiquitous Red Fisher of the *Montreal Star*, who described the coach-goalie dialogue in a memoir, *Hockey, Heroes and Me*.

Blake: "How bad is it?"

Plante: "It's sore."

Blake: "Why don't you wear your mask for the rest of the game?"

Plante: "I don't think I can go back in without it."

Although Blake had never been a proponent of a goalie wearing a mask, the Canadiens' bench boss was suddenly caught between a Jacques and a hard place.

Those were the days, remember, when teams dressed only one goaltender. Without a backup and with a sliced-up starter, practical considerations prevailed. Plante removed the mask from his travelling bag, pressed the shield against his face, and looked in the mirror at seven newly applied stitches that had closed a three-inch gash.

"Doesn't look too bad, eh?" Plante observed, according to Fisher.

"You going to play with that thing for the rest of the game?" Plante was asked.

"Forever," he responded.

Fisher wrote in the *Montreal Gazette* in 1986 that "a buzz ran through Madison Square Garden" when the crowd saw Plante return to the ice and put on (gasp!) a mask, 45 minutes after being beaned by Bathgate.

According to author Hal Bock, one leather-lunged member of the Garden gallery bellowed: "Hey, Plante! Take that thing off! Halloween's over!"

Bathgate was equally unimpressed by the unconventional sight of the Montreal, er, ghoul-tender.

"All of us on the bench thought, 'What the hell is this? You big chicken!'" he told Plante biographer Todd Denault.

NHL president Clarence Campbell, his feathers ruffled by the "chicken" reference, later declared: "It's completely ridiculous for anyone to think a goalie who wants to wear a mask is chicken, because anyone who would stand up to a 100-mile-an-hour projectile is no coward."

One wouldn't blame a goaltender if he cowered after an experience rivalling that of the blood-spattered Plante-Bathgate spat. Yet, the November 1, 1959, game proceeded without further incident or incisions. The Canadiens won 3–1 to increase their unbeaten streak to eight games (six victories, two ties). With Plante steadfastly continuing to wear the mask, the skein eventually swelled to 18 games (15–0–3).

In a different context, Plante could not win—at least in the appraisal of many members of the predominantly maskless goalies' union.

"We thought he was a wimp," legendary goalie Glenn Hall said 60-plus years later. "We looked at the goalkeepers who had played before us and we patterned ourselves after them. They thought they were tough and, when we played, we thought we were tough.

"It was, I believe, the most difficult position in sports in the pre-mask days. We had guys who would shoot at your head and it kind of straightened you up, and then they'd run the next one along the ice. It served a purpose for the forwards to shoot at your head, but you'd force yourself into a crouch. Most of us were lucky. We ended up without an eye injury."

Plante, a teammate of Hall's with the St. Louis Blues from 1968 to 1970, took umbrage to any accusation of being a wimp, a coward, etc.

"They figured a goalie had to be scared to play well," said Plante, as quoted in the *Hockey Hall of Fame's Book of Goalies*. "When shots are coming at you at 100 miles per hour, you're scared whether you have a mask or not."

The flaw in the fear-is-crucial theory has been effectively refuted over time, with Plante being foremost among the objectors.

"If you jump out of a plane without a parachute, does that make you brave?" he was quoted as asking in Hal Bock's book, *Save: Hockey's Brave Goalies*. "No, I think it makes you stupid."

But it was a strange look, indeed, at Madison Square Garden on November 1, 1959. Even now, six-plus decades later, recollection of the scene does not sit entirely well with Fischler.

"I was disgusted with Plante," he said via email in 2021. "My gut told me this would eventually lead to all goalies being masked. I was upset then and still am. The game was revamped from the way it was meant to be played."

Fischler pointed out that until 1959, "more than half a century elapsed without mask use being commonplace," adding, "that's how it should have stayed."

Asked in rebuttal about the issue of player safety, Fischler responded, "Hockey is not a game of 'safety' any more than lacrosse or rugby is." He proceeded to cite the following quotation, which he attributed to Gordie Howe: "Hockey is a man's game."

But what about the advances in stick technology, training, etc., that have led to pucks travelling at greater speeds, often unpredictably?

"It's a risk sport," Fischler countered, "and risk is part of the excitement. With flat, wooden sticks *and* the elimination of the slap shot, goalies could play without a mask...*and* players without helmets."

That said, he demurred, "I'm realistic enough to know that my ideas never will happen. Also, I understand about Baz [Bastien] and other goalies who were badly injured."

Using Bastien as a benchmark, Plante can be considered one of the lucky ones.

"When I first introduced the goaler's mask in 1959, pucks had already carved up my face for 200 stitches," Plante said in O'Brien's authorized biography. "My nose had been broken four times. Both cheekbones and my jaw had been fractured. Also a hairline skull fracture, yet when I donned a mask, I was ridiculed by fearless fellows—including fellow goalies—who hinted broadly that ol' Jacques must be getting puck-shy."

That certainly was not the case on that fateful evening, November 1, 1959. Despite the damage wrought by Bathgate, Plante was able to return to the landmark game against the Rangers without missing as much as a millisecond of on-ice duty.

"After the puck hit me, I didn't think any bones were broken," Plante told a group of reporters, Red Fisher included, after the contest. "But what bothered me the most was that I swallowed some blood. I didn't feel too good and my teeth felt numb."

Rangers head coach Phil Watson, for his part, was feeling discomfort due to the defeat.

"I think Plante played a marvelous game," said Watson, as quoted by Fischler in the November 14, 1959, edition of *The Hockey News*. "The mask was the best thing that ever happened to him." In fact, Watson told Fischler, "it may be the start of a new trend."

Who better to be the trail blazer than someone who was already renowned for revolutionizing the position and, by extension, the sport?

"This was the kind of thing that Jacques Plante would do," observed Hall of Fame goalie and acclaimed author Ken Dryden, who was 12 when Plante suffered his game-changing facial fissure.

"He was the guy who would go outside of his crease. He was the guy who would play the puck. He was the guy who would wear a toque. He was the guy who knitted. He was the guy who in Toronto found difficulty in the hotel the Canadiens stayed at because of his asthma, so he'd stay at some other place.

"All of this was in keeping with what we understood Jacques Plante to be. This was just another example and another expression of it, so I don't know how seriously we took it at the time."

"Jacques Plante will be 'The Man in the Iron Mask' when the Canadiens face off against the New York Rangers in the Forum tonight," a game-day story in the *Montreal Gazette* began on November 5, 1959, as the Canadiens prepared for the rematch.

The article included comments from Blake, who was beginning to moderate his initial disapproval of Plante donning a mask.

"When he was wearing it in preseason training, he wasn't as sharp, and my feeling then was that the mask was to blame," Blake said. "But perhaps it was Jacques himself and not the mask. Anyway, he played very well on our three-game road trip and appeared to have recovered his old form. It was early in the first period in the Sunday game in New York when he was hurt. When he said he wanted to wear the mask, I didn't object. He played another fine game and the mask didn't seem to handicap him. He can wear it as long as he likes, if it doesn't interfere with his goaltending."

Sighs of relief were still audible more than a decade later.

"God help all goaltenders if they'd lost," Hall of Fame netminder Gerry Cheevers wrote in his 1971 book, *Goaltender*. "It might have delayed progress for another generation."

Plante's strong-willed nature also paid long-standing dividends for members of the goaltenders' union.

"He stood up to his coach," said former NHL goalie and long-time broadcaster Kelly Hrudey, who in his autobiography lists Plante and Bernie Parent as his goaltending heroes.

"[Blake] said derogatory comments to Plante for wearing the mask. How ridiculous, right? And yet, Plante was strong-willed enough to continue to wear it, because he knew he was on to something. He knew that it was the right thing to do for the goalies."

In Plante's second game as a masked goalie, he stopped 18 shots in an 8–2 victory over the Rangers. Two nights later, Montreal played to a slightly extended, 2–2 draw with Chicago.

"Jacques Plante held up the game for a few minutes for a visit to the dressing room in the second period," Dink Carroll wrote in the *Gazette*. "The mask he's wearing clouds up and causes him to perspire, but the delay was to have some other part of his equipment fixed."

The Canadiens continued to get their fix of winning. In Plante's first 11 games as a masked minder of the net, he allowed only 13 goals while helping the Habs go undefeated (10 victories, including two shutouts, and one tie).

During that stretch of success, 11-year-old Glenn (Chico) Resch flipped to the sports section of his Saskatchewan-based hometown newspaper, the *Regina Leader-Post*. On Page 41, it was impossible to miss a by-now-familiar photo that was captioned: "His shirt bloodied, Jacques Plante of the Canadiens put on a special plastic mask and returned to the game against the New York Rangers at Madison Square Garden after being treated for a severe facial gash."

As a young goalie himself at the time, Resch took note of the developments.

"Nobody was wearing a mask back then," recalled Resch, whose big-league goaltending career lasted from 1973 to 1987. "The only thing I had seen was some kid playing in minor hockey. He was probably eight or nine, but he had glasses, so he was wearing some type of baseball cage in the Regina Parks League. Aside from that, we didn't think twice about it. Nobody wore a mask. Then Jacques Plante nearly gets his nose torn off and he starts wearing a mask. There was a black-and-white picture in the *Leader-Post*. I was just mesmerized. Well, when this happened to Jacques, then the manufacturers started to come up with something."

All of that was happening around the time that shooters began curving their stick blades in a manner that led to shots that were elevated more routinely and were consequently considerably more difficult for the attacker—let alone the poor, barefaced goaltender—to control or anticipate.

Chicago teammates Bobby Hull and Stan Mikita, for example, were among the first to utilize what was widely dubbed the "banana blade," which quickly increased in appeal. That was not a heel-clicking development for the goaltenders.

"I can't imagine what it would have been like for those guys not to wear a mask," Hrudey said. "Keep in mind that the majority of guys didn't shoot quite as hard, but there were still guys without a mask when Bobby Hull was in the game. It must have been absolutely frightening to see Bobby Hull wind up, knowing that you don't have a mask and that you have very, very little protection."

Meanwhile, the slap shot was gaining popularity, the most prominent practitioners of the day being Hull and Montreal's Bernie Geoffrion.

"When Boom Boom Geoffrion started to slap the puck, there were no big hooks on the sticks," said Red Berenson, a skilled centre whose 17-year NHL playing career concluded in 1978. "You could hardly tell the difference between a right-handed stick and a left-handed stick, and Geoffrion's was no different. It was just a plain, straight stick, but he had a knack of getting some good velocity on it and he had a reputation in the league. At that time, hardly anyone slapped the puck. But as soon as Mikita and Hull started to warp their sticks with a torch, that got everybody going, and that's when the masks came out."

So, too, did the dissenters. A few days after Bathgate plunked Plante, Rangers general manager Muzz Patrick had this to say to *Toronto Star* columnist Milt Dunnell: "Our game has a greater percentage of women fans than any sport I know. I'm talking about real fans—ones who can give you the scoring averages and All-Star lineups. Those women fans want to see men—not masks. They want to see the blondes, the redheads—and the bald spots. That's why I'm against helmets and masks. They rob the players of their individuality. We start out with goalies wearing masks. Every club has a defenceman or two who goes down to smother shots. Soon, they will want masks. All the forwards will wear helmets. The teams will become faceless, headless robots, all of whom look alike to the spectators. We can't afford to take that fan appeal away from hockey."

Dunnell weighed in with his own sentiments on Plante's new look.

"It makes him look like a man who died, from the neck to the top of his head, about the time Chicago last won the Stanley Cup, while the rest of the body decided to carry on," observed the *Star*'s lead sports columnist, referencing a Black Hawks championship drought that, at the time, dated back to 1938. "He knows that he startles the elderly ladies when he leers at them from the screens of their TV sets but all this he feels bound to accept as the price of survival. The selfish fellow simply decided he was too young to die."

There were two noteworthy developments just three days before Plante first donned his mask in a game.

On October 29, 1959, Gordie Bell of the Ontario Hockey Association's Senior A Belleville McFarlands took a shot to an eye during a game against the Whitby Dunlops. He suffered a lacerated eyeball, per research compiled by hockey historian Fred Addis for a 2000 article entitled "The Year of the Mask."

Bell was replaced for a spell by future NHLer Cesare Maniago, who was himself hit in the head versus Whitby on November 7, 1959. According to Addis, the game was delayed 20 minutes while Maniago, who required eight stitches and sacrificed one tooth for the cause, received medical attention.

Once again against Whitby, Bell returned to the competitive hockey scene on December 2, 1959—"wearing a Plante-style face mask," in the words of Addis.

That look also would ultimately be mirrored by Gil Mayer of the AHL's Cleveland Barons, who suffered a fractured jaw during a practice on October 29, 1959. Although it was not uncommon for goalies of that vintage to wear a mask during practices, Mayer was staunchly barefaced.

"I don't like to wear the mask for practice because it doesn't seem natural, and since I don't use one in a regular game," Mayer, a 2007 inductee into the AHL Hall of Fame, explained in a story distributed by the Associated Press.

Following the injury, Mayer travelled to Montreal to have his face fitted for a mask, United Press International reported in mid-November 1959.

He returned to the net on December 30, wearing a mask—one that, as it turned out, was sent to him by Plante—and rang in 1960 by registering a shutout on New Year's Day.

Leading up to Mayer's triumphant return to the net, Toronto Maple Leafs assistant general manager King Clancy had said: "I would like to see someone perfect a face mask to help the goaltender. The game has changed so much and they're getting cut down faster and faster."

Rochester Americans GM Jack Riley subscribed to that line of thinking.

"Who is to say a man should not wear it?" he said. "Suppose you tell a man no, and then he loses an eye?"

But what about the eyesores?

"If my man wanted to use it, I guess it would be OK with me," said Maple Leafs GM and head coach Punch Imlach, as quoted by George Beahon of the *Democrat and Chronicle.* "It's a real tough job, tending goal. But it looks like hell. That thing Plante wears is a spine-chiller. We aren't running a masquerade."

The final few months of 1959 were also eventful, for the purposes of this research, due to the presence of Donald Rich on the New York Rovers' roster. Rich, who played in five games over the span of a month before Plante was plunked, appears in a photograph that was published in the 1959–60 Eastern Hockey League yearbook.

In a posed photo, Rich is shown wearing a motorcycle-style helmet and a clear plastic visor. Tom Telaar, in a 2010 post on theehl.com, aptly labelled Rich as "The First Eastern Hockey League Astronaut."

For reasons that were unrelated to aesthetics, Plante actually dispensed with the mask on one occasion. He appeared barefaced against the host Detroit Red Wings on March 8, 1960. The headline from the *Gazette* reads: "Plante Removes Mask, Canadiens Lose to Red Wings 3–0."

In an Associated Press story, it was written that "the Montreal netminder appeared shaky."

The dispatch from Detroit added that "Plante said he discarded the mask at the request of coach Toe Blake, who never was outspoken in his approval of it. Blake said he doesn't want Plante to wear it in the playoffs and wanted him to get accustomed to playing without it."

By then, Plante was already on to his second game-worn mask, following some tweaking by Bill Burchmore—designer of the original shield. The new model, which had an assortment of holes, was dubbed the "pretzel mask" because, well, it looked like a pretzel (while providing only a slightly greater degree of protection, by the looks of it).

"By January 1960, Burchmore had come up with a new and improved model made of 540 ends of glass yarn," read an excerpt from *The Jacques Plante Story*. "Instead of a solid piece of fibreglass, it was constructed of fibreglass bars. Instead of a 14-ounce mask, Plante was now wearing one weighing only 10.3 ounces. With the bars there was more air circulation; it also looked a little less scary."

Wearing his second mask once again, Plante was unimpressive when he returned to the net following the one final barefaced appearance. Although the Canadiens beat Toronto 9–4, the *Montreal Gazette* reported that the mask "didn't seem to help as he looked weak on at least three Leaf goals." The late-season lemon barely mattered, ultimately. A masked Plante was his customarily stingy self once the playoffs arrived.

Along the way, some compliments were dispensed, with some accompanying incredulity.

"It seems incomprehensible that hockey goalies have persisted for so long in refusing to wear masks; no competitors in sport need them more," *The New York Times* columnist Arthur Daley wrote. "Gump Worsley of the Rangers invested in a mask a while back but the explosive coach, Phil Watson, wouldn't let him wear it, saying: 'Who wants a good-looking goalie?'"

(The Rangers, that's who! Decades later, New York netminder Henrik Lundqvist moonlighted as a model, appearing in several fashion magazines.)

Burchmore downplayed the appearance of Plante's mask, instead touting its efficacy.

"I designed it for protection, not good looks," Burchmore said. "Besides, the mask has all of Jacques Plante's facial features. If it was made for Clark Gable, it would look like Clark Gable."

And if there were dissenters, frankly, Plante didn't give a damn.

His netminding often bordering on the airtight, he backstopped the 1959–60 Canadiens to the franchise's fifth consecutive Stanley Cup title.

In each of those championship seasons, Plante was awarded the Vezina Trophy, which was then presented to the primary netminder on the NHL team that allowed the fewest goals over the course of the regular schedule. (Since 1982, the trophy has been awarded to the goaltender who is subjectively perceived to have been the league's finest during the regular season.)

As the Canadiens' regularly scheduled Cup celebration subsided, Blake met with reporters in the spring of 1960 and made a declaration that would have been beyond his imagination a few months earlier. In a story by the *Gazette*, Blake said: "I wasn't in accord with Jacques Plante's experiments with masks. I wasn't sure a mask was necessary. But he'd had some indifferent games and I figured it was worthwhile going along with his idea. Plante's performances in the two-playoff series have convinced me. I don't care what kind of a mask he wears in the future. As far as I'm concerned, the mask is here to stay."

4

Don of a New Era

Don Simmons, the NHL's second masked goaltender

At a time when nary an NHL team employed a backup goaltender, the identity of the No. 2 man was nonetheless a source of curiosity—at least from one standpoint: Who would be the first to emulate Jacques Plante by donning a mask during a game?

"That's often the example that tells the real tale," Hall of Fame goaltender Ken Dryden reflected. "It's not the first, but is there a second? And if there's a second, when is there a second? You're not a trailblazer unless the trail is blazed for others to follow. You're a quirky accident if it's only you."

For a brief time, beginning on November 1, 1959, Plante was the lone masked NHL goaltender. Some members of the netminders' union simply disregarded the development and continued to go maskless. Some diehards held out into the 1970s. Other goaltenders felt compelled to re-examine the sanity, or lack thereof, of facing flying pucks without the most fundamental form of facial protection. But who would be the next to take the plunge, a la Plante? That was a crucial question.

"It's hard to get to one, but it's really hard to get to two," Dryden said. "Then it becomes much easier to get to five. Once you're at five, 15 is around the corner."

It became easier to get to two—and eventually five, 15, etc.—because a prominent, influential puck-stopper such as Plante was the "one."

"If it had been a second-level goalie, there would been a shrug, along the lines of, 'OK, that's fine, but he's not particularly good, and here's another example of why a mask doesn't work, and look at the last few goals that he let in'—even if he would have let them in before, because he was only a mediocre goalie on a mediocre team," Dryden said. "I suppose the ideal person at a time like that would have been whoever was understood as the mainstream guy, the mainstream star. There were only six goalies in the league, so you didn't have a lot of choice."

Only 15 goaltenders saw duty during the 1959–60 NHL season. That total includes cameo, one-game stints for Montreal's Charlie Hodge (on a scheduled rest day for Plante) and New York's Joe Schaefer (an emergency replacement). Detroit's Gilles Boisvert (three games), Toronto's Ed Chadwick (four), New York's Jack McCartan (four), and Detroit's Dennis Riggin (nine) also had single-digit totals. Al Rollins (10) and Marcel Paille (17), both of the Rangers, were in the low double figures.

Glenn Hall led the way by playing in all 70 of Chicago's games. Plante (69) was next, followed by Toronto's Johnny Bower (66), Detroit's Terry Sawchuk (58), New York's Gump Worsley (39), and the Boston duo of Harry Lumley (42) and Don Simmons (28).

It was commonplace by then for goalies to wear a mask in practice—usually a see-through Plexiglas "windshield." Experimentation had also taken place with variations of Plante's fibreglass model. With the endorsement of general manager Jack Adams, veteran Detroit trainer Ross (Lefty) Wilson had made a plaster cast that was molded to the face of assistant trainer and practice goalie Dan (Ole) Olesevich.

"It's the latest fashion," Wilson, who was scored upon only once in 81 minutes of NHL action over three appearances as an emergency goalie in the 1950s, told Marshall Dann of the *Detroit Free Press* one month after

Plante's landmark game. "I got one of those do-it-yourself kits for making goalie masks. It will be ready in a couple of days.

"Ole is our model. He'll try it in practice. If it works, we'll make one for Sawchuk."

How about it, Terry?

"Don't rush me," an unimpressed Sawchuk told Dann. "I'm not against masks, you understand. I didn't like our big windshield, but Mr. Adams made me wear it. It saved me several injuries in practice. I want to know more about these new masks. I intended to study Plante's last Thursday, but I had to go to the hospital [due to neuritis]. Maybe I can see his [mask] when he comes here Sunday. It's got to be a lot better than our windshield before I'd wear one in a game. I want better visibility and I wonder about the sweat problem."

So why sweat the issue of wearing a mask?

"All this mask talk can get a goalie on edge," Sawchuk continued during his interview with Dann. "If you worry about getting hurt, you can't be a good goalie.

"I've had only one serious injury in the nets and that was 12 years ago at Omaha when I needed three stitches for a cut eyeball. Since then, I've never had a serious cut. Oh sure, I've had lots of little cuts. Maybe for 250 or so stitches. But nothing serious."

Regardless, there was serious talk of Sawchuk possibly wearing a mask. Dann's story of December 15, 1959, was headlined "Sawchuk to Become a Masked Marvel." At practice, anyway.

"Whether Olympia patrons ever get to see his handiwork will depend a lot on Sawchuk's experiments with it this week," wrote Dann, quoting a non-committal Sawchuk as saying: "I'm not for it, but I'm not against it."

Assessing the situation, Dann opined that "all signs point to such masks becoming standard equipment with goalies who like them. Thus, Terry may be wearing one soon. But don't bet on it."

The following day at practice, Sawchuk wore the Lefty Wilson mask for the first time. The grizzled goalie's reviews were hardly effusive.

"It's OK," he told Dann, "except that I can't see."

Sawchuk also complained that the mask pinched his face and was too hot.

"The mask project will not go on the shelf, however," Dann wrote. "Jack Adams wants Terry to continue the experiment in practice. So Terry will carry on. But he also will wear his regular windshield-style plastic mask in practice, too."

Sawchuk remained unconverted, telling Dann: "If I ever have to wear a mask in a game, I'd rather wear the glass one."

A month and a half after Plante shattered the NHL's Plexiglas ceiling, mask-wise, Boston's Don Simmons became the all-important No. 2.

Simmons wore a molded shell during a big-league game—the Bruins' 4–3 loss to the Rangers on December 13, 1959, at Madison Square Garden. The *Boston Globe*'s headline: "Simmons 2nd Goalie in Mask."

"The mask appeared to hinder Simmons on only one of New York's four goals," United Press International reported. "On [Dean] Prentice's second tally, the Boston goalie seemed to lose sight of the puck after stopping a long shot by defenceman Bill Gadsby. The puck dropped in front of him and Prentice swooped in quickly and poked the disc behind Simmons."

Four days earlier, Simmons had worn the mask for the first of two times in practice, leading up to the game in New York. The mask was designed by Gene Long, the trainer of the Hamilton College men's hockey team in Clinton, New York.

"Simmons played well," Bruins head coach Milt Schmidt told the *Boston Globe*. "It certainly wasn't his fault we lost. I'll stay with him."

Simmons, meanwhile, planned to stay with the mask.

"I'm satisfied with the way it worked out in New York," he told the *Globe* as a December 16, 1959, game in Chicago approached. "It rode up on my face once, on the play on which Andy Bathgate scored. But I don't think that will happen again as I become more used to it."

The night after the Boston–Chicago game, George Holmes of the Scotty Bowman–coached Peterborough Petes became the first masked goalie in Ontario Hockey Association Junior A history, according to researcher Fred Addis. Holmes' face and the net behind him were both well-protected. He shut out the Barrie Flyers 3–0.

Also on December 17, 1959, erstwhile NHLer Emile "The Cat" Francis became the first goalie to wear a mask in the old Western Hockey League. Addis noted that Francis, back in action after suffering a shoulder separation, was outfitted with a shoulder harness and a mask for the Spokane Comets in their 4–3 loss to the Seattle Totems.

The 1959–60 Bruins, meanwhile, were once again an also-ran—their 28–34–8 record would be the NHL's second worst—so their 4–0 loss in Chicago on December 16 was hardly surprising. The only goaltender who merited a mention in the game story from the *Boston Globe* was Chicago's Hall, who made 24 saves for the shutout. Simmons' mask, making its second appearance, was not referenced in coverage provided by the *Globe* or *Chicago Tribune*.

The skeptics, however, would not be silenced. Consider the events of January 3, 1960, when the Bruins lost 4–3 in Detroit and Montreal fell 8–3 to a Rangers team that improved to 10–21–6.

"The latest evidence collected Sunday night was unanimously against masked goalies," Dann wrote. "Not only did Plante have his worst night of the season, Don Simmons got into deep trouble because of the mask. Simmons is the Boston goalie who tried a mask a few times in practice and decided it was here to stay. Playing against the Red Wings for the first time since masking his work, Simmons looked bad on three close-in plays. The mask could have resulted in three Detroit goals, although Simmons hotly denies this, of course."

Simmons and Plante would soon cross paths in the NHL's first all-mask game—Montreal's 8–2 victory over Boston at the Forum on January 16, 1960. The teams met again the next evening at Boston Garden, with the Canadiens prevailing once more, 3–1.

By the following season, Simmons had dispensed with the mask. It produced painful consequences for him, but soothing acceptance of masks from the critics.

The painful part: On October 16, 1960, he took an Eric Nesterenko shot in the nose during the third period in Chicago. Bleeding profusely, Simmons headed to the dressing room. Jerry Toppazzini, a right winger, occupied the Boston net (using his regular stick, as opposed to a goalie's paddle) for the final 33 seconds. The Black Hawks, 5–2 victors, did not manage a shot on goal during Toppazzini's cameo—the last appearance in goal by a position player in NHL history—despite the fact that Chicago's top line of Bobby Hull, Bill Hay, and Murray Balfour was on the ice.

Writing about the injury the following day, the *Boston Globe*'s Herb Ralby observed: "If Simmons had been wearing his mask, it wouldn't have happened. But Don has discarded his mask and the bloody nose won't make him put it back on again. There's a very good reason for it, too. With the mask on, Simmons admits he didn't see properly."

Simmons applied that rationale while switching from his initial fibreglass mask to one that resembled a baseball catcher's cage. When neither option was to his liking, he scrapped the mask altogether. While tinkering with the masks, Simmons had chatted with a Major League Baseball catcher—Pete Daley of the Kansas City Athletics—about the situation.

"He told me his vision was partially obscured looking down because he was the standup-type goaler," Daley told Dalby. "A solution I told Simmons might be to switch the bars from horizontal to vertical. It is those bars going across the face that obscured the vision. If they went up and down, the obstacles would be removed—at least I think they would."

Mind you, there is one important difference between a goaltender and a catcher.

"We have an advantage, of course," Daley concluded. "We whip off our mask to catch a foul pop or grab a ball at our feet. The goaltender can't do that. But from having looked through a mask for years, I honestly think making the bars vertical might be the solution."

Simmons had dumped the mask leading up to the 1960–61 season, at the behest of the Bruins' head coach.

"I feel Don may be a better goalkeeper without the mask," Milt Schmidt told the *Boston Globe*. "That's why I asked him to stop wearing it. I've never seen better goaltending than he gave us in the 1958 Stanley Cup playoffs, and he wasn't wearing a mask then."

Schmidt's suggestion did not pay dividends for Simmons, who played in the 1960–61 Bruins' first 18 games—only three of which the team won.

He was then bumped by 22-year-old Bruce Gamble, who played *sans* mask in each of the 52 games that remained.

Gamble had been promoted from the American Hockey League's Providence Reds at the same time Boston called up Willie O'Ree—the NHL's first Black player—from the Hull-Ottawa Canadiens of the Eastern Professional Hockey League. O'Ree's previous big-league experience had consisted of two games with Boston in 1957–58.

With the 1960–61 Bruins, the 25-year-old O'Ree played in what would be his final 43 NHL games, registering four goals and 10 assists. His first big-league goal was scored on January 1, 1961, in a 3–2 victory over Montreal at the Boston Garden.

O'Ree put the puck past Charlie Hodge, who was subbing in net for an injured, ineffective Jacques Plante. Hodge had been wearing a mask in the minor leagues, only to discard it when he was summoned for NHL duty.

Asked about the mask (or lack thereof) by the *Boston Globe*, Hodge told Herb Ralby: "Sure, it impairs your vision a bit. It isn't too bad on shots around your feet. It's bad mostly from the sides—you know, like a horse wearing blinders."

Meanwhile, Simmons' hockey career was in flux. He had been ticketed for Providence, where Gamble had been playing, but refused to join the Bruins' chief minor league affiliate and demanded a trade. According to the *Globe*, Simmons felt he was being made the "scapegoat" for the team's shoddy start.

Simmons relented in early December and off he went to Providence—albeit for only 10 games. He was then returned to Boston by the Reds. The minor league team's owner, Louis Pieri, told the Associated Press that the disgruntled goaltender's play had been unsatisfactory.

All ties with the Bruins organization were severed on January 30, 1961, when Simmons was traded to Toronto for farmhand goalie Ed Chadwick. Simmons balked at the deal when he found out that it entailed playing in the AHL with the Rochester Americans.

"We got into the Stanley Cup finals against Montreal the first two seasons I played for Boston," the 29-year-old Simmons told Hans Tanner of the *Democrat and Chronicle*. "I've got a good record in the NHL and, considering both that and my age, I don't feel I should go to the minors."

As a result, Simmons never played again that season. He returned to action in 1961–62, playing 51 games—without a mask, at least at the outset—for Rochester before being summoned to Toronto to replace an injured Johnny Bower. Simmons was once again wearing a mask by the time he returned to the NHL.

Having embraced facial protection for good, Simmons continued to bounce back and forth between the NHL and the minors until 1969.

At 37, he played in only 10 games—five with the Rangers and five with the AHL's Buffalo Bisons—in 1968–69.

In his first game with Buffalo, he registered his final career shutout by stopping all 27 Providence shots in a 5–0 win.

Simmons made his final NHL appearance on March 1, 1969, replacing maskless Rangers goalie Ed Giacomin at 13:41 of the second period. Giacomin was pulled after allowing a Phil Esposito goal that enabled the Boston star to notch his 98th point and set what was then an NHL single-season record.

Esposito soon increased the total to 99 when Simmons surrendered a goal by Bobby Orr. The 100th point would have to wait, though. There was a close call five minutes into the third period, when Esposito rang a shot off a goal post. Boston went on to win 8–5.

Esposito, with 15 games remaining, eventually fattened the points record to 126. But he settled for 49 goals—the difference between that and the 50 milestone being as minuscule as a shot that found a post, instead of the twine, behind Simmons.

Esposito made his NHL debut with the 1963–64 Black Hawks, at a time when Glenn Hall was a fixture in Chicago's crease.

During one protracted period, Hall played goal in 502 consecutive regular season games—as unbreakable a record as exists in sports.

Goaltending's all-time iron man was actually made of flesh and bone, but the notion of wearing facial protection was anathema at the time—not only for Hall, but also for most goaltenders of the day.

"You wanted to play," he said, matter-of-factly, during an interview for this book. "I played in 1,026 consecutive games. I played five years in the minors, and I never missed a game in junior hockey or in the minors before I got to the National Hockey League, so it's 1,026 straight games that I played."

Today, no right-thinking coach even dreams of having his goaltender play 1,026 consecutive minutes.

"They've got such stupid practices," Hall observed. "We used to play Wednesday, Thursday, Saturday, Sunday, so you were playing four games in five nights. But what made it easy is that we didn't have to practise, and practice is killing the goalkeepers.

"My goodness...they give you free shots in practice. It's nothing but free shots. That's what made the scrimmage so good, because it was like a game, and they used to scrimmage quite a bit in the old days. I don't think they do that very much now."

Hall's streak—be it 502 or 1,026—began on opening night in 1955 and ended November 7, 1962, against Boston. Hall took himself out of the game midway through the first period. In came young Denis DeJordy. These were the days of the one-goalie system, but DeJordy—then of the Buffalo Bisons—was flown to Chicago the day before the Black Hawks battled the Bruins. Chicago general manager Tommy Ivan had ensured that DeJordy was in the stands after discovering that Hall was not 100 per cent.

According to an authorized biography of Hall that was written by Tom Adrahtas, "Glenn was bending over in his locker stall to fasten a toe strap on his leg pads" and "felt a pop in his lower back."

Charles Bartlett of the *Tribune* reported that DeJordy did not initially suit up for the game because Hall had insisted on starting. Hall lasted for 10 minutes 21 seconds, stopping two shots before allowing a goal by Boston's Murray Oliver, on the type of shot that the Black Hawks' netminder ordinarily would have stopped.

"The great Chicago guardian obviously was in pain as he struggled from the ice after trying to make a diving save," Bartlett observed. "He skated slowly below-stairs." (Yes, the old Chicago Stadium was designed in such a manner that players had to descend some stairs to get from the bench to the dressing room.)

The *Tribune* reported that the game was delayed seven minutes while DeJordy, who had been sitting in the stands, strapped on the pads and hurriedly prepared to make his NHL debut.

"In the nine minutes and 39 seconds left of the period, DeJordy proved himself with nine stops, at least five of them of major-league stamp," read another one of Bartlett's quotations. "Denis finished the game with 26 saves and lost no face in either of the two goals scored against him."

The face was preserved, one should note, even though DeJordy did not wear a mask.

The game finished in a 3–3 tie because the NHL did not reintroduce overtime for the regular season until 1983, after a 40-year absence. Chicago was leading 3–2 when, with 1:30 left in the third period, the Bruins' goaltender—"Roly-Poly Bob Perreault," in the words of Bartlett—was pulled for an extra attacker. The move was a success. The Bruins' John Bucyk scored the tying goal with seven seconds left.

The following day, the Black Hawks made it official: Hall's streak was going to end. Destined for Montreal, the team left him behind in Chicago so that he could receive treatment. The *Tribune* reported that Mr. Goalie had "a sharp pain across the hips, just above the sacroiliac region."

Bartlett of the *Tribune* also took some time to do some number crunching. He calculated that Hall had played 31,195 minutes 33 seconds without a respite—dating back to October 6, 1955, when he was in goal for Detroit against his future team, Chicago. The Black Hawks edged the Red Wings 3–2 in the 1955–56 season opener. Seven years, one month and not even a hint of a mask later, the hockey community was left to celebrate a streak that was "one of the great personal feats of modern sport."

After missing only three games, Hall was once again a reliable presence between the pipes, refusing to wear a mask until his 17th season, at age 37.

At the time, Terry Sawchuk was closing in on his first month as a masked goaltender. The venerable Detroit star finally donned facial protection, which to the naked eye offered only a thin layer of resistance, in competition on October 11, 1962.

Sawchuk was approaching his 33rd birthday and entering what would be his 13th full big-league season when, with his grizzled face concealed for the first time, he stopped all but one of the Rangers' 22 shots as the Red Wings won 2–1 at Madison Square Garden.

"It was another breakthrough for the mask," Jim Hynes and Gary Smith wrote in *Saving Face*. "Oddball Jacques Plante was one thing, but once the great Sawchuk started wearing one, the hockey establishment finally started to truly embrace it."

The opposing goalie for Sawchuk's first masked game? Gump Worsley, who had also been in net for the Rangers on November 1, 1959, when Montreal's Jacques Plante made hockey history by concealing his countenance and ultimately putting a new face on goaltending.

Sawchuk kept wearing with the trusty Wilson mask until a few weeks before his untimely, accidental death in 1970. He sported facial protection for his final eight NHL seasons, a span that was highlighted by his stellar play for Toronto in its Stanley Cup run of 1967.

Along the way, Sawchuk had every reason to be thankful for wearing a piece of equipment that he once resisted.

In a 1967 semifinal series versus Chicago, a Bobby Hull slap shot smashed into Sawchuk's masked face. As Bruce McDougall recounted *The Last Hockey Game*, Toronto trainer Bob Haggert rushed on to the ice, made a beeline for Sawchuk, and inquired as to the groggy goaltender's well-being.

McDougall wrote that Sawchuk glared at Haggert—through a mask that the author described as "a bedpan with eyeholes"—and snorted: "I stopped the [bleeping] shot, didn't I?!"

And there was silence.

5

The Holdouts

Maskless goaltenders continue to Gamble

Roger Crozier got his big break—multiple fractures in his left cheekbone—while making his NHL debut.

Pressed into duty for the Detroit Red Wings after one-time mask holdout Terry Sawchuk suffered a wrenched back, Crozier was introduced to big-league hockey on November 30, 1963. He stopped 35 Toronto Maple Leafs shots, including a Frank Mahovlich blast that hit the newbie NHL netminder in the noggin, during a 1–1 tie in Toronto.

The game was delayed 15 minutes while the stricken goalie was examined. The 21-year-old Crozier, a call-up from the AHL's Pittsburgh Hornets, then returned to the game and continued to sparkle. He blanked Toronto until Bob Pulford scored with 4½ minutes left.

Only after the Red Wings returned to Detroit did the severity of Crozier's situation become painfully apparent.

"The doctors were amazed that he had finished the game," Tom Cohen wrote in *Roger Crozier: Daredevil Goalie*. "They operated on him immediately."

Crozier was expected to miss 10 days after having his cheekbone reassembled, Jack Berry reported in the *Detroit Free Press*.

"In the meantime," Berry continued, "the Wings have three games and, even when Crozier does come back, he will have to wear a mask and he's never worn one before. How much of a handicap that will be isn't known yet but the goalies who wear masks and are used to them admit that they have blind spots, especially at their feet."

Crozier didn't have anything but blind spots while being captured in a photo that appeared in the *Free Press* on December 10, 1963. Photographer Jerry Heiman captured the image of Crozier laying on his back on the table of trainer Lefty Wilson. The goalie's face was completely covered with plaster of Paris.

Wilson was in the process of making a plaster cast that would be used as the foundation for Crozier's first form of facial protection.

"He hopes to return to action next weekend—with his new mask," the *Free Press* reported.

Sure enough, Crozier returned on schedule. And he did wear a mask during a 5–4 victory over the visiting Black Hawks on December 14, 1963. The mask was discarded slightly more than seven minutes into the contest and, as Berry put it, Crozier "played barefaced the rest of the way."

Although the gutsy goaltender's face was not well-covered, his net most certainly was. He was undefeated in each of his first five NHL games—the fifth being a 3–0 blanking of Boston.

Why the aversion to wearing a mask?

"No good," Crozier said, as quoted by author Jim Hunt in *The Men in the Nets*. "Too many blind spots."

Too many shots in the head were not enough to sway Crozier's opinion—not for the longest time, anyway.

He was only 16, playing intermediate hockey in Bracebridge, Ontario, when he first felt the consequences of shunning a mask. In his third game of the season, a flying puck opened up a gash on his forehead.

"It didn't hurt too much, but Roger could taste his own blood as it ran down his face," Cohen wrote in his biography of Crozier. "That was frightening. He had never had any stitches before; as the team doctor sewed up his cut in the dressing room, Roger had to fight back the tears. He almost wished he were five years old again and could run home to his parents."

But Roger's hockey career was hardly over and out. He kept climbing the ladder to the junior level, which he cracked as a 17-year-old with the 1959–60 St. Catharines Teepees. He spent three seasons with that Ontario Hockey Association team, with only one interruption.

During the 1960–61 season, the acrobatic Crozier was called up to the AHL's Buffalo Bisons and started three games as an injury replacement. He registered an impressive goals against average (2.31) during that audition.

"His professional debut was a roaring success," Cohen wrote. "It was also a painful one. On Christmas night he suffered his first serious injury in hockey. Halfway through the second period he lost sight of the puck for an instant behind a mass of battling players. He heard the loud crack of a stick connecting with the puck and an instant later he found himself on the ice, his face throbbing with pain. A few seconds later the team doctor was leaning over him, examining his swelling jaw. Roger didn't know how badly he was hurt, and he was a little scared."

X-rays revealed a broken jaw. He was shelved for a week while a mask was made for him.

"When the mask was finished and Roger put it on and skated out on the ice, he was very nervous," Cohen wrote. "He found it difficult to move his head and he felt as if his vision were partially obstructed. But as the game began, and the opposing forwards fired shot after shot at him, he forgot about the injury, the mask, everything but stopping the puck. It wasn't until after the first period was over that he realized what had happened. 'I'm not puck shy,' he thought with relief. He was over one of the biggest hurdles of his hockey career."

Any fears had been shed. Soon enough, so had that annoying mask—with more cuts and consequences to come.

The newly married Crozier was playing in an exhibition game with St. Catharines in 1961 when, as Cohen described it, the goalie's wife "watched in horror as Roger, struggling to find the puck in a pile-up in front of the net, slipped on the ice and fell under the flashing skates of one of his defencemen. The cut on Roger's face required 25 stitches. [Crozier's wife] Arlene was badly shaken."

Crozier suffered another broken jaw during the Teepees' 1961–62 campaign, according to Cohen. The jaw was to be wired shut for six weeks. Over that period, the Daredevil goalie's options for nourishment were pretty much restricted to milkshakes and eggnog.

Having overcome that setback, the unbreakable Crozier would soon become entrenched as the Red Wings' goaltender.

"He could be the find of the century," Red Wings head coach and general manager Sid Abel told Jack Berry of the *Detroit Free Press*.

Despite spending plenty of time flopping to the ice, in proximity to a potentially injurious puck, Crozier continued to brush off suggestions that he wear a mask—although the occasional exception was made in practice.

"I just don't care for it," he told Berry in April 1966. "This one [that is worn in practice] is too small, anyway. But who knows? Maybe someday."

In early November 1967, the emotional and physical toll exacted by playing goal in the pressure-packed pros led a stressed-out Crozier—who was also dealing with a persistent case of pancreatitis and a crisis of confidence—to retire from hockey at age 25.

"I'm headed for the nuthouse if I keep playing," the then-maskless Crozier told Jim McKay of the *Windsor Star*, "so I'm getting out now."

Crozier's decision prompted Joe Falls of the *Free Press* to compose a column that was headlined: "Say a Prayer for Poor Goalie."

"The surprising thing is not that Roger Crozier is quitting hockey—but that more goalies aren't turning in their pads," Falls began. "That is, before they wind up with scrambled eggs in their heads.

"Making a living as a goaltender in professional hockey these days has to be one of the most hazardous professions known to man. And, if you're high-strung, as little Roger is, it's amazing how you can keep any control over your nerves.

"It's a cold fact that those pucks are flying harder and faster than ever. How do you protect yourself against a blue-line deflection off the stick of

Bobby Hull? You don't. You just hope the puck doesn't smash into your face.

"The truly amazing thing is that more goalies aren't hurt...or maimed...or even killed. It's a mystery how any of them can go out there anymore without a mask, as Crozier has done.

"Even a mask is no assurance you won't get hurt. George Gardner took a shot off Dean Prentice's stick in a recent pregame warmup and 18 stitches were needed to close the cut.

"The thing is, a goalie can get hurt almost as easily in practice as he can in a game. When his teammates ride in on him to sharpen their shooting eyes, they don't hold anything back. There is their bread and butter, the way they support their families."

That was also the case for Crozier, who was back in goal by late January 1968.

"My nerves are in much better shape now," he told the *Free Press*. "I guess I just needed some time off to ease the pressure."

Time for reflection did not change his sentiments about a mask. He continued to tinker with facial protection in practice, but left it at that until the 1969–70 season neared.

"If I could get away without wearing a mask, I would," he told Berry in November 1969. "It doesn't give me any more peace of mind. You don't say to yourself, 'Now that you have got a mask on, dive in.' But I'm in the adjusting stage and the longer I wear it, the harder I imagine it will be to dispose of it."

By the time Crozier joined the masked majority, only seven of the 25 goaltenders on big-league rosters were still barefaced, according to a story circulated by the Canadian Press in November 1969.

The magnificent seven were Bruce Gamble (Toronto), Johnny Bower (Toronto), Les Binkley (Pittsburgh Penguins), Denis DeJordy (Chicago Black Hawks), Ed Giacomin (New York Rangers), Wayne Rutledge (Los Angeles Kings), and Gump Worsley (Minnesota North Stars). As well, a maskless Joe Daley had begun the 1969–70 season with Pittsburgh before being dispatched to the minors.

By then, Jacques Plante—pioneer of the modern-day mask—was a 40-year-old member of a third-year franchise, the St. Louis Blues, and still on the cutting edge of innovation.

"Some NASA scientists in Washington are working on a new mask for me," Plante told CP. "They are experimenting with some new lightweight material that can be poured right over your face."

No thanks, said Worsley.

"Anybody who wears a mask," the Gumper told CP, "is scared."

It was actually a brave new world for goaltenders, most of whom had eventually subscribed to Plante's line of thinking.

"At the time I started wearing the mask," he said in the wire story, "I thought it would take about 10 years to accept it."

The degree of acceptance was such that Toronto's Marv Edwards, then a 34-year-old rookie, declared in the CP story that "the mask has come to stay. I will be surprised to see a goalie who is not wearing one by the end of this season."

One by one, goaltenders had emulated Plante. Boston's Gerry Cheevers, for example, unveiled his mask on October 11, 1967—five years to the day after Terry Sawchuk's first game with facial protection. Cheevers would soon become an innovator in his own right, opting to jokingly paint stitches on his face gear. Masks had previously been marked by pucks, as opposed to pen or paint.

Cheevers' goaltending cohort, Ed Johnston, began experimenting with a mask during the 1967–68 season, but was not sold on the merits of facial protection until October 31, 1968. That evening at The Olympia in Detroit, a mask—even one as primitive as the late-1960s models—provided partial protection when he took a shot to the head during the warmup.

Seeing what happened to Johnston, Glenn Hall—Mr. Goalie—began to wonder whether he, too, should join the ranks of the masked goalies. Then 37, and in his 17th big-league season, Hall first wore a mask just two weeks after Johnston was injured.

Hall was actually the youngster in goal for the Blues that season. Plante, the other member of the team's goaltending tandem, turned 40 midway through the 1968–69 campaign, after which the Blues' greying goalkeepers shared the Vezina Trophy.

Two goaltenders next won the Vezina Trophy in 1970–71, when Giacomin and Gilles Villemure took home the hardware on behalf of the Rangers.

For the longest time, Giacomin was resistant to the concept of a mask. In the aforementioned CP story, the popular puck-stopper insisted that he did not harbour any fears of being hit by a puck.

"I'm concerned only with my eyes," Giacomin said, "and with a mask there have to be slits for the eyes so there's no way they can be protected."

Always agile, he reversed course the following season and sported a mask.

"I guess the closest I ever came to a severe injury was the time I took a shot on the jaw from Frank Mahovlich," Giacomin told author-broadcaster Dick Irvin Jr. "I turned a bit at the same time, so the jaw didn't break, but I felt it for months.

"I played 13 years in the National Hockey League and five in the American league. I had a total of 13 stitches and I never lost a tooth."

Not that he was unscathed. While playing for the AHL's Providence Reds, he was forced to leave a January 15, 1965, game against the Rochester Americans after suffering what was reported to be a nose injury, according to the *Athol* (Mass.) *Daily News*. He was back in action four days later against the Quebec Aces, who amassed 56 shots on goal and won 6–2.

A la Giacomin, Binkley wore a mask for the first time in a game on October 10, 1970. How's that for a coincidence?

Giacomin was in goal that night for the Rangers when they lost 3–1 to the host Blues, who sealed the game with an empty-net goal. Binkley, meanwhile, tended the twine for Pittsburgh during a 2–1 road loss to Buffalo in the Sabres' first NHL game.

By then, the 31-year-old Giacomin had been a pro since 1959 and an NHLer since 1966. Binkley, who was 36 when the 1970–71 season dawned, served an even longer apprenticeship. He toiled in the minors from 1955 to 1967 before finally receiving an NHL opportunity when

Pittsburgh became one of the six expansion franchises that hit the ice for the 1967–68 season.

Binkley, like so many of his peers, could tell countless stories about the rigours of the goaltending game. Consider the situation he faced in mid-December 1957, while playing for the Eastern Hockey League's Charlotte Clippers.

"Binkley has survived loss of his contact lenses, sieges of flu, sick stomachs and several dozen stitches to run up his ironman record of 108 consecutive games for Charlotte," Dick Pierce wrote in the *Charlotte Observer*. "He even played almost one entire period at Johnstown last winter—unconscious."

The story, which did not explain how that was possible, included this quote from an incredulous Binkley: "I was the happiest hockey player in the world and didn't know it."

At one point, "hockey player" was only part of the job description. Binkley moonlighted as the Cleveland Barons' trainer in the early 1960s.

"I didn't know anything about being a trainer, but I was told, 'Don't worry about it. We have doctors on staff,'" Binkley recalled in a 2007 interview with Dave Stubbs of the *Montreal Gazette*. "So they sent me all these correspondence courses and I became the fastest scissors in the league, wearing this little holster."

There were times, however, when the trainer required a trainer. On November 3, 1962, for example, Binkley collapsed in the Barons' dressing room following a game against Quebec. He was eventually diagnosed with a concussion that forced him to miss eight games.

Shortly after returning to the lineup, Binkley sustained what the *Baltimore Sun* described as a "severe face injury" against the Baltimore Clippers after being hit by a Sandy McGregor shot from three feet away.

Not long after shaking off that injury, Binkley accompanied the Barons to Buffalo for a game against the Bisons.

"Thanks to Binkley, the underdog Barons were on the verge of a big upset," George Beahon wrote in the December 5, 1962, edition of the *Democrat and Chronicle*. "Binkley fielded one frozen, vulcanized rubber disk with his head, and was felled. Revived on the ice, he was patched up and stayed in the action. Buffalo 'slopped in' a pair and against Binkley, and added some well-earned goals to win easily.

"In the dressing room, right after [the] conclusion of the game, Binkley shouted: 'Nice going, gang. This was a real good win!' His teammates were stunned. So was Binkley, because he had no recollection of anything happening after the stage when his club led and he was injured. It was early the next morning before he began recalling plays after the stunner."

It was that kind of season for Binkley, who was dinged once again on March 31, 1963, in a 14–3 victory over the Pittsburgh Hornets. The Associated Press reported that "Binkley was stunned by a blow in the head by a stick at 13:50 of the first period and was taken out of the game."

Fast forward to March 20, 1964, when Binkley was knocked unconscious by a shot to the forehead in another AHL game against Pittsburgh. He did not regain consciousness until being taken to hospital, where five stitches were applied. He was discharged with "only a headache," according to Albert R. Fischer of the *Baltimore Sun*, and, of course, was soon back between the pipes.

It was back to the hospital on March 16, 1967, when Binkley, then of the Western Hockey League's San Diego Gulls, was concussed as a result of being hit behind an ear with a stick during what United Press International termed "a flurry in front of the nets."

Later that year, Binkley got his long-awaited shot in the big leagues. But one shot was not to his liking.

With the Penguins in 1969–70, Binkley was hit so hard in the jaw that his contact lenses popped out during a game against St. Louis. Having verified that hockey is indeed a contact sport, he left the ice on a stretcher.

The *Pittsburgh Press* published a photo of the messy scene, along with this caption: "LES BINKLEY. Puck mangles mouth."

Bill Heufelder of the *Press* reported that "Binkley escaped without a hitch, but as a doctor told him, a portion of the inside of his mouth 'looked just like hamburger.' Binkley lost one tooth and two others were pushed back, but the team dentist said they may be saved."

(Saves being all-important for a goalie.)

By the time the next season began, Binkley was conspicuously and permanently masked.

In the spring of 1974, by which time Binkley was a 39-year-old member of the World Hockey Association's Toronto Toros, he had a conversation with Trent Frayne for his book, *The Mad Men of Hockey*. The interview commenced with Binkley recounting the toll that had been exacted during the pre-mask years.

Binkley began, briefly: "Couple broken noses."

Frayne asked how those injuries occurred.

"Shots."

Do you remember who shot?

"Let's see. No, I guess I don't. Broke a jaw once."

How did that happen?

"Shot."

Have you got all your teeth?

"Most of 'em."

How many are missing?

"Oh, a few."

Frayne then noted that Binkley pointed toward his upper front bridge.

"These two."

But wearing a mask ended all that?

"You kiddin'? First mask I had, a shot cut me for 15 [stitches] right below the eye. I switched to a different-type mask. Course, who knows, without that mask maybe I lose the eye."

Maskless goaltending could be described as a daredevil's pursuit. It was fitting, then, that Binkley crossed paths with someone who was noted for death-defying feats—Evel Knievel—as part of a publicity stunt at Maple Leaf Gardens on March 25, 1975.

Knievel was to take four shots against Binkley, then of the Toros, with the provision that team owner John F. Bassett would fork over $5,000 for each goal scored during the second intermission of a game against the Vancouver Blazers. Knievel emerged $10,000 richer. Binkley received $2,000—or $1,000 per save.

Binkley became accustomed to the intermission-shootout routine, which also included one showdown with a 12-year-old shooter.

"The kid came in and tried to deke me," Binkley told Stubbs. "When I moved across the crease, his eyes lit up at the space between my pads. He couldn't resist it, and when he shot, my skate flashed across to make the save.

"And I don't think to this day that Wayne Gretzky can believe he didn't score on that one."

Ed Giacomin was reminded of the benefits of a mask while backstopping the Rangers to a 4–1 victory over Chicago on February 9, 1972. One of his 41 saves was a stunner—courtesy of a Dennis Hull blast that left the New York netminder with a cracked mask.

"If I wasn't wearing the mask, I'm sure I would have lost some teeth and gotten a broken nose," Giacomin told reporters. "Maybe my wife will appreciate the mask now. She's always saying she can't tell which goalie is in the nets."

However, the most impactful goalie-related news on that evening in 1972 pertained to the Philadelphia Flyers' Bruce Gamble, who—unbeknownst to himself, or anyone, at the time—had suffered a heart attack while playing against the host Vancouver Canucks on February 8.

Gamble nonetheless finished the contest and, in fact, nearly registered a shutout. Soon after winning 3–1, the Flyers departed for Oakland, where the 33-year-old Gamble was taken to hospital after discomfort persisted. It was there that the heart attack was diagnosed and his NHL career concluded.

Gamble's pro hockey career consisted of 327 NHL regular season games and another 352 appearances in the minors, dating back to the 1957–58 season.

His first full season in the pros included a short, but eventful, stint with the Rangers. Called up, ironically enough, from the Western league's Vancouver Canucks—for whom he would record seven shutouts in 1958–59—he spent much more time in the air than in the crease as a novice NHLer.

With Gump Worsley out for two games with a back injury, a call was put out for Gamble, who was on the other side of the continent at the time.

"Gamble flew all night to get to New York, arrived in the afternoon, and climbed into harness that night," Rangers general manager Muzz Patrick told the *The Province*.

The *New York Daily News* reported that the journey, which took place before jet travel was in vogue, took 29 hours. The Bruins then welcomed him to New York, and the NHL, by winning 5–3.

Gamble was much tougher to solve two nights later, in a 1–0 loss to the host Red Wings. Then it was back to the minor leagues and the joys of life as a goaltender who was minimally compensated and protected.

"Sure, I want to play in the National league. Who don't?" Gamble ungrammatically, but unequivocally, told Dick Beddoes of the *Vancouver Sun* in late March 1959, adding: "I want the National league, because that's where the money is."

The conversation took place shortly after Gamble, back in goal for Vancouver, had suffered a broken nose in a playoff game against the Spokane Spokes after "an errant puck turned his face into a bloody bowl of borscht," as Beddoes so delicately described it.

Gamble's perseverance was rewarded on November 19, 1960, by which time Boston had secured his NHL rights. Promoted from Providence to replace a faltering Don Simmons, Gamble registered his first big-league victory as the Bruins downed Detroit 6–4.

Before too long, Gamble was receiving plaudits from Bruins GM Lynn Patrick, who told Tom Fitzgerald of the *Boston Globe* that "this kid looks like a young Johnny Bower."

Gamble ended up playing in 52 games for the 1960–61 Bruins, a dreadful team, before being supplanted by Don Head to begin the 1961–62 campaign. By mid-season, though, Gamble was back in Boston and Head was headed to the minors as part of a Bruins shake-up, prompting this beauty of a headline in the *Globe*: "B's Ax Falls on Head(s)—Gamble to Mind Goal."

After 28 games with the 1961–62 Bruins, it was back to the minors for Gamble. He would not resurface in the NHL until 1966.

At one point, he opted for a hiatus from hockey, taking off the 1964–65 season instead of playing for the AHL's Springfield Indians and their tyrannical owner, Eddie Shore.

Gamble returned to pro hockey in the fall of 1965, joining the Central League's Tulsa Oilers. Late that season, he was called up to the NHL and sparkled over a 10-game span, thereby alleviating the Maple Leafs' goaltending crisis.

With injuries having shelved Bower (shoulder) and another future Hall of Famer, Terry Sawchuk (back), Gamble registered four shutouts over a five-game, nine-day span in March 1966. Along the way, he shook off a six-inch facial cut that had been opened up in practice by a George Armstrong slap shot.

In another context, Gamble would not be cut...from the Leafs' roster. He stopped the puck so effectively that, following the brief but exceptional introductory stint with the Leafs, he would play another 177 games for Toronto, including 61 in 1968–69 and another 52 the following season. Despite being under the spotlight in the hockey mecca that is Toronto, he was not one to utter any headline-grabbing quotes—or much of anything, for that matter.

"Bruce Gamble is such a dead-panned character that you probably wouldn't know it if somebody put cow-itch in his underwear," Milt Dunnell of the *Toronto Star* wrote of Gamble's taciturn nature.

Dunnell went on to observe that "Gamble, the goalie with the blackjack dealer's sideburns, plays with the stolid fatalism of a man who knows he's a member of the suicide squad and is prepared to await the inevitable."

Such as the conversion to a mask? Gamble was finally swayed in the spring of 1970, having absorbed from a distance the details surrounding an injury suffered by Jacques Plante—then of the St. Louis Blues—in Game 1 of the Stanley Cup Final against Boston.

"I guess I've been lucky," an atypically expansive Gamble told the Canadian Press in May 1970. "I was hit only once this past season and took six stitches. Normally I could expect to be cut three or four times over the season but it happened just once last year. Look what happened to Plante in the playoffs. He says himself the mask saved his life. I think that's fair warning to all the rest of us. I'm wearing a mask next season."

This goalkeeper was also a keeper of his word.

By 1971–72, the NHL's maskless minority had been pared to three—Andy Brown, Joe Daley, and the ageless Gump Worsley.

Daley had actually worn a mask for a brief time after being introduced to the NHL with the expansion Penguins, only to experience a change of heart. Through his final three NHL seasons, Daley was reliably maskless while playing for the Penguins (1969–70), Buffalo Sabres (1970–71), and Red Wings (1971–72).

En route to the NHL, and even after reaching the big leagues, Daley repeatedly crossed paths with a like-minded individual—namely Brown. The two mask-averse goalies were teammates in Baltimore, which was Pittsburgh's AHL affiliate from 1967 to 1970. Brown and Daley were also members of the 1971–72 Red Wings, although not at the same time.

After the 1971–72 season, Daley signed with the Winnipeg Jets, with whom he would play during all seven seasons of the World Hockey Association's existence.

Brown eventually migrated to the WHA after playing in only 62 NHL games over three seasons. He made 10 appearances with the 1971–72 Red Wings and seven more with Detroit the following season before being traded to Pittsburgh on February 25, 1973. He played in nine games with Pittsburgh that season and another 36 with the 1973–74 Penguins.

Brown was a part of barefaced-goalie history in both of his NHL stops.

On December 31, 1972, he was between the pipes for Detroit against Minnesota, which started Worsley for the first time since November 22. That turned out to be the final NHL game in which both goaltenders were maskless. In fact, it was the first time Daley and Worsley faced one another—literally, you might say.

Worsley even notched an assist, his third (and last) as an NHLer, after a J.P. Parisé shot eluded Brown. The Red Wings and North Stars settled for a 4–4 tie. The Gumper made 22 saves, two more than Brown.

Although Worsley was the dean of maskless goalies in the NHL, he was not the last. He ended up wearing a mask during his final big-league season, 1973–74, at the urging of North Stars goaltending cohort Cesare Maniago.

It was Brown, then, who became the final NHL holdout. He was maskless throughout his time in the NHL—an abbreviated tenure that concluded April 7, 1974, when he tended goal for Pittsburgh against the Atlanta (now Calgary) Flames.

(The night before, Brown and the Penguins had defeated Philadelphia 6–1. Brown carried a shutout into the 56th minute before Bill Barber scored for the Flyers.)

Brown's NHL denouement was far from triumphant, as the Flames doubled Pittsburgh 6–3 in Atlanta. (We'll never know, but one can only hope that the organist seized the opportunity to play Sweet Georgia Brown.)

Brown's final NHL game was well-documented by the *Atlanta Journal-Constitution*. The newspaper published a sequence of three photographs, taken by George Clark, showing Brown—labelled in the caption as "the NHL's Only Unmasked Goalie"—making one of his 25 saves, on Butch Deadmarsh of the Flames (a second cousin of future big leaguer Adam Deadmarsh).

For the record, Rey Comeau was the final NHL player to score on an intentionally maskless goalie—that goal coming at 13:41 of the third period. After another 6:19 ticked away, the game was over, and so was Brown's brief time in The Show.

Brown then waddled, as goalies do, to the visiting team's dressing room at The Omni. The omnipresence of barefaced goalies having been rendered a distant memory, the NHL's last link to the old groupthink would no longer appear at the game's highest tier.

PART TWO: GABBING WITH GREATNESS

6

"My Face Is My Mask"

Gump Worsley and the danger of being a Ranger

On the same day Andy Brown became the NHL's last intentionally barefaced goaltender, the most-renowned member of that all-but-extinct fraternity punctuated his hockey career in atypically inconspicuous fashion.

Gump Worsley was on the Minnesota bench on April 7, 1974, for the North Stars' season-ending 6–2 loss to the host Philadelphia Flyers, who ensured that opposing goalie Fern Rivard received plenty of exercise. It was a strenuous weekend overall for Rivard, who the previous evening had been the losing goaltender as the New York Islanders won 4–2 in Uniondale, New York.

A masked Worsley had played his final game as a precursor to the back-to-back, season-ending starts by Rivard. On April 2, 1974, Worsley—six weeks shy of his 45th birthday—was in goal for Minnesota in its 6–3 loss to the visiting Flyers.

"I would have liked to have gone out of here as a winner, but then I would have liked to have gone out in the playoffs, too," Worsley told Chan

Keith of the *Minneapolis Star*. "But you can't have the best of everything, and the way hockey has been good to me, I ain't complaining."

The game was tied 3–3 before Philadelphia erupted for rapid-fire third-period goals by Bill Flett, Ross Lonsberry, and Dave Schultz. The Flyers' sixth goal—the last of 2,398 Worsley surrendered in his NHL career—resonated with the grandfatherly goalie.

"[Schultz] was born the year I played my first pro game in 1949," Worsley wrote in his autobiography, *They Call Me Gump*. "That made me feel old. Probably too old to consider another comeback. Probably."

Schultz was just 3½ months old when Worsley took part in his first training-camp workout with the Rangers, on September 20, 1949, in Lake Placid, New York.

"I certainly must have looked like a sad sack when I showed up at my first Ranger camp in 1949," wrote The Gumper, who spent most of the 1949–50 season with the Eastern Hockey League's New York Rovers. "I was carrying only a single extra pair of slacks and a sport coat in the suitcase my father had loaned me, plus some underwear which I figured to stain as soon as I got a chance to play."

Worsley had grown up in Montreal, not far away from the famous Forum. Initially a forward, he was only 4'11" and 85 pounds at age 14.

"I never got much taller," Worsley told Dick Irvin Jr., "but I got fatter."

The lack of stature prompted a minor hockey coach, Phil Walton, to suggest that Worsley was too small to play any position except goaltender. Even at that young age, Worsley was almost universally known as Gump, as opposed to Lorne.

"George Ferguson, a boyhood friend in Montreal, gets the credit," Worsley recalled in *They Call Me Gump*. "I had a crew cut in those days and my hair stood up like Andy Gump's in the old comic book [The Gumps].

"[Ferguson would] whack the back of my head and say, 'Come on now, Andy Gump, let's get going.' Soon other guys started calling me 'Gump,' and then everyone did.

"At least they didn't call me 'Shorty' or 'Piss Pot.'"

Besides, *They Call Me Piss Pot* would not have been a tasteful title for a memoir.

During a colourful playing career that spanned a quarter-century, The Gumper was known not only for his stellar goaltending—he entered the Hockey Hall of Fame in 1980—but also as an all-time classic character who is fondly remembered by ex-NHLer Marc Habscheid.

"When I was growing up in small-town Saskatchewan, we had an old black-and-white TV and we had only one channel, so Saturday night—hockey night—was a big deal," reflected Habscheid, who was born in 1963. "You'd see Gump Worsley playing for Montreal or the North Stars and you'd be going, 'Wow!'

"He was a scout for Minnesota after he played, and the only time I met him was in Portland, Maine. I didn't get to talk to him too much, but he was just an infectious guy. He was laid-back. He didn't take things too seriously. He just had a good way about him.

"And even though I was in my early 20s when I met him, it was still 'Gump Worsley!'"

He was the same in person as he usually was on the ice—maskless.

"Goalies are a different type, anyway, so that just added to his personality," Habscheid continued. "The goalies back then had incredible personalities. At that time, you'd see goalies with cigarettes and beers in their hand. It was just the uniqueness of the time.

"They weren't too worried about having a kale salad back then."

An ale salad, maybe. Worsley once was accused by a coach of having a beer belly. The garrulous Gumper jokingly took exception, saying: "He should know better than that. He knows I only drink scotch."

And the cigarettes…?

"I've always smoked between two and two-and-one-half packs a day," he acknowledged in *They Call Me Gump*. "A bad habit? I suppose it is, but I've never been able to kick it. Maybe it's because I never really tried."

The only time he vehemently objected to smoking was when fumes were billowing out of an aircraft.

"One of the first plane rides I ever took was with the Rovers. And it was almost my last," Worsley remembered in his autobiography—a collaboration with writer Tim Moriarty. "We had played a game in Milwaukee and were returning to New York on a two-motor prop job. I think it was a Viscount. I was sitting there nervous as hell when one of our guys yelled, 'Hey, there's smoke coming out of the engine.' I figured that was the end. But the pilot managed to extinguish the fire and make an emergency landing in Pittsburgh.

"Perhaps you've heard about my fear of flying. Well, it all began on that night in November 1949."

Worsley's NHL career began on October 9, 1952, shortly after he was hurriedly summoned from the Pacific Coast Hockey League's Saskatoon Quakers as an emergency replacement for Charlie (Chuck) Rayner.

The veteran Rangers goalie sustained a severe charleyhorse—a Charlie-horse, in this case—and was consequently unavailable for the 1952–53 season opener against the defending Stanley Cup champions from Detroit.

An Associated Press story indicated that Worsley was "flown in by plane" from Saskatoon—the other option being, ohhh, a dirigible?

Worsley, who was referenced as "Lorne" in newspaper coverage of the Red Wings' 5–3 home-ice victory, was quickly initiated into the NHL by three players he would eventually join in the Hall of Fame. Ted Lindsay, Alex Delvecchio, and Gordie Howe scored to give Detroit a 3–0 first-period lead.

Although the score hinted at an inauspicious big-league debut for Worsley, Rangers head coach Bill Cook wouldn't have any of that.

"On what he's shown, Worsley is a threat to take Rayner's job, even when Rayner recovers from all his injuries," Cook told the *New York Daily News*.

The case in favour of Worsley was reinforced when, in his second NHL game, he stopped 32 of 34 shots in a 2–0 loss to the host Chicago Black Hawks.

The losing continued, as did the plaudits, when the Rangers lost 3–1 in Montreal. Although Worsley and his team both sported 0–3 records out of the gate, his 34-save gem was touted by the *Daily News* as "one of the best goaltending exhibitions seen here [in Montreal] in years."

Worsley continued to impress, only to be flown back to Saskatoon—by plane, once again—after Rayner recovered. The Gumper's stay in

Saskatchewan was short-lived, however, and he eventually returned to the Rangers and made Cook look prophetic by registering a 3.02 goals against average and two shutouts in 50 games—impressive numbers for a netminder on a bad team, which was 13–29–8 with Worsley in goal.

Perhaps he deserved a medal of valour, but he was forced to settle for the Calder Memorial Trophy, which is annually bestowed upon the NHL's top rookie. The celebration was surprisingly short.

"Gump Worsley was the only goaltender who won a rookie award and spent the entire next season in the minor leagues," Hall of Fame hockey broadcaster/author Dick Irvin Jr. noted.

Upon returning to the NHL in 1954, Worsley customarily shouldered a heavy workload in the days before backup goaltenders.

The tireless efforts were conventionally unrewarded. During 10 seasons with the Rangers, Worsley was 204–271–101 despite reliably registering a save percentage that comfortably exceeded .900. His win percentage: 44.2.

Even then, the number does not tell the entire story. The Rangers actually won a mere 35.4 per cent of those games, the ties having elevated the figure into the 40s.

No wonder Worsley, when asked which team gave him the most trouble, memorably deadpanned: "The Rangers."

He had another pet phrase, a rote reply to inquiries about the lack of a mask in his puck-stopping paraphernalia: "My face is my mask."

And occasionally a mess. The perils of the position were exemplified on February 5, 1961, when André Pronovost of the Bruins fired a shot that was deflected before hitting Worsley near the left eye.

"The Gumper went down holding both hands over his face and rolled over on his back," Jim McCulley reported in the *Daily News*. "It took a couple of minutes for Gump to regain his senses. Then he wobbled off to the dressing room, using two teammates as crutches."

The game was delayed 25 minutes as stitches were applied to gashes above and below the left eye. McCulley noted while documenting the Rangers' 5–2 victory that Worsley "played the final 52 minutes of the contest with only partial vision in the injured orb." He nonetheless carried a shutout bid into the 55th minute.

As was his wont, Worsley made light of the circumstances and occupational hazards.

"I got a beautiful shiner," he told head coach Alf Pike as the Rangers prepared to hit the road, "but my vision's almost normal and I'm making the trip."

Playing for the Rangers was hardly a pleasure trip. By the end of the 1962–63 season, he had appeared in 590 NHL games (only 14 of which were of the playoff variety).

He eventually received a long-overdue reprieve—inclusion in a June 4, 1963, trade that sent him to his hometown Canadiens. Going the other way in the blockbuster was Jacques Plante, who had unveiled his mask while facing Worsley and the Rangers on November 1, 1959.

Plante said several years later that Worsley would have been the first masked goaltender if not for the objections of Rangers head coach Phil Watson.

"Plante is full of hot air," Worsley snorted in a 1971 interview with the *Toronto Star*. "Look, put that in your column. I never heard Watson even mention a mask.

"Only time I ever tried one was when I was with the Rangers. We used to work out at the Iceland rink, which was over Madison Square Garden. The guy who was our practice goalie was a television man. He had this plastic outfit that looked like a welder's mask. One day, I asked if I could try it. It just happened that I picked up the reflection from the lights when I went after a high shot. Couldn't see a thing—so I ducked.

"I threw off the mask. That was it."

When that *was* it for Worsley with the Rangers, it was suddenly Plante's turn to experience the miseries of Manhattan, NHL-wise, whereas the other goalie in the deal had landed in hockey heaven.

On the day of the trade, a giddy Gump revelled in the repetitive radio reports.

"As I sat there listening to that bulletin every 30 minutes, I felt like a man who'd just been let out of prison," Worsley wrote in his autobiography.

That said, he would still face the occasional firing squad—namely the Black Hawks, led by legendary gunner Bobby Hull. The hazards presented by The Golden Jet were all too evident on March 7, 1965, when his searing shot hit Worsley on the right cheekbone during the waning seconds of the Canadiens' 7–0 loss at Chicago Stadium.

"Gump never saw the puck," Jim Hunt wrote in *The Men in the Nets*. "It hit him on the right side of the head and he slumped unconscious to the ice. As the Montreal trainer and the players of both teams gathered around the fallen goalie, a deathly hush fell over the arena.

"Gump was taken to the hospital and when he regained consciousness the first face he saw was that of Hull, who felt this might have been the moment he dreaded [because the Golden Jet had always worried about seriously injuring a goalie]. Gump spent the night in a Chicago hospital. But he was lucky to escape with no more than a severe bruise. The puck, fortunately, had turned in flight and the flat face had caught him rather than the more lethal edge."

Earlier that evening, in an eerie coincidence, Worsley had engaged in a chance pregame conversation with a fan.

"Well, Gump, what do you think?" he was asked.

Gump's priceless response, documented by Pat Curran of the *Montreal Gazette*: "If I could ever think, I'd never have been a goaltender."

By that point, The Gumper had been a goaltender for most of his 35 years. His games-played total, including time spent in the NHL and in the minor leagues, was approaching 1,000. Who knows what the stitch count would have been for the then-maskless Montreal marvel?

"A mask is great for the kids coming up and I guess it has prolonged the careers of some goalies," Worsley told Curran. "Terry Sawchuk figures he's been able to last four more years with the mask. At the same time, I still think that it's tough to follow the puck around your feet."

It was a tough job, period, and not one for the faint of heart.

"Face cuts and stitches shouldn't count as injuries in hockey," Worsley, pointing to a lengthy scar on his right arm, told Curran. "This is from a cut tendon when I got clipped by Bobby Hull's skate and the blood flowed like soup in New York five or six years ago."

By no means was it chicken soup, considering the courage demonstrated by Worsley as, with minimal protection, he faced projectiles launched by elite shooters and, in at least one instance, a gormless spectator at Madison Square Garden.

"Somebody threw an egg from the upper balcony and it came down and hit Gump in the head," said former NHL forward Red Berenson, who was a teammate of Worsley's during that March 12, 1967, meeting with New York.

Worsley was forced to leave the game with a mild concussion. A maskless Rogatien Vachon went the rest of the way in goal in a 2–2 tie.

"The egg-tosser, a 25-year-old fan who had a bag of them when caught by Garden police, got off lucky when Worsley refused to press charges," the *Montreal Gazette* reported.

Worsley was pressing in another sense. Even though he would play for four Stanley Cup winners and share in two Vezina Trophy wins with the Canadiens, a confluence of adverse circumstances was taking its toll on his nerves.

Early in the 1968–69 season, The Gumper was frustrated by a lack of playing time. Vachon, with whom Worsley had shared the Vezina Trophy in 1968, was the far busier of the Canadiens' two goalies. Worsley was not enamoured of the team's new head coach, Claude Ruel. Factor in a fear of flying and, well, it all reached a boiling point in the form of a nervous breakdown.

As Worsley recounted in his autobiography, the first leg of the Canadiens' trip to Los Angeles was a traumatic one. The Gumper got off the plane during a stopover in Chicago and, right then and there, decided to retire.

"I was through with those bumpy plane rides and Claude Ruel and the Montreal fans," read a portion of *They Call Me Gump*. "They could all stuff it."

Not long after travelling back to Montreal via train, Worsley saw a psychiatrist.

It was not a path The Gumper had envisioned back in 1957, when he was featured on the cover of *Hockey Blueline* magazine. The cover story was headlined "I'll Never Crack Up" by Gump Worsley.

The story appeared a few months after Boston goalie Terry Sawchuk stepped away from the game due to a case of nerves.

Worsley's response, told to Dave Anderson in 1957 and excerpted by puckstruck.com in 2016, read in part:

> "When are you going to crack up?" they say. First of all, it's not funny because Sawchuk is a sick guy. Second of all, I'll never crack up.
>
> I don't believe all this talk about "nerves" because a goaltender is under fire all the time. If that's the case, I should be the first one to crack. They shoot more at me than any goaltender in the National Hockey League.

Just over a decade later, Worsley overcame a case of the "nerves" and eventually rejoined the 1968–69 Canadiens. Over the course of the season, he put up customarily solid numbers, registering a 2.26 goals against average, five shutouts and a 19–5–4 regular season record. In the playoffs, he appeared in seven more games, but rode the bench for the entire Stanley Cup Final—a four-game sweep of the St. Louis Blues.

Things didn't get much better in 1969–70. With Vachon entrenched as the No. 1 goaltender, Worsley was asked by general manager Sam Pollock to join the Canadiens' AHL affiliate, the Montreal Voyageurs, for a temporary conditioning stint. A grumpy Gumper balked, declaring once more that he was retiring. He was suspended without pay.

His only action during the next two months was on behalf of a touring Canadiens old-timers team. It was all a prelude to a trade, and a rebirth as an NHLer, at the tender age of 40.

Worsley was dealt to Minnesota for the always-popular "various considerations" (principally cash) on February 27, 1970, by which time he had played only six full games during the 1969–70 campaign. He promptly signed a new contract, calling for a substantial raise, with the North Stars.

One thing did not change. The Gumper was still intractable in his opposition to donning a mask—at least during a game.

"I wear one in workouts when they're not paying me to stop pucks and, believe me, I've got nothing against them," Worsley told author Jim Proudfoot in the early 1970s. "I'm just too old to change. I don't feel comfortable in one, although I know that if they'd come up with them when I was young, I'd have made the switch."

The switch to Minnesota worked out fabulously for a rejuvenated Worsley. Content to play in every second or third game in tandem with workhorse Cesare Maniago, The Gumper continued to excel at stopping pucks while easing into his 40s.

Near the midpoint of the 1972–73 season, the North Stars' brass was pleased with Worsley's play. He did not share that assessment, as demonstrated by the announcement in January 1973 that he was retiring.

"I came to the point where I don't think I can do it anymore," he told reporters. "I don't want to take the club's money under false pretenses."

Unaccepting of that self-appraisal, North Stars general manager Wren Blair opted against filing Worsley's voluntary retirement papers with league headquarters. Good thing, too. The Gumper was bitten once again by the hockey bug and, at 44, returned to the team the following autumn for one more year.

Despite a rekindled enthusiasm for the game, another retirement—by now, we have lost count—was on the horizon. So was the once-jarring sight of The Gumper with a mask.

"The North Stars were training at the Met [Center] one day and Cesare Maniago was being fitted for a new mask," Worsley wrote in *They Call Me Gump*. "He'd been badgering me about wearing one since I'd joined the club in 1970. Now he went to work on me again."

Maniago: Why don't you give it a try, Gumper?

"Naw. Why should I worry about my kisser now? It's my last year."

You say that every year.

"This time I mean it, Cesare."

That's just another reason why you should wear a mask. Why take chances now?

"I'll think about it."

But not for much longer. Maniago's powers of persuasion prevailed.

All Hail Cesare!

"My wife had been begging me to wear one, so I finally surrendered and ordered a mask from the same fellow who was outfitting Cesare," Worsley wrote.

The mask was molded by Bill Cossette of Roseville, Minnesota, in time for the 1973 preseason.

"Aw, I just did it to keep Cesare quiet," Worsley told Dan Stoneking of the *Minneapolis Star*. "I don't know what I'm going to do with it. I really doubt I'll ever wear it."

Not on the ice, anyway.

"Maybe I'll get it and wear it on Halloween night," Worsley quipped.

Stoneking noted in his September 23, 1973, story that Worsley had briefly tinkered with a mask in 1954.

"I had it on for a cup of coffee," he told the *Star* writer. "The first shot came at me with a mask on and I ducked."

Within a few days of being interviewed by Stoneking, Worsley wore a mask during a game—a September 25, 1973, exhibition engagement with Toronto at Maple Leaf Gardens.

That was a prelude to October 13, 1973, when Worsley sported the mask for a regular season game against the Buffalo Sabres.

"Rick Martin and John Gould scored against me in the third period as we lost 4–3," Worsley wrote. "I was having trouble spotting the puck at my feet, so I used a file to widen the eye slits."

Worsley was then idle until October 25, when Minnesota met the Islanders.

"It was a warm night, and during the warmup I had trouble breathing so I decided to play without the mask," Worsley recounted. "The game ended in a 1–1 tie. I drilled more holes in the mask for better ventilation, but this tends to weaken it. So I was now worried about a puck shattering the mask and pieces going into my eyes."

As the season progressed, playing time became increasingly scarce for the venerable goaltender. After starting in goal on November 30, 1973, when the North Stars edged the host Vancouver Canucks 5–4, Worsley did not play again until the new year—January 9, to be precise.

Wearing a mask for the first time since October 13, he made 25 saves in a 2–2 home-ice tie with Detroit. After the game, he told *Minneapolis Star* sports editor Max Nichols that the intent was to continue with the face gear.

The workload soon intensified due to a hand injury sustained by Maniago, who had implored Worsley to give the mask a second chance after the abbreviated early-season makeover.

"The mask wasn't too uncomfortable, so I kept it on and it seemed to give me confidence," Worsley wrote. "I played in eight of our next 10 games, including a stretch of six in a row. It was just like the old days."

It was all a preamble to April 2, 1974, when Worsley played his final NHL game.

The following September, he voluntarily signed his retirement papers...again. But he wasn't finished with the North Stars.

One of the sport's most-beloved players soon transitioned into the role of a highly recognizable scout. And he kept on making stops, appearing (maskless) at arenas throughout North America for 14 years after retiring—for good—as a player.

One scouting excursion took The Gumper to Victoria, British Columbia, where the Western Hockey League's All-Star game was played in 1981.

One of the participants was future NHL goalie Kelly Hrudey, who was then a major-junior player with the Medicine Hat Tigers.

"The day before the game, we have a practice, and Gump Worsley's there," Hrudey recalled. "He's in the stands and I recognize him.

"The puck was at the other end of the ice and I think I may have even been leaning on my crossbar with my arm. And I hear, 'Hey, hey, Kelly!' I look up in the stands and there's Gump, motioning for me to come out of my crease."

Fortuitously, the whistle soon blew, and a water break ensued—enabling Hrudey to meet one of his idols, who had some sage advice to impart.

"He comes down and says, 'Kelly, always make sure that you're outside your crease so that when the play turns over and they start coming at you, you're already in good position. You don't have to skate out seven feet and get ready now. You're already in the position you need to be in,'" continued Hrudey, a 1980 Islanders draftee.

"That was a 'wow' moment for me, because he didn't need to do that. He's scouting for a different team. He doesn't need to give me any pro goalie tips.

"I thanked him immensely—and I thought, 'Wow, was that ever gracious of him to give me a pro tip, for no other reason than he was just a nice man.'"

7

Hull-abaloo

Facing Bobby Hull: Even an owner needed a mask

Appearance-wise, Cesare Maniago was the antithesis of Minnesota North Stars goaltending cohort Gump Worsley. Whereas Worsley was a compact 5'7", Maniago stood 6'2½" and was therefore a towering figure in the goaltending fraternity.

In fact, Maniago was labelled as "the tallest of all professional goaltenders" by Dana Mozley in the January 8, 1966, edition of the *New York Daily News*. Today, a goalie in the 6'2" range would be slightly on the shorter side. Someone of Worsley's shrunken stature? Unthinkable.

The Gumper's longevity is also a throwback. He did not retire as a player until 1974, when he was pushing 45. By then, Maniago was comfortably into the masked portion of his lengthy NHL career.

Maniago had flirted with facial protection during the 1962–63 season after being called up from the minors by the Montreal Canadiens due to Jacques Plante's recurring asthma attacks.

"Cesare came out to practice and he's skating around with a mask on. Toe Blake, the coach, just glared at him," broadcaster/author Dick Irvin Jr.

said. "Cesare didn't say anything. One of the players said to him, 'Cesare, you'd better take that thing off or you're going to be in trouble,' so he did, and he never wore it, because Blake hated the concept of it."

Maniago played in only 14 games with the 1962–63 Canadiens. He then toiled in the minors until 1965, after Montreal traded him to the New York Rangers. Maniago began the 1965–66 season in the minor leagues, because the Rangers had opted to retain Ed Giacomin and Don Simmons. Early in 1966, however, New York called up Maniago from its farm club in Maryland and bumped Giacomin to Baltimore. Gone by then was the mask with which Maniago had tinkered while with the Canadiens and as a minor leaguer.

"Unlike Zorro, The Lone Ranger, and Jacques Plante, who became famous when they put their masks on, Cesare Maniago didn't get ahead until he took his off," Red Foley wrote in the *Daily News* on January 6, 1966, adding that Maniago "isn't anti-face mask. He agrees they do afford protection, but feels his vision is partially blocked."

Maniago played in 28 games with New York over the second half of the 1965–66 season. Noteworthy was a March 12, 1966, game in Chicago, where Maniago was in net when Bobby Hull became the first NHLer to score more than 50 goals in a season.

Early in the following season, a maskless Maniago lost two teeth during a game against the Toronto Maple Leafs. He did not play again for 2½ weeks. Even then, it was a rare appearance in the crease for Maniago, who also experienced back problems during a 1966–67 season in which he played in only six NHL games. Giacomin's stellar play also rendered Maniago expendable.

Maniago received a long-awaited break in June 1967, when the 28-year-old netminder was Minnesota's top pick (fourth overall) in the expansion draft. Chosen ahead of Maniago were three future Hall of Fame goaltenders—Terry Sawchuk (claimed from Toronto by the Los Angeles Kings), Bernie Parent (Philadelphia Flyers, from the Boston Bruins), and Glenn Hall (St. Louis Blues, from Chicago).

Never again would Maniago play in the minors. His career reborn in Minnesota, Maniago began the 1967–68 season without a mask. There wasn't any concealing his brilliance, as evidenced by a December stretch in which he became the first big leaguer since Hall, with Detroit in 1955, to register three consecutive shutouts.

As a North Star, Maniago was becoming increasingly amenable to wearing a mask, which he did from time to time.

"In the two seasons Maniago has been patrolling the Minnesota net, Cesare has only used the mask for special occasions—in practice sessions and against the Chicago Black Hawks," Dan Stoneking wrote in the *Minneapolis Star* on October 14, 1969. "The Hawks [known to most NHL goalies as those headhunters from Chicago] seem to believe the best way to score goals is to bank the puck in off a goaltender's chin."

Maniago explained the rationale in a story that appeared in the *Minneapolis Tribune* on September 28, 1968. Staff writer Dwayne Netland began the article by noting that Maniago had just worn a "helmet" (i.e., mask) for the first time in nearly 10 months.

"Anytime we are playing the Chicago Black Hawks, the helmet goes on," Maniago explained. "I don't like to wear one, but against that club I believe it's the only sensible thing to do."

Hull's blistering blasts weren't the only reason Maniago donned the extra armour versus Chicago.

"They all fire the puck high on that team," he told Netland. "It's strange that there are so many of them with one club. Usually, a team has four or five guys you've got to worry about, but with the Black Hawks you can go right down the line...Bob and Dennis Hull, Stan Mikita and Kenny Wharram, Doug Jarrett, Pat Stapleton...the works."

Netland went on to cite a home game from the 1967–68 season, in which a blast by Hull "caromed off [Maniago's head], ripped into the stands and broke a fan's nose."

The Golden Jet also struck twice that season when Garry Bauman was in goal for Minnesota. He was injured by a Hull howitzer on back-to-back Sundays.

In the first instance, the masked Minnesota 'minder stopped a shot with his collarbone and was knocked out of the game. Enter Maniago, who was promptly pelted by Hull.

"Bobby hit him from far and near, wrist and slap," Ted Damata wrote in the *Chicago Tribune* after the Black Hawks won 2–1 on November 26, 1967. "Maniago even gloved a couple of bullets, considered foolhardy if not impossible."

One week later, Bauman started again against Chicago and survived what was described by Damata "as a glancing blow to the top of the head," compliments of Hull.

An unruffled Bauman remained in the game and backstopped Minnesota to a 4–3 victory. Bauman's opposite number, barefaced Denis DeJordy, was not as fortunate. He took a puck on the chin in the first period and was forced to leave the game—but not before facing one more shot. DeJordy's day was done after he allowed a 50' goal by Ray Cullen, who had also unleashed the shot that found the goalie's chin. While 12 stitches were being applied to DeJordy, Dave Dryden finished up in goal for Chicago.

"When I saw Garry get hit, I made up my mind to try a mask next time we played Chicago," Maniago told Stoneking during the 1968 preseason. "If it works well during these exhibition games, I'll wear it when we face the Hawks during the regular season."

Maniago went several steps further, in fact, sporting a mask throughout his final 10 NHL seasons—eight more with Minnesota, followed by two with the Vancouver Canucks.

Always congenial and candid, Maniago was a logical candidate to be interviewed for a *Sport* magazine story about Hull.

"Someday, he'll kill somebody, whether it's a goalie, a defenceman, or a fan," Maniago said in 1969. "Someone's going to get it, because a lot of his shots not only go wild around the rink but into the stands."

Pittsburgh Penguins goalie Les Binkley added: "I've always thought that somebody's going to get killed by his shot."

Oakland Seals goaler Charlie Hodge chimed in: "If Hull ever hits anyone dead-on with his shot, there's a good chance of killing him, because that puck moves something terrible."

And there was this from the Kings' Gerry Desjardins: "I'm frightened of Hull. Of course, there isn't a goaltender around who isn't scared."

So, what was it like to face Bobby Hull?

"I was afraid you'd ask that question," Parent said with a laugh, "but I'll answer your question.

"I remember when he would come down the ice, between the blue line and the faceoff circle. He was a big guy with big shoulders and he had the curved blade. He would wind up and I would put my hand in front of my face and say, 'God, please let him score!'

"My God, he was dangerous. Anybody else, let him shoot, but as far as Bobby Hull was concerned, do whatever you can to not let him shoot. As a matter of fact, his shot was clocked at 118, 120 miles per hour."

More than a few goalies were clocked in the cranium by The Golden Jet's blistering blasts.

"Bobby Hull hit me in Chicago, and it ricocheted off the top of my head," former Boston Bruins goalie Ed Johnston said. "It ripped the skin off. A half-an-inch more and he would have killed me. Thank God it didn't hit me an inch or so below that."

That sentiment wasn't exclusive to Johnston. Jim Hunt, who authored *The Men in the Nets*, asked Worsley: "What would happen if a goalie got hit in the head with the full force of a Hull slap shot?" Gumper's blunt retort: "They'd get out the box and put them in it. There's no way he could survive."

It never came to that, thankfully, but during the 1960s an increasing number of goaltenders realized that all possible precautions needed to be taken. In a 2011 book, *The Devil and Bobby Hull*, author Gare Joyce noted that "Hull did more than any player to popularize face masks for goalies, more even than Plante."

Consider the case of Maniago, who shelved his reservations about wearing a mask when he encountered Hull, who played for Chicago from 1957 to 1972 before joining the Winnipeg Jets of the nascent World Hockey Association. He starred in the WHA—to which his arrival lent instant credibility—for all seven seasons of its existence after signing a 10-year, $2.75-million mega-contract.

Hull's best years in Winnipeg were spent on a legendary line with Swedish sensations Anders Hedberg and Ulf Nilsson. The Hull–

Hedberg–Nilsson troika, which left opponents dizzied and demoralized from 1974 to 1978, revolutionized the game with its free-wheeling, criss-crossing style.

"You'd follow Hedberg and Nilsson toward the net and then you'd look back and there was Bobby, winding up with his 150-miles-per-hour shot," said former WHA star forward Dennis Sobchuk, exaggerating only slightly. "You'd just stand there and cringe. When you heard the puck hit the glass, then you could open your eyes again.

"Could you imagine being a goalie and facing Bobby Hull without a mask?"

Moreover, imagine being Harold Ballard—the irascible Toronto owner who habitually watched his team's home games alongside a dear friend, King Clancy, at Maple Leaf Gardens.

"They looked like the Muppets up in their little box," said former Chicago gunner Dennis Hull, The Golden Jet's brother. "One time, Bobby shot one off the crossbar and hit Harold Ballard in the head. He had a big cut on his forehead or around his eye.

"Billy Reay was our coach and it was Harold Ballard who had fired Billy when he was in Toronto, so now Harold Ballard wanted to come into our dressing room to show Bobby what had happened to him. And when he walked in the door, Billy grabbed him and said, 'Get out of here!'"

Dennis Hull, no slouch himself, scored 303 goals—coincidentally, the same number that his big brother registered in the WHA—over 959 NHL games, most of which were spent with Chicago.

The younger Hull, who assisted on his brother's 1,000th NHL point, peaked at 40 goals with the 1970–71 Black Hawks and added 39 two years later.

The Hulls, teammates with Chicago for eight seasons, boasted searing slap shots that made rival goaltenders go, "Oh, brother…"

"The difference between Bobby's shot and my shot was obvious, though," Dennis, the uncle of Hall of Fame marksman Brett Hull, wrote in a 1998 autobiography, *The Third Best Hull*. "Bobby could shoot a puck through a car wash without getting it wet. I couldn't hit the car wash."

Dennis Hull's shot was therefore more unpredictable and, in a sense, of greater danger.

"I always said with Bobby and Dennis Hull, who had the two hardest shots in hockey, that Dennis would scare you a little bit, but I wasn't too worried about Bobby because he'd usually score," Hall of Fame netminder Gerry Cheevers said. "That means it didn't hit me."

Such was the case when Cheevers allowed two of Hull's milestone NHL goals—his 400th (January 7, 1968) and 600th (March 25, 1972). Additionally, Hull scored twice against Cheevers on March 20, 1969. That evening at Boston Garden, Hull tied and broke his own NHL single-season goal-scoring record of 54, set in 1965–66. He finished the 1968–69 campaign with 58 goals, while scoring on 14 per cent of his shots. Dennis, who scored 30 times, had a shooting percentage of 12.9.

Bobby's career accuracy rate, taking into account his time in the NHL and WHA, was 14.8—3.2 per cent higher than that of his brother.

"The one I used to sort of enjoy and fear at the same time was Dennis Hull, because Dennis, I thought, had an even harder shot than Bobby," former NHL and WHA goalie Dave Dryden noted. "But with Dennis, it took him longer to release it. He'd get the stick back and then he'd come down and, by the time he actually made contact with the puck, I could be 20 feet out of the net, almost right in front of him, and he would drive it right into my pads. But it was intriguing, because the era with Bobby and Dennis and Stan Mikita was the big boomerang stick era."

Yet, a number of goalies continued to stare down the Hull brothers, Bernie (Boom Boom) Geoffrion, et al, while either going maskless or wearing a form of facial coverage that provided only a thin layer of protection, if it could be so termed.

Complicating matters, they faced shooters, such as Hull, whose stick blades were bent as much as three inches before the NHL intervened and took steps to flatten the curve. The maximum curve was limited to an inch and a half, effective in the 1967–68 season. The limit was subsequently changed to one inch, then a half-inch, before an enduring compromise was reached at three-quarters of an inch more than 50 years ago.

"No one in sports in the late '60s was more courageous than goalies when you had sticks with the big banana hooks," former NHL goalie Glenn (Chico) Resch said. "There was just a lack of control. On bad angles, guys would say, 'The goalie's playing really well tonight. If you get a sharp-angle shot where you're not going to score anyway, down by the goalie, just try to hit him right in the face. Try to hit him in the head.'

"Bobby Hull was very good about blasting high. Oh, he shot that puck! You had no idea where it was. You didn't see it. He had that hook. But Dennis was more jovial and, on bad angles, he would waste them. And then he'd chuckle and say, 'Oh, that one just about got you, didn't it?'

"Mickey Redmond also had one of those great shots. His was heavy and hard. And you can't blame them. They're thinking, 'If I can get an edge and get this goalie scared...'"

That isn't just a shell-shocked goalie talking.

"That was part of the deal," Dennis Hull acknowledged. "Rogie Vachon, the goalie in Montreal, used to watch us during the warmup or our morning skate, so Billy Reay would say, 'Shoot some high ones off the crossbar.' So we would do that, and poor old Rogie was shaking even before he got to the game that night."

For years, the debate raged: Which Hull had the hardest shot?

In 1968, *Popular Mechanics* magazine did a story in which Bobby Hull's slap shot was reported to have a peak velocity of 118.3 miles per hour. The Sports College, based in Toronto, once recorded a Hull blast at 119.5 mph.

"Even Hull's backhand, clocked at 96 miles an hour, is 10 miles faster than the average NHL player's forehand," Jim Hunt wrote in his 1966 biography of Hull, whose skating speed with the puck was once measured at 28.3 mph.

"Hull's own forehand has been timed at 105 mph. The goalies don't stand a chance when he lets fly from close to the net. The average netminder, according to the tests Sports College has conducted, needs 2/10ths of a second to start his hand moving; 4/10ths to get his leg going. A Hull shot from 20 feet out, or less, is travelling so fast that it is in the net before the goalie can move."

Hunt went on to observe that Hull's slap shot was "so powerful that it has knocked down goalies and ripped the gloves off clutching hands."

In conversation with Hunt, Johnny Bower described a Hull shot from the vantage point of a goalie who was situated 60 feet away from firing range.

"It was a black blur heading straight for my right ear," the Maple Leafs' netminding legend said. "I straightened up and tried to take it on my chest but it was too fast and caromed in off my forearm. It felt like I had been seared by a branding iron."

The Black Hawks' boomer was so feared, in fact, that a chapter in an authorized biography—*The Jacques Plante Story*—is titled "When Hull Shoots, I Must Not Blink."

"Exaggeration? Not a bit," Plante told collaborator Andy O'Brien. "If you blink when he belts a slap shot, even from the blue line, you have to pick up the black blur of rubber again and it's too late unless he hits you. And hitting you can really hurt, despite a goaler's padding.

"A Hull shot has left my arm numb and useless for several minutes, forcing me to skate to the bench for relief. In catching his shot, I try to take the puck in the webbing of my glove; if it hits fingers or palm, a shock goes up in my arm like when you grab one of those electrical gadgets in an amusement park."

Exacerbating the challenge, a Hull shot did not travel at a reliable trajectory.

"Sometimes it drops four or five inches," Plante noted. "You have to see it to believe it."

The problem was that goalies couldn't see it—or believe it, for that matter. But, oh, could it be heard!

"One day at the Chicago Stadium at practice, there was a group of kids who were blind," Dennis Hull recalled. "Billy Reay said, 'You and Bobby shoot up against the glass, because they want to hear it, and they can tell you who has the hardest shot.' So we shot up against the glass and the kids said, 'The second shot.' That was mine."

Also worth noting is the fact that non-goalies—most of whom opted not to wear helmets—were hardly immune from the rigours of the game.

"[With] the amount of ice time, the style of game he played, the equipment, everything, I have no doubt that Bobby Hull took more punishment on the ice than anyone who ever played the game," ex-Black Hawks forward Jim Pappin told author Gare Joyce.

"He didn't start things and he didn't retaliate, so a lot of the toughest guys in the league took liberties with him. He figured if he stayed in the game, rather than end up in the penalty box, he gave his team the best chance of winning."

Hull entered the 1963 Stanley Cup playoffs with an injured shoulder. That turned out to be the least of his worries. In Game 2 of a semifinal series, Hull was accidentally clipped in the face by the stick of the Detroit Red Wings' Bruce MacGregor. Black Hawks team physician Dr. Myron J. Tremaine told the *Chicago Tribune* that Hull had "a fracture of the orbital bone along the left side of his nose and rather extensive internal injuries of the nose." He also required 10 stitches on the bridge of his thrice-damaged nose.

The headline from the *Tribune*: "STAR'S NOSE IS MANGLED IN 5–2 STANLEY CUP VICTORY."

Hull missed the series' third game, which Detroit won 4–2 to reduce Chicago's lead to 2–1. He was back in the lineup for Game 4, won 4–1 by the Red Wings. Ted Damata from the *Tribune* wrote that Hull's return was "a surprise move," considering that "the man with the smashed nose" had a fractured orbital bone and a bruised right shoulder in addition to being weakened by a loss of blood. Nonetheless, Hull scored Chicago's only goal in Game 4.

Hull tallied once more in the fifth game, a 4–2 Detroit victory at Chicago Stadium. (The *Tribune* referred to the Black Hawks' loss in supposedly advantageous surroundings as "Home-icide.")

Detroit won 7–4 on April 7, 1963, to end the best-of-seven series in six games. Hull figured in all four Chicago goals, scoring three times and adding an assist.

"It was a remarkable display of hockey guts and ability because Hull should have been in a Chicago hospital," read a portion of the editor's note in The Golden Jet's eponymous autobiography, published in 1967.

"In a previous game, his nose had been smashed up so badly the fracture reached up to his skull. Although the doctors advised against it, Bobby left the hospital and flew alone to Detroit to join his team. Chicago's coach pleaded with him not to play, but he wouldn't listen. While Bobby played, one eyeball was totally red with blood and a nose cast restricted his vision. An injured shoulder cut down his shooting effectiveness, but with skill and courage he scored enough goals to win a normal game."

Fast forward to December 25, 1968, when Hull did not enjoy a Merry Christmas. Instead, he suffered a broken jaw in a 4–3 home-ice loss to Toronto.

"I missed one game while playing six weeks with a wired jaw," Hull wrote in *The Golden Jet*, published in 2010. He wore a protective helmet, with a football-style face guard, during the recuperative period.

"Why did this athlete, the greatest shooter in hockey, jeopardize not only his brilliant career but also possibly his life to play in a game against the wishes of the doctor and of management?" Damata wrote after the Hulls combined for three goals—two by Dennis and one by Bobby—in a 4–1 victory over Los Angeles.

"Because," The Golden Jet managed to say through gritted teeth, "they're starting to call me Dennis' brother."

A more serious explanation was offered in a 1969 interview with Lee Mueller of the Newspaper Enterprise Association.

"When you turn out for the team, you grab a position and hold it," Bobby Hull said. "Nothing keeps you from showing up for the game each week, not even if you're hurt—broken bones or anything. There are 15 kids waiting to take your place, so you'd better be there."

How many goaltenders, barefaced or not, had echoed those sentiments over the years?

"You can't even let 'hurt' enter your mind," Hull, who died at 84 on January 30, 2023, told Mueller, in that 1969 interview, emphasizing the need to mask the pain.

8

Bower Power

Ageless Toronto goalie finally turns over a new Leaf

Johnny Bower—known as The China Wall—took an unforgettable shot to the face in the 1960 Stanley Cup Final.

An image of the save is accessible via YouTube, to which "videobutch1" posted a 9½-minute clip titled "Montreal Canadiens win 5th consecutive Stanley Cup—1960 color film."

Fast forward to 1:41, when you can see Bower's left cheek absorb the impact of a rebound shot from Marcel Bonin, moments after the Toronto goalie foiled the initial attempt by Dickie Moore.

"Right in the face!" wrote a commenter, using the handle of RK Larkin. "But China Wall just nods it off and looks to make the next save."

Sprawling in the crease, Bower barely blinked while doing his utmost to prevent Bonin from scoring on another rebound. The Montreal attacker's follow-up backhand attempt sailed just wide of the net in the fourth and final game of the championship series.

"That is exactly the play that Brent Butt references in his stand-up," the goalie's grandson, John Bower III, said of the popular Canadian comedian. "He had a routine from years ago where he talked about hockey and he talks about J.B. He said, 'You see him stick his head out like a tortoise to stop the puck with his face.' That is so true.

"It's unbelievable and unfathomable to me that somebody would have played hockey without a mask."

Bower's opposite number in that 1960 game, Jacques Plante, registered a shutout as Montreal won 4–0 and celebrated NHL supremacy for an unprecedented fifth consecutive season. Plante therefore became the first masked goalie to win a title.

Bower, for his part, remained among the unconverted for most of the 1960s, even as other goalies, one by one, were opting for a modicum of facial protection.

"Grandpa just decided that, playing goal, he was going to lose his teeth," Bower III said, "and he was fine with that."

By the time Bower wrapped up a career that made him an automatic enshrinee in the Hockey Hall of Fame, he had sacrificed his teeth and accumulated an estimated 250 stitches.

"As long as I knew Grandpa, he always had false teeth—all of them," said Bower III, who was born in 1974. "When I was a kid, he used to pop them out of his mouth and we'd laugh. He'd let us play with his dentures."

Some of the dental damage was done on January 28, 1953, when Bower, then of the Cleveland Barons, was hit in the mouth by a John McLellan shot during an American Hockey League game against the Pittsburgh Hornets.

"The flesh was torn inside and outside of my mouth, as my teeth cut right through it," Bower told Bob Duff when they collaborated on the goalie's autobiography, *The China Wall*. "A four-foot bridge was knocked out, a pivot tooth crumbled, a front bridge was destroyed, one anchor tooth was knocked out and another cracked. Another front tooth fractured at the gum line.

"It took 12 stitches to patch me up and plastic surgery in the summer to make me beautiful again. Dr. Philip Faix, who treated me, called it the worst injury to a goaltender that he'd ever seen. I'd lost eight teeth and taken 40 stitches to my face by this point in my career."

Regardless, Bower wanted to go back into the game after receiving medical treatment, "but I was overcome by dizziness from the loss of blood when I tried to return."

That was three games later.

"When I came back," he told Duff, "I did so with this giant white bandage across my upper lip that resembled an oversized moustache."

Another day in the life of a barefaced goaltender.

"People always marvel at how we goaltenders take a shot in the face like that and frequently, after getting stitched up, come right back in to continue facing the barrage of rubber, but we never thought it was that big of a deal," Bower continued. "When you get cut, it's numb anyway for the first 30 minutes. You might feel it a bit while they're doing the stitches, maybe a little more the next day, but that's all. Then they put you back in there.

"It was a way to test you, in a sense, I guess. Then they find out if you're puck-shy or not. If you can play with injuries, if you don't pull up on shots after something like that, then they know they've got themselves a pretty good guy in the nets.

"On the other hand, maybe people have been right all these years. When I think about all the punishment I took, it could be that you have to be nuts to be a goaltender.

"Honest to God, we didn't even think of putting on a mask back then. I never would have thought of that at the time when I was a kid. I just learned to duck, I guess, that's about all.

"I got knocked out a few times. I had my nose broken five times. I got hit in the mouth. When you get hit in the mouth and over the eyes, that's a little scary. It happened mostly on deflected shots.

"You'd get hit over the eye, it'd swell, there'd be a lump. So they'd put the leech on. The trainer kept them in a solution on the infirmary shelf and he'd take one out with a pair of tweezers and place it next to the lump. The leech would edge over, examine the lump, then clamp on to it and have a meal. It would get fatter and fatter and then, pop, down he'd go and the swelling around the cut would go, too."

Such were the times. The harsh realities of the era were underlined when Bower was plunked in Pittsburgh.

With Bower out of the equation, Floyd Perras—the Barons' promotional manager and occasional practice goalie—was summoned from the stands to take over in net. Back in Cleveland, Bower's wife was understandably worried while listening to the broadcast.

"Nancy was still waiting for news on the radio," Dan Robson wrote in *Bower: A Legendary Life*. "She hoped the team would have the sense to take Johnny to a hospital in Pittsburgh. When Nancy got a call saying her husband was travelling home on the team bus that night, she was incredulous. She waited and waited for him to arrive. Hours later, when he finally walked in the door, Johnny held a filthy-looking towel to his face, covered in blood."

The bloodied red Baron was in such a bad way that, at 3:00 AM, Nancy successfully implored her husband to seek immediate medical assistance.

"He almost bled out that night," said Bower III, whose grandfather remained in hospital for several days.

Bower was quite a sight when he returned to the lineup. He was modelling a brace on his jaw and a bandage that covered his upper lip.

"Johnny simply viewed it as a test," Robson wrote. "If he didn't get right back in the net—or if he did but flinched when a puck was shot at him—it would show that he was scared to play. He had to show that he wasn't.

"At the time, wearing a mask in a game didn't cross his mind. Sometimes he wore one in practice. It was a clear piece of Plexiglas that looked like something a welder would wear.

"Johnny hated it. Every time he wore it, it would fog up and he wouldn't be able to see anything. So, despite his missing teeth, Johnny wasn't about to start wearing a mask in games."

That philosophy was unalterable even when, in March 1953, Bower underwent a procedure to remove a bone chip from his upper jaw. Only then was it determined that he had also suffered a broken jaw on that injurious evening in Pittsburgh.

"My grandfather's tolerance for pain was incredible," Bower's grandson said.

The same description—incredible—was applicable to Bower's play with the 1952–53 Barons.

"That season, Geoffrey Fisher, a reporter from the *Cleveland News*, started to refer to Johnny as 'the China Wall' in his reports," Robson wrote. "Fisher first used the reference to describe how impenetrable the Barons goalie was after he'd posted a couple of shutouts. Johnny picked up the paper one morning and saw Fisher's 'China Wall' reference. He loved it."

The eighth-year Baron was then pushing 30 and had played 450-plus games of professional hockey without spending as much as a millisecond in the NHL. That would soon change.

In July 1953, the New York Rangers acquired Bower's rights from Cleveland. The deal was made even though Rangers goalie Gump Worsley had just won the Calder Trophy as the NHL's top rookie.

The Rangers were obviously enticed by the fact that Bower had been named the AHL's top goaltender in 1951, 1952, and 1953. At the time of the trade, he had also backstopped the Barons to two of the past four league titles.

"If Cleveland wasn't an independent team, Johnny would have been in the NHL long ago," an unidentified *New York Daily News* staff writer opined on July 21, 1953, adding: "Bower is bigger and steadier than little Gump Worsley, whom he'll have to beat out of the Rangers' job."

Mission accomplished. The Rangers dispatched Worsley, then 24, to the Vancouver Canucks of the old Western league. Bower proceeded to play every minute of all 70 games with the 1953–54 Rangers, only to be supplanted by Worsley the following year.

"My grandpa always hoped that he could get a shot in the NHL with the Rangers, and he had a great season," Bower III said. "But he came to camp the next year and rested on his laurels. It was one of the few times that he kind of lived high on the hog. Gumper came back into camp in better shape."

So it was Bower's turn to be optioned to Vancouver.

"When I finished that [1953–54] season, I thought, 'Oh boy. It took me a long time to get here, but I've made it,'" Bower told Dick Irvin Jr. "Then when they sent me down the next season, it hurt quite a bit. I felt, 'Jeepers, what did I do wrong?'

"But I didn't give up, because it was my life. As a kid, I wanted my name engraved on the Stanley Cup so much, and even after all those years I kept figuring that someday I was going to get a break. Finally I did."

But it took a while. Although he did make five appearances with the 1954–55 Rangers, most of that season was spent in Vancouver. For the next two seasons, he stopped pucks on behalf of the AHL's Providence Reds, save for a two-game stint with New York in 1956–57. Then it was back to Cleveland for the 1957–58 campaign.

Well into his 30s, Bower could have given up. But he loved the game, the money was good by the standards of the day, and his goaltending was even better.

Hence, the Maple Leafs claimed him from the Al Sutphin-owned Barons on June 3, 1958.

"Even though Grandpa was selected in the intra-league draft, he was under no obligation to sign with the Leafs," Bower III noted. "He chose to sign with the Leafs after Mr. Sutphin guaranteed that he'd have a place with the Barons if he got cut. That's what kept him going."

At 34, Bower quickly became a mainstay with the Maple Leafs, helping them win Stanley Cup titles in 1962, 1963, 1964, and 1967 and becoming as popular as he was identifiable.

"The fact that he didn't wear a mask is important, because people could recognize his picture," Bower III said. "We've got a lot of *Hockey Night in Canada* videos where they zoom in. There's J.B. tapping the goal posts, and you could clearly see his face. A lot of it has to do with the fact that they were maskless, helmetless, at the time. It's also a testament to the fact that player safety is focused on a lot more than it was back when Grandpa played."

Bower made a series of brilliant saves in Game 2 of the 1967 championship series, recording a 3–0 shutout in Montreal despite suffering (just like Bower, you'll never see this one coming) an inadvertent face wound.

Diving for a loose puck, Bower was hit in the mug by John Ferguson's stick. The Montreal enforcer had accidentally clipped the personable puck-stopper while being checked by defenceman Larry Hillman. Toronto trainer Bob Haggert quickly dashed out on to the Montreal Forum ice.

"Blood poured from Johnny's nose," Robson wrote. "He tried to dab out the bleeding with his glove."

The trainer asked if Bower wanted to leave the game. The response: "I'm hot! Just leave me alone! Don't bother me!"

In response to a similar inquiry from head coach Punch Imlach, Bower said: "I'm OK. Just give me something to wipe away the blood."

Bower ended up stopping all 31 shots he faced. After the game, reporters quizzed him about the facial wound.

"Nothing serious," Bower responded while sitting next to goaltending cohort Terry Sawchuk. "It's like Punch Imlach says: 'A hurting nose doesn't hurt anybody.' Right, Terry?"

Sawchuk's lighthearted retort: "Not unless you get knocked out."

Bower saw his personal stitch tally increase only two days after he blanked Montreal in the 1967 Stanley Cup final. During practice, a Frank Mahovlich shot bonked Bower in the chin. Undaunted, he played in Game 3, which Toronto won 3–2 in double overtime at Maple Leaf Gardens. The 42-year-old marvel was credited with 61 saves.

"Johnny Bower has to be the world's greatest athlete," Imlach told reporters after Toronto assumed a 2–1 lead in the best-of-seven series. "Bower is the oldest guy, playing the toughest position of all in the fastest game there is. Sure, he's amazing. Name me somebody in any sport who compares to him."

As luck would have it, Bower would not make another appearance in the 1967 final. In the warmup before Game 4, he pulled a muscle in his left thigh. Sawchuk took over and played the final three games of the series, including the clincher—a 3–1 Toronto home-ice victory on May 2, 1967.

When Bower returned to the net the following autumn, he was wearing a mask. It had been designed, according to Robson, by "a young dentist named Richard Bell—who, Johnny said, had actually tragically died that summer."

Robson expounded that, shortly before Bell lost his life in a car accident, he and Bower "had been working on making the nose smaller so Johnny could see the puck better beneath him."

Robson continued: "The mask was made of fibreglass. Johnny hated wearing it. The sweat pads in the helmet were soaked after every practice. Whenever he wore it, sweat rolled down his face and into his eyes. Then he struggled to locate distant shots and to see the puck in scrambles around his net.

"During an exhibition game against the Rochester Americans, he made a stick save without even reacting because he hadn't seen the shot. When the puck hit him he was visibly startled, and the crowd broke out laughing. Johnny came out for the second period without the mask. He managed to put off the shielded visage for another year."

Then he put it off some more, buoyed by a new contract with the Leafs.

"Grandpa was one of the lowest-paid Leafs," Bower III said. "Punch Imlach basically said, 'You're here because I'm here, and I can get rid of you,' even though he would never get rid of Grandpa. J.B. always had this fear that he was always going to get cut."

Well, he did get cut, but only by flying pucks, errant sticks, and other foreign objects.

Despite his value to the organization, Bower continued to perform *sans* mask during the 1968–69 regular season, although he was warming up to the idea.

"I never liked masks," the Saskatchewan-born Bower wrote in his autobiography. "When I was a kid growing up in Prince Albert, I played a little baseball. I was the catcher, but I didn't like a mask at all, so I went behind the plate without one.

"To be honest, I only got hit a couple of times on top of the head with foul tips. After a short time, though, I came to my senses and thought, 'Hey, I better start wearing a mask.'"

At least in baseball, anyway.

"It didn't happen so quickly in hockey," Bower continued in *The China Wall*. "It was dangerous, for sure. One game, I got a skate blade in the mouth, which took two molars out through my cheek. I needed 45 stitches to close the gash.

"Still, I was always reluctant to wear a mask in net. I tried one during several practices, but I found it fogged up and I couldn't see. It also kept falling down my face and I had to bend my head to see the puck. Then I was hit on the top of the head and cut for eight stitches, so I put the mask idea behind me for quite some time, but after nearly a quarter-century of facing pucks barefaced, it finally happened."

By then, even the seemingly ageless goaler was 44 and no longer at his peak. He had been relegated to backup duty behind 30-year-old Bruce Gamble, who was in his 12th season of pro hockey.

Gamble continued to gamble by playing without a mask and consequently paid a painful price on January 19, 1969. With 13:53 remaining in a game in Boston, Ken Hodge deflected a Phil Esposito shot off the goalie's head.

"Gamble, blood spurting from a cut that would require six stitches to close, staggered off the ice," Ray Fitzgerald wrote in the *Boston Globe*.

Enter Bower—an old goalie with a new look. He was wearing a mask for the first time in a regular season game.

"He is maybe 23 years too late," Fitzgerald opined, "because John Bower's face looks like a road map of Toronto. Stitch marks, angry red welts and white-lined scars fight for attention on Bower's mug. He did not win all the battles with the enemy, the well-struck hockey puck."

Bower was in goal for a span of 7:40 in the third period before a patched-up Gamble returned to the net. It was Bower's 533rd NHL appearance, but only his 15th of the season. Nonetheless, it was a career landmark due to the rare disguise, worn in compliance with Imlach's wishes.

"As he put me in, he said, 'From now on, you've got to wear a mask,'" Bower wrote in *The China Wall*. "I wore it for 17 games in the regular season, but I never did like it.

"Sure, I'd used one in practice for years, but that was simply as a precaution. In Cleveland, I'd used one that was a clear fibreglass mask simply for protection to keep me from getting cut or hurt. When I went to Toronto, I kept wearing it, but I didn't like the looks of it. Punch told me I'd better go to Boston and get one made like the rest of the goalies were doing at the time."

Next stop: St. Louis, where the Maple Leafs battled the Blues in the second leg of a seven-game road swing. Gamble started again and, for the second consecutive game, required medical attention after taking a puck in the head. Cue a second-period cameo by Bower, who saw duty for three minutes eight seconds before Gamble resurfaced.

Bower would appear in only 20 games during the 1968–69 season, registering a 2.86 goals against average—his highest as an NHLer—and two shutouts.

On April 2, 1969, the Maple Leafs began the playoffs by losing 10–0 in Boston. A masked Bower relieved Gamble after two periods.

The Bruins breezily swept the Maple Leafs in a best-of-seven quarter-final, after which Imlach was fired. Bower played in all four games against Boston, making two starts.

Gamble was again the workhorse for the Leafs during the 1969–70 season, making 52 appearances. Marv Edwards tended the twine for Toronto in 25 contests. Bower, for his part, continued to practise with the Maple Leafs but did not see any live combat through the first 24 games.

The first start finally arrived on December 10, 1969, when the Leafs lost 6–3 in Montreal. Even though it was his first action for the first time since the Leafs' intra-squad game, he stopped 33 shots by the Canadiens, whose final goal was an empty netter.

Bower continued to serve as a backup before injuring a knee during practice on December 29, 1969.

"I tried to come back from my knee injury, but things just weren't going my way," he wrote. "I came home one day and I told Nancy, 'I can't go on any longer. I'm letting in a lot of long shots in practice that I shouldn't be and I think it could be because my eyes are going.'"

Bower's retirement became official on March 19, 1970. He made the announcement at a media conference, in tandem with Leafs general manager Jim Gregory.

A story distributed by the Canadian Press noted that Bower, 45, was "the only player in the NHL who became eligible to collect his pension while still an active player."

A fixture in the professional hockey ranks since 1945, Bower was at peace with the decision.

"I don't feel too bad about bowing out of active playing," he told reporters. "I thought it would be worse than it is. I felt better when Mr. Gregory offered me a job with the organization, because I'm still going to be with the players. I'm going to enjoy it real [sic] well."

The reference to "job" in the singular was somewhat deceiving. Bower had actually transitioned into a dual role—that of scout and goaltending coach.

The newly appointed assistant joined a Maple Leafs coaching staff that was headed by the very same John McLellan who, during a 1953 minor league game, unleashed a shot that unintentionally, but injuriously, hit Bower in the mouth.

9

Life of a Legend

Sawchuk surname still symbolizes greatness

Jerry Sawchuk is as talkative as his famous father was taciturn.

And why wouldn't that be the case? People around Detroit are still talking about Jerry's famous dad—a man as intriguing and sometimes controversial as he was legendary.

As one who resides in White Lake, Michigan, within an hour's drive of Detroit, Jerry carries a surname that is especially recognizable in that region. In fact, the Sawchuk name—prominent in hockey circles for more than 70 years—still resonates with fans whose grandparents are too young to have seen him play.

"It blows my mind," Jerry Sawchuk marvelled. "There's a goalie on my grandson's team. He's out there flopping around and the coach says, 'What are you doing?' He says, 'I'm playing like Terry Sawchuk.'

"This is a 10-year-old kid. Where did he get that?"

Jerry Sawchuk was quick to answer his own question.

"What amazes me is, that after all these years, his popularity is coming back," he continued. "With the Internet, these young kids are researching everything."

If someone is conducting even the most perfunctory research into the history of goaltending, or of hockey in general, it does not take long for "Terry Sawchuk" to pop up on a computer screen or in a book.

There are various contexts in which he can be studied, ranging from staggering successes to suffocating stresses to the saddest of endings.

At the time of Sawchuk's death—in 1970 at age 40—he was the NHL's all-time leader in regular season victories (445) and shutouts (103). If he had retired from the game at, say, age 30, he still would have been a mortal lock for enshrinement in the Hockey Hall of Fame.

Sawchuk, inducted in 1971, is one of only 10 players for whom the Hall's three-year waiting period has been waived. The others: Dit Clapper (1947), Maurice Richard (1961), Ted Lindsay (1966), Red Kelly (1969), Jean Béliveau (1972), Gordie Howe (1972), Bobby Orr (1979), Mario Lemieux (1997), and Wayne Gretzky (1999).

The same year Sawchuk posthumously entered the Hall, he was named the recipient of the Lester Patrick Trophy in recognition of myriad contributions to hockey in the United States.

Sawchuk made that lasting imprint while enduring the physical and mental toll that was exacted by a gruelling game.

The rigours of the sport and a most unforgiving position had been underlined just four years before Sawchuk's death, when he posed for a *Life* magazine photo.

"They were just trying to show what a brutal position it was, or what he went through," Jerry said. "I don't think there's anybody in the National Hockey League who went through what he did and still performed."

Life enlisted a makeup professional and a physician to, well, doctor the appearance of a man who, even without the artistic liberties, was still battle-scarred.

What was going on inside that head, no one knows for sure. Neither mental health issues nor the notion of acquired brain injuries were much considered back then. Facial injuries, accumulated over a generation in the NHL, were much more visible.

Jim Hynes and Gary Smith wrote in *Saving Face* that "according to some sources, [Sawchuk] received as many as 600 stitches in his face as well as two broken noses, punctured lungs, a broken instep, and ruptured discs in his back as a result of playing goal."

The authors' take on the portrayal by *Life* of Sawchuk was that he "looked something like an early sci-fi villain: Half-human, half-alien, and brutally unhappy."

"I always felt he was a victim of his profession," Joe Falls wrote in the *Detroit Free Press* after Sawchuk died, "and so I always felt a little sorry for him."

Falls had squabbles with Sawchuk, not unlike many other members of the media, but the columnist's last word on the oft-troubled goaltender was one of compassion.

"They've always said it takes a special kind of person to be a hockey goalie," Falls observed in his column on June 1, 1970. "Well, Terry Sawchuk was a special kind of person.

"Hockey held an overpowering lure to him. He was like the moth and hockey was like the flame. He knew that the flame would consume him if he got too close to it, and yet he was unable to stay away from it.

"Actually the only time Sawchuk was happy...completely, totally happy...was when he was in those big, brown, bulging pads, with his legs dangling over the trainer's table and a cigarette dangling from his lips, and he was exchanging insults with his teammates."

Those were the days when nobody talked about sports psychologists or was attuned to mental-health issues. Sawchuk's state of mind was well-documented, but did anyone reach out in the hope of helping the man? Hindsight being infallible, it seems that he was left to suffer in virtual solitude. In that respect, he was far from alone.

"Of all the stormy and troubled occupations of man, none is filled with more ups and downs than that of the goalkeeper for a professional hockey team," Trent Frayne wrote in a December 19, 1959, *Maclean's* magazine story that was headlined "The awful ups and downs of Terry Sawchuk."

"The mere physical nature of the job compels its tenant to hurl himself, legs and arms asprawl, to a concrete-hard sheet of ice as many as thirty times in a sixty-minute game, then spring erect in the next split-second in the uncertain hope that a steel-hard rubber disc is not about to clunk him on the head at a speed of a hundred and twenty miles an hour.

"Emotionally and psychologically, the big-league goaler faces even greater and more perilous shifts of fortune. His single mistake can cost his teammates the victory that represents thousands of dollars in playoff money, a charge that can never be made so strongly against the forward who misses an open net or the defenceman who misses a check. These mistakes can be amended; a goalkeeper's never can. He either stops the puck or the red light goes on.

"Of all the great members of the craft, none has ever suffered more ups and downs than Terry Sawchuk, the masterful and complicated young man who guards the padded cell for the Detroit Red Wings."

The article was prefaced by a description of Sawchuk as "a moody veteran"—and "the greatest goalie of all"—whose "life on the ice and off is just one crisis after another."

Early on, there was the aforementioned, potentially career-ending shot to the face that resulted in three stitches being applied to the right eyeball of an 18-year-old Sawchuk.

The stress encountered in the intervening years was such that Sawchuk's weight fluctuated from a low of 162 pounds to a peak of 219. After reporting to the Red Wings' training camp at the latter weight, he soon dropped 40 pounds, but at a greater cost.

"By then, the pressure of the job had got to Sawchuk and he was never able to regain the lost weight," Jim Hunt wrote in *The Men in the Nets*. "If there was a point in his career at which Sawchuk changed for the worse it was when he was forced to take off all that weight. Sawchuk's pleasant disposition seemed to vanish with the fat. Where he had once been jolly and care-free he became grim and morose."

Hunt noted that a case of the nerves forced Sawchuk to sit out three games in 1955. John McGourty of nhl.com wrote in 2009 that Sawchuk suffered "at least two nervous breakdowns." On top of depression, he endured a struggle with alcohol, a divorce, and a litany of injuries and ailments.

By age 22, Sawchuk had already undergone three operations on an elbow. One surgical procedure involved the removal of 60 bone fragments.

"I've been collecting all the parts they take out of me," he told a reporter in 1954, the same year in which Jerry was born. "I have one bottle for the teeth I've lost, another for bone chips, and another for my appendix.

"I know it sounds odd, but what's the difference between that and collecting stamps or old coins? Not many people have the chance to get the collection I have of old pieces of me."

Sawchuk also collected accolades, uncomfortable as he was in the spotlight.

Through it all, he was able to play for 21 seasons and win four Stanley Cups—three with Detroit (in 1952, 1954, and 1955) and one with Toronto (1967).

In 1952, he helped Detroit win all eight of its playoff games. His postseason shutout total (four) approached the number of goals he allowed (five) during an 8–0 postseason that is unmatched by any goaltender. The goals against average: 0.63.

Fifteen years later, Sawchuk's already-tender left shoulder absorbed a scorcher from Chicago's Bobby Hull in the Stanley Cup Final. Leafs trainer Bob Haggert rushed on to the ice, surveyed the damage, and eventually asked Sawchuk if he could remain in the game.

"I stopped the [bleeping] shot, didn't I?" he growled, as recalled by legendary Toronto sportswriter Dick Beddoes. "Help me up and I'll stone those sons of bitches."

That was business as usual for someone who won or shared in four Vezina Trophies (in 1952, 1953, 1955, and 1965) and was named a first- or second-team NHL All-Star seven times.

The outset of Sawchuk's NHL career has few parallels. The goals against average was under 2.00 in each of his first five seasons, all with Detroit. He boasted a double-digit shutout total in four of those seasons.

If ever there was a franchise goaltender, a young Sawchuk seemed to fit that description. What's more, he was the template for such a player.

Nonetheless, he was dealt to the Boston Bruins in 1955 by a ruthless Red Wings boss.

"Jack Adams ruined him," Jerry Sawchuk said. "The son of a bitch treated him terribly and made him lose the weight and put the pressure on him. He was just never the same after that. He still performed and did well, but he wasn't the same. Jack Adams did a number on him. When he got traded to Boston, that killed him."

Things were so bad that in January 1957, Sawchuk walked out on the Bruins and declared that he was finished with hockey, to the chagrin of general manager Lynn Patrick and head coach Milt Schmidt.

Sawchuk—at 27, already one of the game's all-time goaltending greats—was spent, having encountered a strength-sapping case of mononucleosis and reaching the brink of a nervous breakdown.

"Neither Schmidt nor Patrick appeared capable of grasping what should have been obvious: Terry Sawchuk was an emotionally troubled and physically sick young man who deserved to be cut some slack," Brian Kendall wrote in *Shutout: The Legend of Terry Sawchuk.*

"In his eagerness to help his team, Terry had damaged his health first by coming out of the hospital too soon, and then by continuing to play to the point of breakdown—all because he didn't want to disappoint his general manager, coach, and teammates."

Sawchuk met the media on January 21, 1957, and read from a prepared statement, noting that his nerves were shot, his sleep was fractured, and his appetite was non-existent.

"I'm still under contract to the Boston hockey club, which has always treated me very well," he said. "But my health, for my family's sake, is certainly more important than any monetary consideration."

Although Sawchuk had kind things to say about the Bruins organization, he never got over the June 3, 1955, shocker of a swap with Boston—even though he would be dealt back to Detroit following a 1956–57 campaign that, for him, had ended around mid-season. By the fall of 1957, however, he was back in goal with the Red Wings—for better or worse, the latter scenario often applying.

"Goaltending can be hell," Jacques Plante once said. "How would you like it if every time you made a mistake in your job, someone turned on a red light so 20,000 people knew you had made a mistake and could criticize you?"

The stress was such that, not unlike Sawchuk, prominent puck-stoppers such as Gump Worsley and Roger Crozier later stepped away from the game for brief periods due to frayed nerves.

Bill Durnan, who won six Vezina Trophies with the Canadiens, retired for good—due to jangled nerves—in the midst of the 1950 playoffs. Durnan was succeeded in the Montreal net by Gerry McNeil, whose fine career was also shortened by anxiety.

Not to be forgotten is erstwhile Maple Leafs goalie Frank McCool, who was descriptively nicknamed "Ulcers."

"No wonder some of those guys had ulcers. Who wouldn't, right?" said Kelly Hrudey, a mental health advocate who tended goal in the NHL from 1983 to 1998.

"I can't imagine Glenn Hall playing over 500 consecutive games and the fear that he would have had. No wonder he threw up before every game. It would be terrifying to go into a game not wearing a mask and knowing the potential for injury is high."

Hall himself spoke to the issue in an interview with author/broadcaster Dick Irvin.

"There is a fear factor to playing goal," Mr. Goalie said. "I obviously can't speak for anybody else but, boy, is there ever."

Some coaches regarded fear as a positive emotion, as counterproductive as that may seem.

"When Jacques Plante put the first mask on, coaches and people around the league were like, 'Well, that's not a good idea. He's going to play without the fear,'" said Martin Biron, an NHL goalie from 1995 to 2014. "The goalies needed to have that fear to be at their best. [Many coaches and GMs] wanted them to be scared that they were going to get hit in the face so they would be very, very focused on the game. And then if you put a mask on, you're not going to be as focused, because you don't have that fear."

Jerry Sawchuk acknowledged the fear factor in a broader sense.

"Everything that motivated my father was based on fear," he told Bob Kravitz of espn.com in 1998. "Fear of injury. Fear of losing his job. Fear of life after hockey. Fear of somebody not being able to support a wife and seven kids.

"A hard life. A very hard life. Dad's death seemed almost natural. His hockey career was finished, and life off the ice had never been easy."

But Terry Sawchuk's adjustment to a mask was easier than expected. Once adamant that he would not cover his face, he eventually became the second prominent goalie—after Plante—to do just that. Why the eventual acquiescence?

"Did you ever hear of a guy by the name of Bobby Hull?" Jerry Sawchuk said with a chuckle, referencing the Chicago superstar—one of the first practitioners of a booming slap shot. "The sticks got curvier. The shots got harder. They got higher. It was time for a mask."

The transformation was not universally applauded—not even in the Sawchuk household.

"Even when I played goalie, I didn't wear a mask," Jerry said. "It's just what you did. You didn't think about it."

Terry Sawchuk's first game-used mask, manufactured by Red Wings trainer Lefty Wilson, can now be found in the Hockey Hall of Fame.

Jerry and his son, Jon, both carry an image of the original Sawchuk mask everywhere they go—thanks to Brent Davis, a tattoo artist from Hartland, Michigan.

The mask, or a likeness thereof, is now emblazoned in ink on Jerry's back. He also carries with him other reminders of life between the pipes.

"Teeth gone...stitches," Jerry began. "I had my sinuses shattered. They're screwed up to this day. I had multiple concussions from getting hit in the head.

"But you didn't think anything of it. You got hit. You got stitched. Away you went. That's just the way it was."

It didn't help that the protection in general was essentially a rumour.

"Black and blue marks were constantly there," Jerry said. "They had no padding on the arms. They had no padding in the chest. The catching glove was just a worn-out baseball mitt, with no padding. Even with the blocker, you'd have puck marks on your hand."

The Sawchuks, father and son, found a way to mitigate some of the damage that could be incurred by flying, and possibly errant, pucks.

"I used to hate practice," Jerry said. "My dad wouldn't practise. Oh, he'd show up and dress, but he'd stand next to the post and wave his stick at them.

"I asked him, 'Dad, why?' He said that he gets paid to play games, not to practise. He used to drive the coaches nuts, because he wouldn't work at his art. I don't know how he did it, but he did it."

But again...why? Considering the risks of playing the position, along with remuneration that pales in comparison to the stratospheric salaries commanded by today's players, both magnificent and marginal, who in their right mind would aspire to be a goalie?

"I don't know," Jerry said, the inquiry having elicited a chuckle. "Good question.

"Most of them, it was the kid who couldn't skate, but you had to be a good skater to be a good goalie. I don't know. It was just something I did. I started out doing it and it was my passion.

"With my father, his older brother [Mike] had passed [after suffering a heart attack at age 17], and he was a goalie. That's probably most of the reason he picked up his pads and went on.

"My dad always said, 'There are 80 forwards and four goalies at tryouts,' so the odds were in his favour."

In one respect, anyway. Remember, though, that there were only six teams in the NHL until 1967. For most of the pre-expansion era, there were only six big-league goaltending jobs, period.

"You didn't want to be out of the lineup," Jerry said. "There was always somebody to replace you. There was a lot of pressure.

"My dad got traded real quick, early in his career, and I don't think he ever forgot that. You're out. You're gone. The owners just abused these guys something terrible. If you got a career-ending injury, you were on your own."

So the gutsy goalies forged ahead, with periodic stoppages for stitches and bandages, and longer respites when the nerves became unbearable—and faces were far from un-bare-able.

"Life was different," Jerry reflected. "Life was hard-working. People were tougher. It's not like where you've got to have woke rooms now and everything like that. It was just a different breed of people."

Terry Sawchuk's toughness was such that he withstood flying pucks, persistent pressure, a 1953 car crash in which he sustained chest injuries, an appendix that ruptured and burst, imperious general managers, and cantankerous coaches.

He absorbed the hardest shots that were unleashed during NHL's Original Six era—first without a mask, and then with a face shield that was marginally protective—and did so while being treated like an item, as opposed to an icon. There were three stints with Detroit to go with stays in Toronto, Los Angeles, and New York, and the accustomed uprooting of a young family.

"We were kids," Jerry recalled. "We ran around the arena, like kids would do. In California, it was a little different. You always rooted for him and hoped he did well. You'd be nervous as hell for him. But it was just what he did. It was his job. You didn't look at it like he was the first star or anything special. It was just like your dad went to work every day."

An unforgiving vocation could shut down Sawchuk mentally and punish him physically. He endured the dangers and daggers of high-stakes professional hockey to the tune of 1,000-plus games and lived to tell about it, only to have a freak accident ultimately end his life.

Shortly after the 1969–70 season, Sawchuk and Rangers teammate Ron Stewart were involved in a dispute relating to the residence they rented on Long Island. The disagreement began at a pub and carried over into the players' backyard in East Atlantic Beach, New York.

During an alcohol-fuelled scuffle on April 29, 1970, Sawchuk took a spill and immediately writhed in agony while clutching his stomach.

Stewart eventually persuaded Sawchuk that medical attention was required. An ambulance was called and the great goalie was soon hospitalized, with three surgeries resulting.

Sawchuk's condition would improve as May neared an end, but he then encountered an irreversible decline. He died of a pulmonary embolism—a blood clot that lodged in an artery—on May 31, 1970, just 47 days after his final appearance in an NHL game.

Tributes poured in as the shocking news circulated about Sawchuk's death. The compliments were typically accompanied by reminiscences about a complicated man.

"He was the greatest goalie I ever saw, and the most troubled athlete I ever knew," Joe Falls wrote. "The first time I met Terry Sawchuk he was raging with anger and shouting obscenities and throwing skates at a reporter. This was in 1953. In all the years to follow, he never really changed."

Stewart, who was among the honorary pallbearers at Sawchuk's funeral, was eventually absolved of responsibility when a grand jury deemed the death to be accidental.

"Terry just kept coming after me," Stewart told the *New York Post*. "He fell on me, that's for sure, but all his lifetime, Terry took much worse falls on the ice and he always bounced back...and then he trips on me and suddenly his life is ended.

"It doesn't make sense. A fall like that, just like a thousand he's taken on that hard ice, and nothing ever happened to him. And this thing happened and Terry is gone. It's all like a bad dream when I look back now."

Imagine being a teenaged Jerry Sawchuk at the time.

"Don't forget, I'm a 15-year-old kid when my dad passed," he said. "I was just a young kid.

"That summer, I went to Kitchener [to play junior B hockey in Ontario] and it was intense. I put up with all the papers and the whole thing with my dad's death and being a superstar. I just wanted to be left alone.

"There was the pressure of playing goal. I played very well, but it was taxing. I played a couple of years and then, right in midstream, I went to forward. I got out of the goal.

"You've got to figure that everything I did ended up in the papers. I'm a 15-year-old kid. My dad just passed. It just wasn't fun—and there was a lot of pressure, especially when I was doing well. They put you way up on top [of a pedestal] and it just wasn't worth it.

"If he would have been alive, with the WHA coming in, who knows what would have happened? What better mentor to have?"

While the World Hockey Association was in its formative years, Jerry Sawchuk was a left winger with the Southern Ontario League's Detroit Junior Red Wings. He left the game after spending the 1975–76 season with the United States Hockey League's Traverse City Bays.

All these years later, Jerry is immensely proud of the Sawchuk surname—which belongs on a Mount Rushmore of Michigan sporting greats. With that in mind, he was asked what it is like to introduce himself as a Sawchuk in Detroit.

"I don't," he responded. "I sort of stay hidden. I just keep to myself a bit.

"My grandkids have got to live with that. I have a new grandbaby. We just sort of protect them. I protected my daughter when she played college. It's just something you don't go screaming about."

From what is he protecting them?

"I know what it's like to have the pressure on you," Jerry Sawchuk concluded, "and I won't let that happen to them."

10

Something's Bruin

Bernie Parent, Gerry Cheevers, and Ed Johnston

A parent of Parent was a notable influence in the area of facial protection.

In 1959, future Hall of Famer Bernie Parent—who won back-to-back Vezina Trophies while leading the Philadelphia Flyers to Stanley Cup championships in 1974 and 1975—was 14 and honing his prodigious goaltending skills in the Montreal minor hockey system.

A couple of cuts around young Parent's eyes had been a cause for concern even before his eventual mentor, Jacques Plante, first donned a mask in a game on November 1, 1959. Attentive to the landmark events of the day, Claude Parent issued an ultimatum to his son: "If you want to keep playing goal, you have to wear a mask."

Father knew best.

"I wore a mask all throughout my career," said Parent, who played in the NHL from 1965 to 1979 and, in fact, was the first regular NHL goalie to wear a mask for the entirety of his big-league career. (The first non-regular, in case you want to split hairs: Bob Champoux.)

Parent made his NHL debut on November 3, 1965, when he played for the Boston Bruins in a 2–2 tie with the host Chicago Black Hawks. He had been called up after only three minor league games with the Oklahoma City Blazers.

Injuries to Ed Johnston and Gerry Cheevers had left Boston without a goaltender. Cue the elevation of the 20-year-old Parent, who made 40 saves in his introductory NHL game.

Parent celebrated a milestone just 11 days later, registering his first NHL shutout—a 2–0 victory over the Toronto Maple Leafs.

"The occasion, naturally, was a great one for young Parent, who was grinning after he removed his mask and was mobbed by his exultant colleagues," Tom Fitzgerald wrote in the *Boston Globe*.

Parent's opposite number in that game was a still-maskless Johnny Bower. Parent, unlike Bower, did not sustain any serious injuries in the pre-mask period.

"I was very fortunate," Parent said at age 75. "This is why I'm so good-looking today.

"I got hit a few times, like all goalies, but I believed in the way the masks were designed."

When Parent was introduced to the NHL, however, there were still resolute anti-maskers.

"When the transition came, the goalies in the National Hockey League were used to performing without the mask and they had difficulty adjusting," Parent said. "If you look at guys like Terry Sawchuk, Gump Worsley, and Glenn Hall, they were great goalies, but you had some goalies who paid a big price for not wearing a mask. They had a lot of injuries, with deflections and shots.

"They eventually realized that wearing a mask was a lot better than not wearing one."

Parent—of a different vintage and possessing a comparatively unscathed visage—never gave the issue of wearing a mask a second thought after adhering to his dad's decree.

"I recall that there weren't any challenges as far as the mask was concerned," he said. "It was welcome.

"At the same time, it was rewarding, because every time they scored a goal, I would blame the mask. So at the beginning, it was a good asset on my part.

"I don't recall anybody objecting to me wearing a mask. It just made sense to everybody."

Not that the masks were the cure-all. Early models provided only moderate protection, especially in comparison to the current shells. But at least it was, well, something.

"At the beginning, anything that could save some injuries was good," Parent said. "Even that [original Plante mask] would save a lot of goalies from getting cut. In the beginning, it was still good protection. But they redesigned the mask and it was a blessing.

"Today's masks have a lot more protection. They've come a long way. Very seldom do you see goaltenders getting hurt these days. It's virtually non-existent."

During the 1966–67 season—Parent's last with Boston—two other goaltenders in the Bruins chain suffered serious injuries after being hit by a puck. And one of them was wearing a mask at the time.

Claude Dufour was early in his 11th minor league season when, on October 3, 1966, he suffered what turned out to be a career-ending injury in a non-game situation with the Hershey Bears.

"Dufour was brushed across the face by a puck in practice two weeks ago," the *Lancaster* (Pa.) *New Era* reported on October 19, 1966. "He did not complain, said [head coach Frank] Mathers, and he played in Hershey's first two games. His left eye started to bother him yesterday, so he was taken to a specialist who diagnosed the detached retina."

By February 1967, the 30-year-old Dufour had undergone three surgical procedures at Wills Eye Hospital in Philadelphia. Hans Tanner of the *Democrat and Chronicle* reported that "doctors now are hoping they can save just 50 per cent of the sight in the eye. His playing days are over."

Official confirmation from doctors was provided the following April.

The Bruins played a benefit game for Dufour on October 7, 1967, at the Hershey Sports Arena. Ted Gress of the *Lebanon (PA) Daily News* reported in the October 9 edition that nearly 4,000 fans turned out to watch the Bruins defeat the Bears 7–3. Contemporaneous newspaper reports noted that the amount of money raised for the prematurely retired goalie was still being tabulated.

"Dufour expressed his thanks to the crowd, which gave him a standing ovation," Gress wrote in reference to a tribute that was held during the first intermission. "Players of both squads were lined up on the blue lines during the ceremony and expressed their approval by banging the ice with their sticks."

The gifts included a plaque for Dufour and a bouquet of roses for his wife.

Bouquets were not in order for some media types after Gerry Cheevers' first big-league game—a 35-save effort for Toronto in its 6–4 victory over Chicago on December 2, 1961.

"The Black Hawks, playing listless hockey for the first two periods, nearly salvaged a tie against Bob Cheevers, rookie goalie, who was making his National League debut," read a portion of a United Press International report that was filed from Maple Leaf Gardens.

If that gaffe wasn't enough, a wire-service statistical summary of the game referred to the Toronto goalie—then five days shy of his 21st birthday—as "Cheerers."

There were, ahem, cheerers aplenty in the years ahead, especially among the ranks of the Bruins' fan base. Cheevers—first name: Gerry—became a popular figure as he backstopped Boston to Cup-clinching victories in 1970 and 1972 en route to being enshrined in the Hall of Fame, where a replica of his mask is prominently displayed.

That piece of equipment, designed by Ernie Higgins, has long been known as the "Cheevers mask" due to the *faux* stitches that were painted on the fibreglass.

One doesn't need to have seen Cheevers play in order to appreciate the mask and the character behind it.

"The Gerry Cheevers mask is something that's unique and that stood out," said former Western Hockey League goalie Carl Stankowski, who was born in 2000—20 years after Cheevers retired as a player.

"It caught my eye, because I used to be a big hockey card collector. I remember there was this one card of Gerry Cheevers that I really wanted. I was in Grade 4 and checking out eBay. I think it was five bucks or something. I was like, 'Aw, man, I can't get it!' But I ended up getting it and I was the happiest kid in the world.

"That mask is something pretty cool—and I think it would have been pretty cool to be the first goalie to have something on your mask back in the day."

Nowadays, it is rare to see a pro hockey goaltender whose mask isn't a work of art. How often does one spy a plain white mask? But, in the 1960s, those goalies who did don face gear were of the "basic is beautiful" persuasion until Cheevers injected some imagination, not to mention some humour, into the equation.

All these years later, he still fields questions about the unique on-ice appearance.

"The basic topic is why or how or when the stitches came on to the mask," Cheevers began.

"First of all, masks were white at the time, and I didn't even wear white socks when we played. Under my pads, I wore black socks. I hated to have white anywhere on my uniform, so I kept driving into practice thinking, 'How am I doing to decorate this mask or do something different with it?'

"Also, in the back of my mind, it was, 'How am I going to get out of practice?' I wasn't a very good practice goalie.

"This one time, the puck flipped up. It would have cut me if I didn't have a mask on, but I feigned being seriously hurt and went into the dressing room. I'm trying to get out of practice, but [head coach] Harry Sinden walked in and said, 'Gerry, you're not even hurt. Get out there!'

"Our trainer, Frosty Forristall, said, 'Hold it,' and he painted about a six-stitch cut with a magic marker over my eye [hole]. In essence, that's all there was to it. We all got a giggle out of it when I went back on the ice. I said, 'See? I'm seriously hurt.'

"From there, we decided to keep track of where I might have got stitches if I didn't have a mask on. I would go in after a period and say to Frosty, 'That looked like about a six-stitcher if I didn't have a mask on.'

"That's how it all started. It was very simple, very easy. I got my way with being able to decorate my mask. I got a lot of notoriety because of that."

Cheevers had actually flirted with such a concept earlier in his NHL career. The book *Saving Face*, by Jim Hynes and Gary Smith, includes a close-up photograph of a younger Cheevers wearing a Terry Sawchuk/Lefty Wilson-style mask. The image clearly shows, as described by Hynes and Smith, "several black stitch marks and a long red one over its left eye."

Hynes and Smith added: "So Cheevers had tried the stitches gag at least once before he added a little colour to his Higgins mask." Colour in the form of black ink, anyway.

The merits of a mask had become evident to Cheevers when he made his second NHL appearance, substituting for an injured Johnny Bower. One night after helping Toronto defeat Chicago, Cheevers was between the pipes in Detroit, where the Red Wings won 3–1.

"I'll never forget it," Cheevers wrote in the foreword to *Saving Face*. "Gordie Howe came down the wing and wasted what I figured was a routine shot. Well, that routine shot knocked the stick out of my hand. Even though it took me a few years and a few near-misses to go out and get one, I finally realized that if I wanted to play in the NHL I would need to wear a mask."

There had been previous reminders, such as one that was delivered during a 1961 preseason game in which he played for Toronto against his future team, Boston.

"Early in the game, Bruin[s] defenceman Leo Boivin rifled a shot that grazed off Tim Horton's pants in front of me and took off," Cheevers recalled in his 1971 book, *Goaltender*. "The puck whacked me above the eye, knocking me down, dazing me, and requiring 10 stitches."

Friendly fire was also dangerous.

"One morning at practice, Frank Mahovlich let go a blast that just grazed the side of my head," Cheevers continued in *Goaltender*. "I'm glad it only grazed me; it opened a slice of my scalp that sent me to hospital for more stitching...but you still didn't catch me wearing a mask. Too much vanity."

Too much waiting. After those two 1961 regular season appearances with the Leafs, he did not return to the big leagues until the 1965–66 season. By then, he belonged to the Bruins, having been claimed from Toronto in the intra-league draft. It was one step closer to becoming a full-time NHLer, and to wearing a mask.

One particularly influential day was January 25, 1965, when Cheevers became a father a few hours before helping the Rochester Americans post a 10–1 American Hockey League victory over the Quebec Aces.

"Only 10:45 had gone by when Red Berenson's rising shot caught Cheevers in the face—snapping off half of two upper teeth and three lowers," Hans Tanner wrote in the *Democrat and Chronicle*. "Twelve stitches were required to close slices inside his lips.

"The popular Amerk goalie amazingly had never lost a tooth or had one broken before he had to be aided from the rink on rubbery legs. Play was held up for 20 minutes while he was administered to in the dressing room. With no pro spare available, Cheevers was given several shots of Novocaine and returned to duty."

The next day, Cheevers was a stand-up goalie in a different sense—serving as the best man at the wedding of Americans teammate Red Armstrong.

"He'd caught a stick in the eye for five stitches in the Quebec game," Cheevers wrote in *Goaltender*. "His eye was swollen and bruised, my mouth was swollen and bruised, and I was missing six teeth in front when the ceremony began.

"I don't know what Red's in-laws and his wife's friends thought the girl was getting into."

Getting into a mask soon became a serious consideration.

"Cheevers recently visited Toronto for a fitting of a brand-new plastic mask, and has used it in workouts," George Beahon wrote in the *Democrat and Chronicle* on January 29, 1965. "It's unlikely he'll use it tonight because Cheevers is a firm believer in the old psychological bit about getting right back up on the horse after he's thrown you, or taking another trip in the flying machine after the near-miss."

There was also the imperative of playing, period, because the Americans lacked a second option. Cheevers played in all 72 games for the Rochester team of 1964–65.

Most of the following two seasons were also spent in the minors, with Oklahoma City. The exception was a seven-game stint with the 1965–66 Bruins.

Cheevers was maskless for each of those seven games, and in all 22 of his appearances on behalf of the 1966–67 Bruins—a weak team that, to the goalie's chagrin, could not be described as Hap-less.

"We played in Montreal and they beat us 10–2," Cheevers recalled in conversation with author/broadcaster Dick Irvin Jr. "Hap Emms was our general manager and, I don't care what anyone thinks of him, he was no good. There might be two people I've met in all of hockey that I'd say that about, and he's one of them. I hated him.

"After the game he comes in, looks me in the eye, and says, 'What happened?'"

Cheevers responded with a poem:

Roses are red,

Violets are blue.

They got 10,

And we got two.

Emms, the Bruins' GM for two seasons, left the team after the 1966–67 season. Cheevers remained with Boston, but with a new look. He sported a mask for the 1967–68 season opener—a 4–4 tie with Detroit at Boston Garden.

"Thinking about the protection of the mask was all up to you," Cheevers said. "If you said you were 100 per cent protected even though you weren't, it made a difference.

"Even though the early masks were nothing like the later masks or present-day masks, most goalies had to have 100 per cent confidence to make it work. That's the way I felt. Even with the old Lefty Wilson mask, which really didn't do a good job, it felt better.

"A perfect shot could have got in my eye slot, but it would have had to have been a million-to-one shot to fit in there. Usually, the puck would have a little flip to it or a little waver to it, so it couldn't get in there. So I felt 100 per cent confident.

"I don't know how anyone played without a mask after I put one on."

Ed Johnston still shakes his head while pondering that notion.

Cheevers' long-time goaltending cohort with the Bruins, Johnston—who made his NHL debut in 1962—was maskless until 1967. Even when he finally made the switch, he wasn't initially sold on the new look.

The indecision is interesting, in hindsight, considering the degree to which Johnston was pelted with pucks as the bold, beleaguered goaltender with brutally bad Bruins teams before Bobby Orr's arrival as an 18-year-old prodigy in 1966.

The 1963–64 Bruins, for example, posted an 18–40–12 record—the worst in what was then a six-team league. One of the few bright spots happened to be Johnston, who played in 4,200 minutes over all 70 games. Not since then has an NHL goalie played in every minute of every one of his team's regular season games.

Despite the lack of a respite, Johnston nonetheless received several breaks.

"I remember breaking my nose on a Wednesday in New York," he recalled. "They said they'd stop the game and fix it. Then I re-broke it again on Saturday night in Montreal. And when I came off the plane, because my eye was shut, I went to the hospital and they put in leeches—which they still use today—and I was able to play the next night.

"We talk about stupidity. The number on my back was Number 1, and that was basically most of the goalkeepers' IQ."

Jacques Plante, by contrast, was "the first smart guy" in the assessment of Johnston.

"Nobody even thought about a mask until Plante got hurt," he said. "I was brought up in the Montreal organization. When I played for the Montreal Junior Canadiens, I was their practice goalkeeper nine times out of 10, and nobody had a mask on back then.

"Back then, it was just automatic. You played without a mask."

And prayed that puck wouldn't connect with, say, the temple.

"If you thought about it, that would be the worst thing," Johnston went on to say. "Then you'd be afraid and that's when you're going to get hurt."

Johnston played...and played...and played in the minors until he finally got a shot, as his 27th birthday loomed.

He was a veteran of 374 games of professional hockey until breaking in at the big-league level on October 25, 1962, and starring in the Bruins' 3–3 tie with Detroit.

By that point, the battle-hardened Johnston was already referring to himself as "Scarface." That was *before* he suffered a broken nose in three consecutive games.

A one-time boxer, the Montreal-born Johnston was experienced at absorbing pucks and punches to the face.

"I fought in the Golden Gloves," he told Bud Collins of the *Boston Globe* in 1964. "Wasn't too good, but I didn't get knocked down. I got knocked down plenty in the street, though.

"Hockey was the thing there, of course. My brothers made me the goalie when I was six because I couldn't skate, and I've been there ever since.

"I got my first stitches—six in the forehead—when I was 10, but nothing bothers you when you're a kid. I guess I've got 60 or 70 stitches in my head. But I've never lost a tooth."

Johnston did lose his patience early in the 1967–68 season, after first sporting a mask in a game.

"One of the few goalies in the NHL who doesn't wear a mask, Ed experimented with one in training camp because of two facial injuries suffered a year ago," read a portion of a profile that appeared in the *Globe* on December 10, 1967. "The first time Coach Harry Sinden sent him into action was at the start of the second period at Toronto. Johnston hadn't expected to play so he didn't bring his mask out with him. Rather than waste time, he played without it. The next few games, however, he wore the mask but then discarded it because of poor lateral vision."

Johnston overcame those reservations by the time the 1968–69 season arrived. The change of heart may very well have saved his life.

He was seriously injured on October 31, 1968, in Detroit, where the Bruins were readying themselves for a game. According to Marvin Pave of the *Globe*, a shot taken by Orr during the warmup deflected off the goalie's stick and slammed into his right temple.

"The puck hit just outside the area of his face mask, but the mask did absorb some of the shock," Bruins trainer Dan Canney told Tom Fitzgerald of the *Globe*. "It could have been worse if he had not been wearing the mask."

Johnston was rushed to the hospital. Although the injury was initially described as a concussion, Johnston said he actually ended up in a coma.

"The injury was so severe that Johnston lost 40 pounds in two days, and blood clots formed in his head," *The Hockey News* wrote in 2018, when it rated Johnston 87th on its list of the top 100 goalies in NHL history.

"During the time he was in the coma, he didn't realize that his family came to visit or that a priest showed up for two weeks."

Nor was he aware that there was one other visitor of note—Glenn Hall.

While the St. Louis Blues were on a road trip in November 1968, Mr. Goalie dropped by Johnston's hospital room to check on his well-being. The 37-year-old Hall, it turned out, would soon become the next prominent NHL goalie to switch to a mask.

11

Seniors of St. Louis

Glenn Hall and Jacques Plante start anew with the Blues

GLENN HALL NEVER KICKED OUT A SHOT BEFORE BEING KICKED OUT OF his first game as a masked goaltender.

Mr. Goalie was ejected just 2:01 into a November 13, 1968, matchup between his St. Louis Blues and the New York Rangers at Madison Square Garden.

The catalyst for the expulsion was a delay-of-game penalty that had been assessed to Blues defenceman Noel Picard with St. Louis already trailing 1–0 on a goal by Vic Hadfield just 1:16 into the first period.

Having faced only the shot that eluded him, Hall angrily articulated his displeasure with the penalty call to Vern Buffey. The veteran official responded by issuing a 10-minute misconduct.

When Hall persisted—to the point where he "pushed the referee lightly," in the words of the Wally Cross of the *St. Louis Post-Dispatch*—the grumpy goalie was dispatched to the dressing room, having received a game misconduct for the first time in a storied NHL career that dated back to 1951.

Hall could laugh about it afterward, because the Blues won 3–1.

"How do you like that?" he told Cross. "Every time I wear a mask, I get a misconduct."

A one-time goaltending iron man was soon replaced by a man named Irons. Robbie Irons, that is.

Whereas Hall had once played in 502 consecutive regular season games, Irons' big-league "career" consisted of the 2:59 he spent in the Blues' goal before 39-year-old Jacques Plante became the third St. Louis netminder of the rather eventful evening.

Cross noted in his chronicle of the game that Irons had suffered a "convenient leg injury" while warming up to replace Hall, "meaning that Coach Scotty Bowman was free under the rules to call in Plante."

The cagey coach took advantage of a soon-to-be-scrapped rule that stated: "If both listed goaltenders are incapacitated, the team shall be entitled to dress any available goaltender who is not on the reserve list of another NHL member club."

So, while Plante rushed from the press box to the dressing room and frantically changed into his goaltending garb, Irons was flawless in his cameo. He turned back one Rangers shot before being waved back to the bench. Plante proceeded to stop all 22 shots he faced.

Afterward, Irons quipped: "Too bad I don't get credit for the shutout."

(Four nights later, Hall made his first save as a masked goaltender. He stopped 26 shots in a 3–3 tie with the Minnesota North Stars.)

The three-goalie night by the Blues impelled the NHL brass to quickly close the loophole. A team would soon be limited to using only the two goaltenders it had dressed for the game. In the event that injuries shelved them both, the replacement would have to be an unlucky—and presumably masked—defenceman or forward.

We are still waiting for the lineup to form, although defenceman Jamie Allison did back up Nashville Predators goalie Brian Finley on December 13, 2005.

In terms of mask-wearing, Hall's train of thought changed while he rode the railway.

While the Blues were travelling from Boston to New York, the old-fashioned way, star centre Red Berenson bluntly told the team's goaltender: "You're stupid not to be wearing a mask."

Hall was smart enough to grasp the wisdom of Berenson's words.

"I didn't have an answer for him," Hall, then 37, told Cross.

That conversation was the clincher when it came to Hall's decision to relent and, at long last, unveil a mask.

Like Hall, Plante was a throwback to a time when each NHL team employed only one goaltender, as was the custom for much of the Original Six era.

When expansion took effect in the fall of 1967 and doubled the ranks of big-league hockey to 12 teams, changes were on the horizon for two well-established goaltending legends.

Having weathered a painful second season with the Rangers, Plante retired after the 1964–65 campaign. Hall remained with the Chicago Black Hawks, who were grooming Denis DeJordy as a successor.

The writing was on the wall for Hall, who was left unprotected in the expansion draft. The Blues happily claimed him on June 6, 1967.

Hall again became a workhorse, appearing in 49 games during the Blues' maiden season. His understudy, Seth Martin, played in 30 games and devoted some of his spare time to mask manufacturing.

Martin was an ex-Blue by the 1968–69 season, but his influence was nonetheless evident when the mask he designed was worn by Hall. The milestone was marked by a *Hockey News* story that was touted by a blaring, front-page headline: "Look Who's Wearing a Mask!"

The sudden change was not the result of an emerging fear, Hall asserted in an interview with the *Post-Dispatch.*

"I've always been afraid," he told Cross. "You know, it smarts a little when you catch one in the mouth. No, it just makes better sense to wear one now. With all the jamming in front of the net and screened shots, a goalie doesn't know where the puck is coming from half the time. I'm surprised more goalies haven't been seriously hurt because of this."

One could argue that Hall had, in fact, been seriously hurt, albeit not to the extent that he was forced to miss significant playing time.

"I had been hit hard three times—really, really hard," he said in an interview for this book, responding to a question about the impetus for putting on a mask.

"I was getting close to 40 years old. I thought, 'Boy, it would be stupid to lose an eye,' and a few of the goalies when I played had lost an eye. That was the biggest concern—the eye injuries."

Those, he had avoided.

"You have to be lucky," Hall continued. "When I was hit hard with the puck, it was not the eyes that had it, although I got a couple that were close. I got one between the eyes higher than the nose and that left a little bit of an X. I remember another shot that I got. It was in practice and it left an X."

Hall ultimately left a legacy as one of the game's greats. Ditto for Terry Sawchuk, whose misfortune had paved the way for Hall to make his NHL debut.

Hall had been summoned from the Western Hockey League's Edmonton Flyers after Sawchuk suffered a broken bone on the inside of his right instep during a practice on December 2, 1952. The injured foot was placed in a cast and three weeks of rest were prescribed.

Farmhand goalie Ralph (Red) Almas made one start for Detroit while Hall was in transit.

When he did arrive, it was in advance of his equipment, which wasn't anywhere to be found when he landed in Montreal as a game against the Canadiens beckoned.

Therefore, Hall was forced to borrow equipment from Detroit trainer Lefty Wilson, who doubled as the Red Wings' practice goalie.

With a looming initiation to the NHL, and equipment that was unfamiliar, Hall embraced normalcy in one respect. He threw up before the game.

"The guys didn't realize it was part of my routine," he told biographer Tom Adrahtas. "So as everyone was getting dressed and taping their sticks, I ran into the bathroom and got sick. I'm sure it was loud enough for all the players to hear. When I came out, I was white as a ghost."

Hall whitewashed the Canadiens for the opening 23:33 on December 27, 1952, before allowing his first NHL goal. It was scored by Doug Harvey—a legendary defenceman who, coincidentally, concluded his playing career as a teammate of Hall's with the 1968–69 Blues.

After the Red Wings played the Canadiens to a 2–2 tie, Detroit head coach Tommy Ivan told Dink Carroll of the *Montreal Gazette* that "we'll probably keep Hall until Sawchuk returns, if he stands up the way we think he will."

That he did. While Sawchuk was unavailable, the 22-year-old Hall played in five games—one of which was a 15-save, 4–0 blanking of Boston on January 8, 1953. By that point, Hall had allowed only eight goals in five NHL games. He made one more start, celebrating a 5–2 victory over Toronto, and was rewarded for his excellence by being sent back to Edmonton—presumably in the good company of his equipment.

Hall would not return to the NHL until the 1954–55 season, allowing only one goal in each of his two appearances.

Even though Hall possessed just eight games of NHL experience, the Red Wings' brass had seen enough to know that he was a keeper, in more ways than one.

Red Wings boss Jack Adams consummated a shocker of a swap on June 3, 1955, sending Sawchuk, Lorne Davis, Vic Stasiuk, and Marcel Bonin to Detroit for a generally anonymous quintet consisting of Gilles Boisvert, Réal Chevrefils, Norm Corcoran, Warren Godfrey, and Ed Sanford.

The deal was a forehead-slapper at the time, considering that Sawchuk, only 25, had just backstopped Detroit to its fourth championship in six years.

Adams' rationale was outlined by the *Detroit Free Press* in a story headlined "Goalie Hall Key to Wings' Trade." As Adams put it in an interview with Marshall Dann, "Hall is more advanced now than Sawchuk when he joined us and all the players insist that Glenn has been NHL material for the past year."

Hall validated the decision by boasting seven shutouts at the midpoint of his first season as a starter.

With the increased duty came an elevated risk, as was obvious during the 1956–57 season. In regular season play, he had been hit near the eyes and sustained wounds that necessitated 10 and eight stitches. And it would get uglier.

In Game 2 of a 1957 semifinal series against Boston, Hall took a Stasiuk sizzler in the face and required 18 stitches—four inside the mouth and 14 beneath the nose.

"I got up, not because I was tough or anything, but because Charlie Rayner and Turk Broda and Frank Brimsek and all of those guys prior to me, that's what they did," Hall told Adrahtas.

"The goalkeeper considered himself tough. That was foremost in his mind: 'Don't let the tradition down.' Boy, you go in the closet and cry. Don't cry on centre ice. I think that you didn't get up for yourself. You got up because of all the old goaltenders."

In that spirit, Hall returned to the crease and finished the game. Detroit won 7–2 to even the best-of-seven series at 1–1. Boston won the final three games, however, and that was it for Detroit's season—and for Hall's time with the Red Wings.

Hall was traded on July 23, 1957, in a deal that also sent a fellow NHL All-Star, left-winger Ted Lindsay, to Chicago. The Red Wings received Johnny Wilson, Hank Bassen, Forbes Kennedy, Bill Preston, and cash in what the *Free Press* termed "one of the most startling deals in Detroit hockey history."

Once again, Adams was called upon to explain his decision to trade a premier puck-stopper, having unloaded Sawchuk two years earlier.

"Glenn changed after the Stasiuk shot," Jolly Jack said, according to Adrahtas' biography of Hall. "He was puck-shy and just wasn't effective after that."

Hall was so, er, ineffective in Chicago that he spent 10 seasons with the Black Hawks, earning first-team All-Star distinction in 1958, 1960, 1963, 1964, and 1966. Additionally, he helped the 1960–61 Black Hawks win the team's first Stanley Cup title since 1938.

So maybe, as Adams asserted, Hall *did* change after the Stasiuk shot. He got even better.

"Glenn was *the* goalie," former Chicago teammate Bill Hay said. "His reactions were outstanding, and he had the quickness. He was so smart that he could tell where a guy was going to shoot based on where he had shot before, and he knew what the shooters were used to. He understood the thinking of most of the shooters and he had outstanding ability."

He also had the ability to withstand what he once referred to as "60 minutes of hell."

"Certainly, there was pressure to play well," Hall reflected. "I would put myself into a position to throw up before the games. I simply felt I played better when I forced myself to play at that level.

"Anybody can play at a lower level. In fact, they used to put the fat kids or the kid who couldn't skate in goal. If you could skate and you were in reasonably good shape, you were in the top 10 per cent automatically."

Hall wasn't portly, ponderous, or porous. Skating was one of the many attributes he demonstrated while cementing his status as a sure-fire Hall of Famer. Any discomfort came with the territory—and not just because he was resolutely maskless throughout his tenure in the Windy City.

"Like I say, 'Pain hurts,'" Hall said. "You didn't have much protection. You would try and tell the equipment people what you wanted, but they'd say, 'Oh no, you want it like this,' and they had no idea what they were doing, so everybody fixed their equipment a little bit.

"The greatest thing that ever happened to the goalkeeper was those bubbles that they used in packing. You could put it on the inside of the arm."

All the resourcefulness in the world could not compensate for the fact that, as Hall put it, "we just had bad equipment."

And some accompanying bad days.

"I sometimes ask myself 'what the hell I am doing out here?' but it's the only way I can support my family," Hall said in the 1960s, as quoted by author Trent Frayne. "If I could do it some other way, I wouldn't be playing goal."

Even though Hall left his stamp on the sport, he told Dick Irvin Jr. that, given a chance for a do-over, he would have worked at the post office instead of being a goalie.

"At my age right now," the 60-something Hall noted in the mid-1990s, "I'd have a pension you couldn't believe."

Joking aside, Mr. Goalie wanted to make one point clear.

"There's a perception sometimes that I didn't like playing hockey, what with my so-called nerves and everything," he told Irvin. "That's an interpretation. Of course, I liked playing hockey, but only one way: The game had to be played well."

Few played it so well, or for so long.

In Hall's 10th and final season with Chicago, he became a Vezina Trophy winner for the second time, sharing the award with Denis DeJordy.

Hall's last four seasons in the NHL were spent with the Blues, with whom he enjoyed a renaissance.

Improbably, he won a third Vezina Trophy despite playing for an expansion team that was in its second season of existence.

Hall was 37 when he helped St. Louis allow by far the fewest goals (157 in 76 games) in the 12-team NHL. Although Hall was a hockey warhorse at that point, he wasn't even the oldest goalie on his own team.

The Blues' other netminder, Jacques Plante, turned 40 during the 1968–69 campaign.

Hall had once dismissed Plante as "a wimp" for wearing a mask. By 1968, he was a teammate.

Plante had supposedly retired on June 7, 1965, with six Vezina Trophies, an equal number of Stanley Cup championships, and one history-making mask to his credit.

A month before the announcement of his retirement, Plante had undergone surgery to repair a troublesome right knee. He attributed the decision to leave the game not to the injury, but instead to a desire to spend more time with his family.

"The operation was successful and has no bearing on my decision to retire," the 36-year-old Plante said while addressing the media. "I feel fine and maybe I could play another four or five years."

Concerns about Plante's knee had prompted the Rangers to acquire (maskless) Ed Giacomin the previous February. Plante had seen some

Jacques Plante, who helped the Montreal Canadiens win five consecutive Stanley Cup titles, was a multifaceted goaltending pioneer.

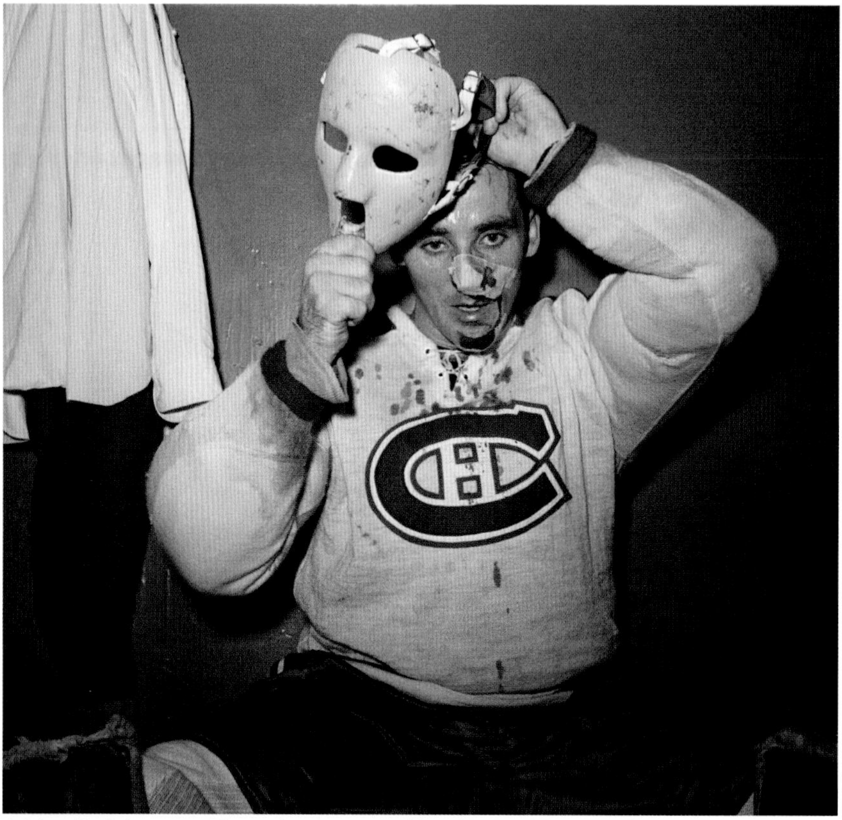

A bloodied Jacques Plante is shown at New York's Madison Square Garden on November 1, 1959—a night that changed the face of goaltending.

Before joining the Detroit Red Wings, a maskless Terry Sawchuk suffered a career-threatening eye injury on his 20th birthday.

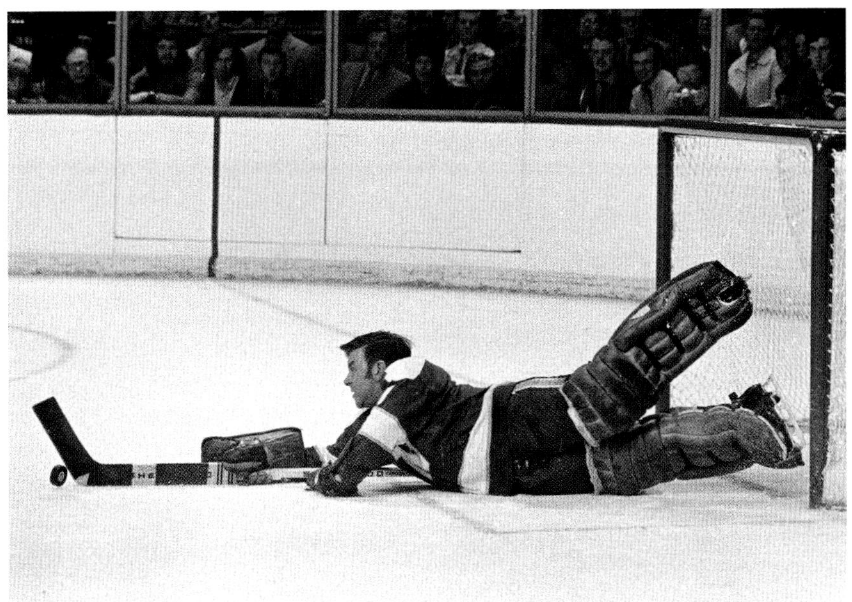

Gump Worsley, one of the final maskless holdouts, famously commented, “My face is my mask.”

Cesare Maniago began wearing a mask as a member of the Minnesota North Stars, initially in games against the run-and-gun Chicago Black Hawks.

Toronto Maple Leafs goaltending great Johnny Bower wore a mask for the first time in a game on January 19, 1969, at age 44.

The faux stitches on the mask of Boston Bruins goaltender Gerry Cheevers were a trademark. To this day, replicas of that mask are popular with hockey fans.

Glenn Hall, shown with St. Louis, wore a Blues uniform when he donned a mask for the first time in a game—on November 13, 1968. With Chicago, "Mr. Goalie" had played in an astonishing 502 consecutive regular-season games...all without a mask!

Bob Perreault, shown with the Rochester Americans, played maskless into his forties.

(American Hockey League Hall of Fame)

The New York Rangers' Ed Giacomin was one of the final NHL goalies to switch to a mask.

Bruce Gamble, who emerged as a bona fide NHL goalie with the Toronto Maple Leafs, was forced to retire from hockey after suffering a heart attack while playing for the Philadelphia Flyers on February 8, 1972.

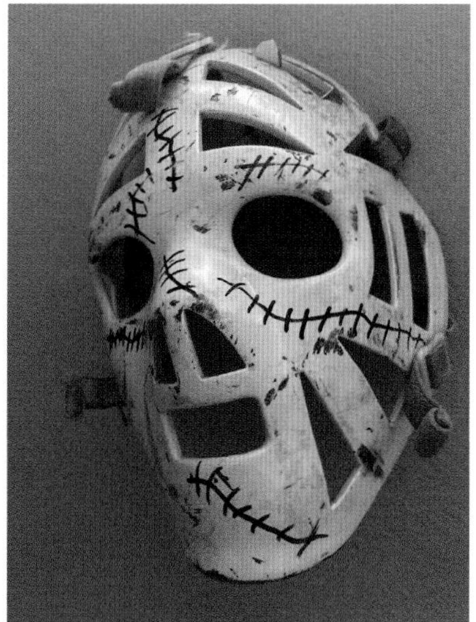

Russ Gillow—who painted stitches on his mask, à la Gerry Cheevers—was an NHLer for one night (February 9, 1972). (Russ Gillow)

Gaye Cooley, who starred in the NCAA ranks with the Michigan State Spartans, was reliably, colourfully maskless until the mid-1970s. (Michigan State University Sports Information Dept.)

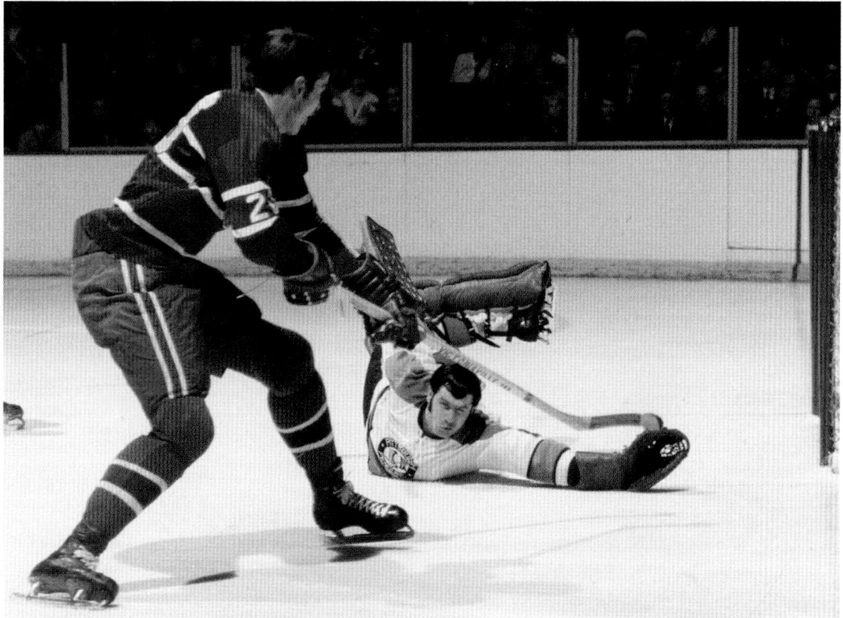

Andy Brown, shown with the Pittsburgh Penguins, was the final goalie in NHL history to begin a game without a mask. He played his final big-league game on April 7, 1974, against the host Atlanta Flames. (Jim Shields)

Jim Shields took this photo of Indianapolis Racers goalie Andy Brown before a March 31, 1975, WHA game against the host Winnipeg Jets.

Dave Dryden is pictured in 2021 wearing one of the masks he donned during a lengthy career as a goalie in pro hockey. By the time he retired as a player, he was also a pioneer in mask design. (Dave Dryden)

The puck-marked mask of Winnipeg Ice goalie Carl Stankowski is shown after the Western Hockey League team's practice on April 4, 2021. A puck hit Stankowski in the forehead with such velocity that the puck's logo left an imprint on the mask. (Carl Stankowski)

minor league duty, for conditioning purposes, while contending with knee issues during the 1964–65 campaign—his second and last with New York.

With the Rangers' permission, Plante suited up for the Montreal Junior Canadiens for a December 15, 1965, exhibition game against a touring Russian team. He stole the show as the Montreal juniors won 2–1, eliciting a prolonged, passionate standing ovation from a Forum crowd of 14,981.

Plante was out of hockey for the subsequent two seasons, except for appearances with an old-timers team and some sessions as a clinician, while working as goodwill ambassador for Molson Breweries. He resurfaced in the NHL in the fall of 1967 as a special assistant to Oakland Seals head coach and GM Bert Olmstead.

"The immediate reaction among newshounds was that [Plante] would be lured out of retirement, where Charlie Hodge seemed to be going as a salary holdout," Pat Curran wrote in the *Montreal Gazette* on October 3, 1967.

"After all, Jacques claimed that the mask would keep him in the game until he was 40 and he won't be 39 until January. Plante stayed with the Seals for two weeks with the pads on and was by far the best of their netminders."

But the rumoured comeback was not signed, sealed or delivered. He soon returned to Montreal, telling Curran: "It's the same story as two years ago. I've retired."

A likely story. Plante was suitably enticed after being claimed by St. Louis from the Rangers' reserve list on June 12, 1968.

"The news floored me," Plante told Red Fisher of the *Montreal Star*. "I was buffaloed by it."

Plante was added by the Blues after Seth Martin, Hall's understudy during the 1967–68 season, retired.

"They need another working man," Fisher wrote, "because Hall doesn't want to play more than one-half a season."

Wearing the patented "pretzel mask," Plante returned to the NHL and registered three rapid-fire shutouts over his first 11 games. The third goose-egg was a 44-save gem against Bobby Hull and the high-powered Black Hawks.

Plante finished the 1968–69 season with a 1.96 goals against average and five shutouts in 37 appearances. Hall, who played in 41 games, fashioned a 2.17 GAA and eight shutouts while performing at such a high level that he was named a first-team All-Star for the seventh time. Just like that, the geezer goalies were once again Vezina Trophy recipients.

The following season, the Blues relied on a netminding triumvirate. Plante appeared in 32 games, posting a 2.19 GAA and five shutouts. Injuries limited Hall to 18 games, over which he recorded a 2.91 GAA and one shutout. Ernie Wakely, at 29 and therefore embryonic in comparison to Hall and Plante, was called upon 30 times with the 1969–70 Blues. Wakely registered a 2.11 GAA and four shutouts.

Effective that season, Plante introduced his third mask—a more-protective model that had been developed by David Britt. The timing was fortuitous, given the events of the 1970 Stanley Cup playoffs.

Plante was called upon to start Game 1 of the championship series against the formidable Bruins. It would be his final appearance in a league final, due to a steamer of a shot that was taken by Phil Esposito and deflected by Boston teammate Fred Stanfield before smashing into the face of the St. Louis goalie.

"It really nailed him, and the mask he was wearing was a contact mask," then-teammate Red Berenson recalled. "They made a mask right over his face, so it touched him everywhere. Wherever it hit you, it split you open pretty good."

The impact of the puck also split Plante's mask and rendered him unconscious for two minutes, according to the May 4, 1970, edition of the *St. Louis Post-Dispatch*.

"The next thing that happens, all I know is the pain," Plante told author Hal Bock. "It's like somebody coming up behind you and hitting you with a sledgehammer. The pain...and then I open my eyes and see all those legs around me. Something is squeezing my tongue. It's burning. I didn't know what was happening. The cool air is in my mouth and that was the oxygen they had brought on the ice."

Plante then paused before declaring: "The mask saved my life."

He was quickly taken to Barnes-Jewish Hospital in St. Louis and diagnosed with a concussion, several decades before any sporting federation had established a protocol regarding head injuries.

"Too bad we'll lose you for the series this time, Mr. Plante," a nurse told the 41-year-old patient, according to *The Jacques Plante Story*. "Your mask didn't save you this time, did it?"

To which he responded: "My dear young lady, if it wasn't for my mask you would now be gazing on me in a funeral home, not a hospital."

According to Dick Irvin Jr., "Plante compared the sudden impact on his brain when the shot hit him to that of a car's engine going from zero to 800 miles per hour in one second."

The Bruins never applied the brakes, sweeping St. Louis in four games. The punctuation mark was a classic overtime goal scored on Hall by Bobby Orr on May 10, 1970—Mother's Day.

What was then the mother of all mask-related innovations was then foremost in Plante's fertile mind. His convalescence was used most constructively to conceptualize "the mask I had been trying to design for a dozen years," Plante told Andy O'Brien, the two having collaborated on the aforementioned biography.

As O'Brien wrote of Plante, "He had learned the hard way—by being shot at and hit—the weaknesses of the wired mask and the plastic mask. Enter the design with fibreglass and high-resistant epoxy resins able to bounce away, undented, air cannon shots worse than anything Bobby Hull can slapshoot."

One of hockey's greatest pioneers had something else up his sleeve, or on his face. Plante devoted the summer of 1970 to developing a new mask, in partnership with an expert on plastics and with members of the engineering faculty at the University of Sherbrooke in Quebec.

A 51 per cent owner of the fledgling Fibrosport company, Plante kept refining his latest invention.

"The safety factor was upped in a creation of fibreglass with ridges plus a pointed nose piece to deflect the puck and prevent solid impact," read a portion of *The Jacques Plante Story*. "It also had protrusions to protect his ears. Engineering tests with pucks shot out of an air cannon at 120 mph have failed to dent his mask and one puck split on impact."

O'Brien added that "Plante has even heard from Washington that some NASA scientists are working on a new mask for him. He explains what the space men have in mind: 'They are experimenting with some new lightweight material that can be poured into a mold right over your face. The fibreglass mask I've used is molded like that, but it weighs 22 ounces. I have already tried the space mask and it weighs only seven ounces. Of course, there's a slight catch. The space mask will cost anywhere from $300 to $500. Mine are a lot less costly, although maybe not quite as comfortable.'"

Plante thought the new mask was out of this world. Other prominent goaltenders, such as Bernie Parent and Roger Crozier, were quick to agree. The Fibrosport mask, and derivatives thereof, remained in use into the early 1990s.

As for Plante, he joined the Maple Leafs after two seasons in St. Louis and remained in Toronto until late in the 1972–73 campaign, when he was dispatched to Boston.

Plante then accepted a 10-year, $1 million offer to become the head coach and general manager of the Quebec Nordiques, with whom he spent the 1973–74 World Hockey Association season.

The gig was not to his liking, so he stepped down after one season. But he wasn't finished with hockey, despite one more "retirement."

During the 1974–75 season, Plante played in 31 WHA games with the Edmonton Oilers.

At the tender age of 46 years and 73 days, he made his final appearance in goal when he started against the San Diego Mariners on March 31, 1975.

He allowed five goals, the last of which was scored by Joe Hardy at 14:18 of the second period, before pulling himself from the game due to a sore hand. Ken Brown mopped up in goal as San Diego won 5–2 before perhaps 6,000 spectators at Edmonton Coliseum.

A more fitting punctuation mark was applied on June 13, 1978, when Plante was elected to the Hockey Hall of Fame during his first year of eligibility.

A fellow 1978 inductee was none other than Andy Bathgate, whose shot to the face of Plante on November 1, 1959, had forever changed the game.

PART THREE: UNSUNG AND UNMASKED

12

One Fateful Night in Oshawa

Ian Young, Mickey Redmond, and success after setbacks

IAN YOUNG WAS FAR TOO YOUNG FOR HIS BIG-LEAGUE DREAM TO BE DASHED.

He was only 20 when, in an instant, irreparable harm was done to his left eye and, by extension, his aspirations of playing for the Boston Bruins.

"He was an exceptionally good goalkeeper," said Ed Johnston, who was a mainstay in goal for the Bruins when Young was in the team's system. "If he didn't get hurt, he definitely would have been in the NHL."

A maskless Young was injured on January 21, 1967, while playing with the Oshawa Generals in an Ontario Hockey Association junior game against the Peterborough Petes.

"I remember it distinctly," he said more than 50 years later. "Mickey Redmond, who had one of the best shots in the league, came in on the left-wing side. He just got inside the faceoff circle and took his shot.

"I was out high in the net, cutting off the angle, and the puck hit me right in the eye.

"I didn't reach for the shot. I never moved."

Except to fall to the ice.

"I never lost consciousness," Young continued. "It felt like my eye was in the back of my head.

"It was fairly sore."

There was an eerie silence at Oshawa Civic Auditorium as Young was tended to on the ice.

"I ended up being carried off on a stretcher and into the trainer's room," he recalled. "I only required eight stitches, but the stitches were both above and below the eye.

"My left eye had puffed up, so our trainer forced the eye open a bit and shone a flashlight in my eye, from about a foot away. He asked me, 'Do you see anything?' I saw nothing—total black.

"When that happened to me, I just barfed. It just hit me."

Young then returned to a virtually deserted Generals dressing room, where he waited to be taken to the hospital.

"They had called for my dad," he said. "I looked up when he came into the dressing room. I saw his face and I knew that this was serious.

"It just was a pretty good career snuffed out."

That was the ultimate outcome, but not one that was assured for the first few months after the injury.

"When I was released from the hospital, I did not know about my career being over," Young said. "I knew it was serious, but I always believed that I would regain the vision over time.

"Then I went to an eye specialist and he explained that the macula in the back of my eye had blown out and there was nothing surgery-wise that could be done to bring back the vision.

"I was fortunate in a way that it cut me above and below the eye and I didn't lose the eye, but I ended up with four per cent peripheral vision."

Redmond's first question, before the formal interview even began, was: "How is Ian doing?"

He was pleased, but hardly surprised, to discover that Young's story is one of success. Great things were envisioned for both Young and

Redmond when they starred in the OHA and, sure enough, they ended up excelling in the game of life—despite some unexpected detours.

"Ian Young was tasked to go to Boston," Redmond said. "He was going to be the heir apparent [to Johnston and Gerry Cheevers].

"Ian was very, very good, so it had to be devastating, with that kind of future in front of him, for something like that to happen out of nowhere."

At the time the 6'2" Young was stricken, the 19-year-old Redmond was in the midst of a sensational season in which he would amass 51 goals in just 48 games.

He was not one whose shots typically went awry. But, on that January day in 1967, the puck did not end up anywhere near the target.

"Ian was a tall goalie, so I remember trying to go low to the glove side with a straight stick," said Redmond, who had not been swept up in hockey's curved-blade craze.

"I believe that, just as I was releasing the puck, it caught a rut or a bump and it fluttered. Instead of going low, it accidentally went high and that's how it hit him in the left eye."

Given a different turn of events, their careers could have connected in a different fashion.

"I'll give you an interesting twist to all of this," Redmond offered, flashing back to 1958 and a story involving his father.

Back then, Eddie Redmond—whose sons Mickey and Dick would eventually play in the NHL—was a member of an Ontario-based senior A team, the Whitby Dunlops, that represented Canada at the world men's championship in Oslo, Norway. In fact, the final game of Eddie's hockey career was the gold-medal final, in which the Dunlops doubled the Soviet Union 4–2.

Dunlops general manager Wren Blair would soon play an integral role in bringing junior hockey back to Oshawa. The Generals had been on hiatus from 1953, when Oshawa's Hambly Arena burned down, until the team was revived in 1962.

Once the Generals were re-established, Blair remained on-board in a scouting role. It was he, in fact, who found Bobby Orr, who debuted for Oshawa at age 14 and excelled with the Generals before joining the Bruins at 18, on the fast track to superstardom.

Blair's keen eye for talent also put Redmond in the crosshairs.

"Before I turned 15, Wren Blair called my parents and said, 'I'd like to bring Mickey into Oshawa. He doesn't have to practise. He just has to come to the games. It's only 35 miles away. And alongside him, I'm bringing in this kid from Parry Sound named Bobby Orr,'" Mickey Redmond noted.

"If I had gone to Oshawa and signed what they called a C Form, I would have belonged to the Boston Bruins, and I probably would have been playing with Ian Young.

"But my mother stepped in and said, 'He's 14 years old. He doesn't even weigh 100 pounds. I'm not letting my son go in against guys who are 20 and 21 and weigh 220 pounds. He'll get killed. You can't do it,' so I didn't do it.

"The next year, somebody got hurt in Peterborough during training camp and I filled in and made the team at 15. I signed a C Form and therefore belonged to the Montreal Canadiens.

"That's how crazy this world is as far as destiny."

Redmond had 38 points (including 21 goals) in 53 games on the path toward being named the OHA's rookie of the year for 1963–64.

Seasons of 23, 41, and 51 goals followed for Redmond, who was named the league's most valuable and most gentlemanly player for the 1966–67 campaign.

Redmond's junior career was further honoured in 1981, when he was enshrined in the Peterborough & District Sports Hall of Fame, of which his father and younger brother are also members.

Comparably, Young has been celebrated by the community in which he played junior hockey. He entered the Oshawa Sports Hall of Fame in 1996.

Born in Glasgow, Scotland, on August 18, 1946, Young moved to Canada with his family when he was 22 months old. He grew up in Scarborough, Ontario, where he played minor hockey, before being introduced to the junior loop during a three-game stint with the 1963–64 Generals.

The promising puck-stopper spent 1964–65 in junior B with—here's another Young-Redmond link—the Whitby Dunlops. Then it was back to Oshawa, where Young was a standout for the remainder of a junior career that was cut short by a few months.

With Young entrenched in goal, the 1965–66 Generals reached the best-of-seven Memorial Cup championship series, won in six games by the Edmonton Oil Kings.

The following season, Young was named MVP for the Generals, even though he did not play for them beyond January 21, 1967.

The question looms: Would the outcome have been different if facial protection had been worn?

"The Bruins asked the Generals to get me a mask, but they went to a sporting goods store in town and picked one off the wall," Young said. "I put it on and I couldn't see anything at my feet, so I still hadn't worn it in a game.

"It was just the beginning of the era of a transition to everybody wearing a mask. In retrospect, I would have had no problem wearing a mask. It's just that we didn't do it back then."

Young estimates that "40 to 50 per cent" of the opposing goaltenders were masked, so his appearance could not be deemed anomalous.

Another consideration was the frequency and severity of the facial blows he had absorbed.

"You get hit all the time but, frankly, when you get hit by the puck in the head, it doesn't really hurt," Young said.

"I know it sounds funny. It stung, but it wasn't painful, and you get stitched while you are still sort of numb from the hit. Even then, you'd get stitched and then come back and play.

"Over the four years of my junior career, I probably had to get stitches about four or five times. That was about it."

Considering the design of the early-era fibreglass models, Young isn't certain that a minimal buffer between the face and the projectile would have mattered in his situation.

"I have a feeling that some of these masks were made without reference to a puck hitting the eye," he said. "In some cases, I'm sure that a direct hit on some of those masks would have injured the eye."

Essentially, what it came down to was this: wrong place, wrong time. If there is someone to blame, Lady Luck should assume responsibility.

"There has never been any grudge against Mickey," Young emphasized. "He was a great player and a fine gentleman.

"It was a shot. There was nothing personal."

But there was nonetheless a personal touch—a nice gesture by Redmond, not long after the accident.

"He sent me a card when I was recovering at home, wishing me well and saying sorry that it happened," Young said.

It says something that Redmond's gesture stands out, after all these years, because there was a lengthy list of well-wishers and good deeds.

"I could have opened up a grocery store with all the fruits and vegetables that were sent to my house," Young said. "I became a banana addict.

"I was stuck in the house and they didn't want me moving or running or doing anything, so I'm getting all these deliveries. All of a sudden, you look in your living room and there's 20 floral arrangements.

"I appreciated them. Don't get me wrong. All these teams, including ones from the NHL, were sending them to me. I admittedly couldn't eat it all, and I couldn't give it away."

Young had returned home after being hospitalized for 10 days that felt more like 10 years.

"The team doctor drove me to the hospital," he recalled. "My first reaction when I got into that car was, 'Could you turn the game on? I want to see how the boys are doing.' That was my mindset. I was a team guy my whole life.

"When I got to the hospital, they put me into a private room. They didn't want any light to get into my eyes, so I spent 10 days with patches on my eyes. One of the team's directors got me a transistor radio so I could listen to the games.

"After the 10th day, the patch on my bad eye had been pulled off only for a second. They said, 'Do you see this?' I didn't see the little flashlight that they were using.

"It took me about five minutes to get acclimatized to the light after they took the patches off."

It was then that he received a lasting lesson in perspective.

"I sat up on the side of the bed and asked if I could have a shave, because my girlfriend was going to pick me up at the hospital and drive me home," Young recalled.

"I sat up to shave and I looked at the doorway and there was this young boy in a wheelchair staring at me. I said to the nurse, 'Who's this young lad?' I was told, 'You're his hero. He asked if he could talk to you, and we wouldn't let anybody in,' because nobody was allowed in to see me except family.

"They didn't want me talking to him in case it caused any sudden movements of my head, so they had said to the boy, 'You can sit there, but don't say anything and don't go in the room.'

"I was getting ready to leave, so I said to him, 'Come on in,' and he came in on his wheelchair. He asked for my autograph and we talked for a little bit. He told me how much he thought of me, and I was touched by it.

"But here's the climax to this: When I was leaving, I said to the nurse, 'When's that little fella getting out?' She said, 'He's not…'

"He had terminal cancer. He was eight years old."

Young could not get that little boy out of his mind. In fact, he still can't.

"After I went home from hospital, I couldn't really do anything," Young said. "Every morning I covered my good eye and tried to look out of my bad eye, and the vision was never, ever coming back.

"In those moments, and anytime I've had any adversity, I think of that little boy. I think, 'Don't you ever complain about losing millions of dollars in hockey when you know what people like that little boy are going through.' I've always used that.

"To this day, I always remember the sight of that boy and his story. Sports is everything, but it's nothing. It's a dream, and 99 per cent of the people who have that dream are never going to make it.

"You just can't put importance on sports over life. You have a wife. You have a family. You bring up children. You earn money to support the family. That's life. It's not getting a cheque that's a net of $300,000 every two weeks."

Cashing in around the net was Redmond's forte, as the Bruins discovered on December 3, 1967—24 days before he turned 20.

The first two of his 233 NHL goals were scored at Boston Garden, which was once expected to become Young's hockey home, at the expense of Ed Johnston.

Redmond had played in five early-season games with the 1967–68 Canadiens before being sent to the Central League's Houston Apollos. After being recalled by Montreal in early December, he proceeded to score the Canadiens' first two goals in their 5–3 loss to Boston.

The Canadiens returned to action four nights later, tying Detroit 2–2 at the Forum. Redmond's tally gave him three goals in a span of two games. His first three NHL goals, by the way, were against maskless goaltenders—Johnston and the Red Wings' Roy Edwards.

Redmond became a full-time NHLer in 1969–70, scoring 27 goals in 75 regular season games.

The following season, he had 14 goals in 40 games before being traded to Detroit in a January 13, 1971, blockbuster that resulted in future Hall of Famer Frank Mahovlich joining the Canadiens.

Redmond had only six goals in 21 games with the 1970–71 Red Wings, but fans in the Motor City would soon become accustomed to his blistering drives.

He scored 42 times for the 1971–72 Red Wings and followed up the following season by scoring 52 goals—topping the previous franchise record of 49, set by Gordie Howe in 1952–53—and being named a first-team All-Star. Then came a 51-goal season in 1973–74.

Just 26, and already the proud owner of back-to-back 50-goal seasons, Redmond seemed to be nicely on track for a 500-goal, Hall of Fame career.

However, a back injury limited him to 29 games in 1974–75. The discomfort carried into the following season, during which he played in only 37 games before being forced into retirement.

Only 28 at the time, Redmond could relate to Young, in that both players were forced to leave the game prematurely.

"Without knowing Ian personally, I'd have to say, 'What a great inner being he has, to be able to deal with that and then move on,'" Redmond marvelled. "He had to figure out, 'OK, now what am I going to do?'

"In a strange way, I had to do a similar kind of thing when I had back surgery. I had to walk away from the game in the prime of my career. That was devastating for me, so I can only imagine what it was like for Ian.

"What are you going to do? You've got no training. Your education's not there. There's no background in any other things to do. All you want to do is be a hockey player. It's like, 'Whoa! Where do I go?' Talk about being lost. That can really eat you up.

"It took me a good two years or so to try to get around it, so I can only imagine what Ian went through as a younger hockey player. He already knew that he was a really good goaltender and probably knew that he was destined to go to Boston, which is even more devastating."

Devastating, yes, but not defining. Young and Redmond both overcame injury-related setbacks and became immensely successful in the hockey world outside of a playing capacity.

Redmond transitioned into a much-decorated career as a broadcaster following an abbreviated comeback attempt in 1979. He started out doing part-time colour commentary for Red Wings telecasts and, all these years later, is still in the booth.

His post-playing career was recognized at the highest level when, in 2011, he received the Hockey Hall of Fame's Foster Hewitt Memorial Award for outstanding contributions as a broadcaster. By that time, he had worked as an analyst for ESPN, ABC, CBC, Fox Sports Detroit, and the USA Network. As of this writing, he was part of Bally Sports Detroit's Red Wings television coverage team.

As for Young, he put the eye injury behind him by going into coaching and writing books on goaltending—once he was finished playing, that is. Not even being legally blind in one eye could derail or deter him.

Long after minding a hockey net, Young can attest to the value of a safety net.

"Whenever I speak to kids, I stress the importance of education, because while everyone was playing poker on the bus, I was one of those guys who was reading chemistry books," he said.

"I always took my education seriously. Then, when I got hit, I could suddenly get into any university I wanted."

He chose the University of Waterloo and took a four-year arts course with a major in finance. As a bonus, he was welcomed with open arms by members of the Ontario-based university's hockey team. From 1967 to 1970, he was an assistant coach with the Waterloo Warriors.

"They took me into the team and that helped me through it all," Young said. "The guys on the team were always after me to 'try it again.' I'd been told that I couldn't play anymore, but for some reason, in my fourth year at school I decided to give it a shot."

As a masked goalie for the first time, Young protected his face and his net with comparable effectiveness.

In one season with the Warriors, he helped them win the league title and was named the team's MVP for 1970–71. He was also a first-team Canadian university All-Star.

After graduating from Waterloo, Young worked for the Thorne Riddell accounting firm from 1971 to 1975. For the first two years, he moonlighted by playing for the Oakville Oaks, an OHA senior team.

Young had also maintained his ties to the game by keeping in touch with Orr and Wayne Cashman—former Oshawa teammates who had become mainstays with the Bruins.

"I used to always go down to Boston and stay with Orr and Cashman," Young said. "One night after a Bruins game, we're back at Bobby's apartment and a bunch of the Bruins are there. Of course, people are always kind of hesitant to talk to me about the injury, but it finally came up that night. I told them about being a first-team All-Star and coming back and playing a little bit."

Those conversations were the catalyst for an even more ambitious comeback. In the autumn of 1974, Young attended a combined Bruins-Rochester Americans training camp in Fitchburg, Massachusetts.

"Bobby called up [Bruins general manager] Harry Sinden and got me the tryout, so I took a leave of absence from work," Young said. "I wasn't really sure if I should be doing it, because look at what I was risking. But I was still young enough at the time, so I gave it a shot.

"So here I am at an NHL camp, with one eye. I played in several games for Rochester and had a great camp, so they offered me a contract, but it was a two-way deal.

"I thought to myself, 'At 28, I want to play in the big leagues. I don't want to be going to the American league for $15,000 a year,' so I asked them to let me go to the Kansas City Scouts."

The Scouts, an expansion team, were then coached by Bep Guidolin, who had been the Generals' bench boss when Young played in Oshawa.

"The Bruins wouldn't release me, so I said, 'That's it. I'm not going to go and play at Rochester,'" he said. "I asked them, 'What are my chances of getting a shot to play with the Bruins?' They said, 'Well, frankly, we can't believe you did what you did and we want to see if you can continue it. If you can, you could get a shot.'

"Well, I just wasn't into doing that. At the time, I had proved to myself that I would have made it had I had the two eyes."

Eyeing the future, Young obtained a Certified Professional Accounting degree while working from 1975 to 1990 as the assistant controller with Oxford Properties and Cambridge Properties. He was subsequently a vice-president and investment advisor with RBC Dominion Securities (1990–2003) and Scotia McLeod (2003–2012).

While becoming enormously successful in his professional life, Young still found time to contribute to the game of hockey. In addition to writing three books on netminding, he founded a goaltending school.

Moreover, he returned to the Generals and spent 13 seasons as the Ontario Hockey League team's goaltending coach—including the 1989–90 campaign, which was punctuated by Oshawa's Memorial Cup title.

So, despite that dark day in 1967, there has been a happy ending.

"In life in general, a lot of times there's tension, but look back on all the things that have been tense for you and that have brought you down," reflected Young, who has settled in Whitby. "What were the results of that tension going forward? How tense, really, was it?

"In many cases, you get tensed up over stuff that you have no right to be depressed about, but you've made it into that mountain.

"You tend to over-worry and manufacture a worst-case scenario. It's not worth it."

Take it from Young, who in 1967 faced what he thought was a worst-case scenario and went on to lead an exemplary, accomplished life.

"After my injury, I was forced to be mentally tough going forward," he reflected. "I'm looking at all the success that I had in hockey, playing despite my one eye, and I don't know how I ever did it.

"I look back on it now and I say, 'Maybe I shouldn't have even done that,' but I did do it. It something that I did that I'll cherish."

13

"Have Plate, Will Travel"

Bob Perreault and a lasting legacy of laughter

Bob Perreault looked more like an avuncular uncle than a professional athlete.

Media reports conventionally referred to him as "pudgy" and "balding," among other descriptions that would disqualify him as cover-page material for GQ—Goaltenders' Quarterly.

The burgeoning bald spot was especially conspicuous because he did not wear any form of headgear for the entirety of a professional hockey career that spanned nearly a quarter-century.

Most netminders who played in his era caved in and opted to wear a mask at some point. Johnny Bower and Gump Worsley, two of the most notable holdouts, eventually concealed their familiar, mid-40ish mugs during their farewell seasons.

Perreault, by contrast, was maskless at the end—although there is evidence that he did wear a face shield, at least for a brief spell, for the Des Moines Oak Leafs during the 1970–71 International Hockey League season.

The Oak Leafs were one of 13 teams, in seven different leagues, for which Perreault toiled from 1951 to 1974.

Cumulatively, he played in 987 games—only 31 of which were in the NHL—and accumulated innumerable stitches.

In the American Hockey League, he was third all-time in shutouts (37) and sixth in victories (229), in addition to being a member of four championship teams.

Through it all, he maintained an air of joviality, endearing himself to teammates and fans.

"Bobby was a funny, funny man, and so down-to-earth," recalled Norm Fong, who worked closely with Los Angeles Sharks head trainer Larry Oldes when Perreault spent part of the 1972–73 season with that World Hockey Association team.

"This one trip, we were in Houston and the head trainer, myself, and Bobby went to a mall. We were looking at dress shirts and I hear this screaming: 'Larry! Larry! Call the police!' I'm thinking, 'Holy crap! Are they getting held up? What's going on?'

"Here was Bobby showing Larry the shirt, and the price was outrageous. That was Bobby's way of telling Larry, 'Don't buy the shirt! They're charging way too much!'"

Everyone certainly got a charge out of Perreault, wherever he happened to be.

"He's a great man to have on a team," head coach Phil Watson told Herb Ralby of the *Boston Globe* during Perreault's 22-game stay with the 1962–63 Bruins. "Besides being a capable goaltender, he's the type of fellow who keeps the team relaxed with his funny cracks."

Not to mention his quirks, such as routinely removing his goalie glove during a stoppage in play to kiss a ring or a medal, following a save.

"He has medals taped to his fingers, medals in his pads, all over the place," Des Moines Oak Leafs teammate Luc Tessier told Buck Turnbull of the *Des Moines Tribune* early in the 1971–72 IHL season. "He's been doing that for years. In fact, the first time I heard of Bobby was when he was a softball catcher—and he was good at that, too. Someone pointed him out to me and said, 'That's the guy who kisses medals.'"

And about the bling…

"It's a religious ring a kid gave me back in 1948," Perreault, then 42, told Al Slater of the *Long Beach Press-Telegram* after backstopping the Sharks to a 4–2 victory over the Quebec Nordiques on February 24, 1973. "I've worn it every time I've played. It was blessed by the pope. The minute the game's over, I put it back in the safe."

Perreault's line of work was anything but safe, especially in light of his bare-bones equipment—a contrast to Sharks goaltending cohorts George Gardner and Russ Gillow.

"With Russ and George, the equipment was new, with bulky shoulder pads and big chest pads," Fong remembered. "Bobby didn't have any of that. His little chest pad looked like a baseball catcher's chest pad—a tiny little thing.

"We'd go on the road and the other two goalies each had two bags of stuff. Well, we could get all of Bobby's equipment in a regular player's bag.

"When you say 'basics,' it was truly basic. He just had enough equipment to say that he was the goalie, and that was it.

"To play with that sparse equipment when you know that there's newer stuff, better stuff, lighter stuff, it was something. But he was used to that and that's what he was going to do."

Above the neck, Perreault's equipment went from being sparse to non-existent.

"He wouldn't even think of putting a mask on," Fong said. "He was very old-school. I don't think he would even let them fit him for a mask. That was out of his realm of possibilities. He was so confident in himself. You can't teach an old dog new tricks.

"Those guys who played without masks, I don't know how they did it. It just blows me away."

The early years of Perreault's goaltending career began accidentally enough.

"At 12, I was in the stands in Three Rivers watching my cousin play goal," he told the Turnbull of the *Tribune* in 1972. "All of a sudden, he got mad and hit the referee on the head with his stick. He was kicked out of the game. In fact, he was suspended and never played again, so his team needed a goalie right away to finish the game and I agreed to do it. That's how I got my start. We went all the way to the finals of the playoffs that year.

"Do you know what happened to my cousin? I should have been so lucky. He became a doctor and now has more money than he knows what to do with."

Perreault also became familiar with modern medicine due to his many doctor's appointments—the result of dedicated, distinguished and, yes, dangerous service between the pipes.

He was introduced to professional hockey on May 30, 1951, when he signed with the AHL's Providence Reds. He not only saw duty during the 1951–52 season with the Reds, but also with the Quebec Senior Hockey League's Sherbrooke Saints. The following two seasons were spent in the Quebec Hockey League, with the Montreal Royals (1953–54) and Shawinigan Falls Cataracts (1954–55).

In fact, Perreault spent the better part of three seasons with Shawinigan, the most notable exception being a six-game stint with the 1955–56 Montreal Canadiens.

Perreault was called up after Canadiens goalie Jacques Plante suffered facial injuries in practice on December 16, 1955. While recuperating in hospital, remember, Plante had an epiphany—realizing all too well that the injuries could have been prevented, or at least mitigated, had he been wearing a mask.

In Plante's absence, Perreault prevented goals—especially in a spotless NHL debut. On December 17, 1955, he helped Montreal blank Chicago 5–0 at the Forum.

"Hawks fed Perreault with 18 shots which he gobbled up like a ravenous resident of skid row at a Christmas dinner," Baz O'Meara wrote in the *Montreal Star*. "Few of them were hard shots, but Perreault handled those with veteran aplomb. He answered the burning question of whether he would be an adequate replacement for Jacques Plante while the latter is recovering from a nose fracture in practice."

Montreal won three games and lost three with Perreault pinch-hitting for Plante. Over those six games, Perreault boasted a 2.00 goals against average and a .931 save percentage, including the shutout.

That carried little capital in the depth-deprived days of the NHL's one-goalie system. Perreault shuffled back to Shawinigan Falls as soon as Plante recovered.

The following season, Perreault played 41 more games with the Cataracts and another 24 with the AHL's Rochester Americans. He then began a lengthy residency in Hershey, Pennsylvania, playing in 279 AHL games over five seasons with the Bears.

Included in that span was a three-game look-see with Detroit. With Terry Sawchuk on the shelf after being hit by a puck on the point of a shoulder during a warmup, Perreault minded the crease.

He began his truncated tenure with the Red Wings by registering back-to-back victories over Chicago—3–2 (on January 21, 1959) and 2–0 (January 24). During the latter game, Perreault made 24 saves for his second shutout in a span of eight big-league appearances.

Even better, the game was nationally televised in the United States. An Associated Press report on the whitewash referred to Perreault, who was then four days shy of turning 28, as "a balding minor league veteran."

Perreault made one more start with Detroit, losing 7–3 to Montreal one night after the shutout. By that point, Sawchuk was poised to resume his career, having returned to practice the day after the drubbing versus Montreal.

"His shoulder protected by a big pair of hated shoulder pads, Sawchuk gingerly tried his first bit of hockey action in a week," Marshall Dann reported in the *Detroit Free Press* on January 27, 1959.

Growled Sawchuk: "Never will know whether I'm ready or not wearing this straitjacket."

As Dann pointed out: "He never wears shoulder pads when he plays, but general manager Jack Adams ordered this set for the practices this week."

Red Wings head coach Sid Abel was not the least bit rankled by Sawchuk's irascibility, observing: "You can tell Terry's getting well by the way he's complaining."

Very soon, Sawchuk got the nod.

"As a result, travelling orders were written for Bobby Perreault, the chubby little veteran from Hershey," Dann wrote. "He headed back to that American League base carrying a paycheque from Adams and a wide assortment of memories from his service as a Red Wing. Detroit ended a nine-game non-winning streak while he was here. Perreault was a winner in his first two starts against Chicago, 3–2 and 2–0, but absorbed a 7–3 pasting Sunday night from Montreal. No one blamed Bobby. Sawchuk probably could not have done much better against hockey's finest team."

Perreault would have to wait another 1,355 days for a third, and ultimately final, shot at the NHL.

When Perreault finally resurfaced in The Show, with the Bruins, he was 31 and the oldest rookie in the league—as noted by no less of an authority than *Sports Illustrated* on November 5, 1962.

"They call me chubby in Cleveland and portly in Buffalo, but in Hershey they call me '*le chat*'—quick hands," Perreault told *SI* writer Gilbert Rogin.

The 5'8" Perreault, whose weight was generously listed at between 180 and 190 pounds, attracted the magazine's attention after returning to the NHL with a flourish. In his first game with Boston, he blanked Montreal 5–0. It was his third shutout in just 10 career NHL games.

"All you have to do to play goal is be fast and close your eyes," Perreault told *SI.* "I don't know how I shut out Montreal the first game of the season. I have my eyes shut tight all the time.

"Follow the puck—that's how you play goal. Soon as it's hit, you make the move. You make the good move, it's a stop. You make the bad move, it's in, eh?

"In Providence, two years I sit on the bench, taking it nice and easy. I look good on the bench.

"I put on a few pounds. It's good for a goalie to be fat. The puck don't hurt so much."

The lengthy wait between NHL stints was more painful, to the extent that he pleaded with Bruins head coach Phil Watson for one more opportunity.

Watson had been scouting a second-round AHL playoff series between the Buffalo Bisons and Perreault's Hershey Bears. After Buffalo won the best-of-five series in four games, Watson conversed with Perreault and inquired about whether he would like to play for the Bruins.

"Just give me a chance," Perreault pleaded, according to Ralby, "and I'll make good for you."

Those words were proven to be prophetic in the 1962–63 season opener. Perreault stopped all 28 Montreal shots, including prime chances by future Hall of Famers Jean Béliveau and Henri Richard.

"Following the rotund rookie's rousing shutout versus the Canadiens here Thursday night, elated B's addicts traffic-jammed the east lobby at the Garden, waiting to give Perreault a close-up ovation when he emerged from the dressing room," Jerry Nason wrote in the *Globe*. "He emerged and walked right through them unrecognized. They thought he was a bar bouncer on his night off."

They weren't wrong. It was noted by Prescott Sullivan of the *San Francisco Examiner* in a 1963 article that Perreault "serves as his own bouncer in the waterfront bar he operates in Three Rivers, Quebec."

It helped to have a bouncer who once boxed as an amateur while carrying the nickname of Kid Flamingo.

Perreault had also bounced around—from league to league, team to team—during his itinerant professional hockey career.

Had he finally found a home in Boston? That appeared to be so, based on results that were achieved early in the 1962–63 season. After the opening-night victory, the Bruins returned to their traditional non-winning ways, although the swoon was hardly attributable to the goaltending.

"In the Bruins' last five games, in which they have gained only two ties, the opposition has blitzed Perreault with 201 shots," Ralby reported on October 22, 1962. "That only five goals were scored against him last night and but 21 in the five games is due solely to the balding goalkeeper's fine play."

He continued to perform commendably until December when, once again, he experienced bad luck. He injured a knee on December 15, 1962, against Toronto and was replaced by Ed Johnston with 7:12 elapsed in the third period.

The severity of the injury was such that Perreault never played another millisecond in the NHL. With Johnston entrenched in goal for Boston, Perreault was loaned to Rochester in late February 1963. He was in such a slump, in terms of things going his way, that even the trip to the minors was a major hassle—to the extent that he was late for his first practice with the Americans.

What should have been a six- or seven-hour drive became a nine-hour excursion that concluded at 5:00 AM. The team was to practise at 10:00 AM.

"The road was really bad and I had a flat tire on the way, and I get lost somewhere on the thruway and find myself near Watertown," Perreault explained to Hans Tanner of the *Democrat and Chronicle*. "I must think I'm on my way home to Three Rivers."

Perreault's last, and longest, NHL stint consisted of 22 games, during which he registered a 3.73 goals against average and the season-opening shutout on behalf of the Bruins. As a member of the Americans, he played in 10 more games that season, after which the travellin' man was on the move once more.

Next stop: San Francisco.

The San Francisco Seals of the Western Hockey League sealed a deal for Perreault on June 4, 1963, purchasing his contract from Boston for $25,000—"an enormous sum in hockey circles," according to Paul Lippman of the *San Francisco Examiner*.

Lippman interviewed Bruins general manager Lynn Patrick, who offered this scouting report of Perreault: "He's round, but he can really move. They'll like him out there."

That they did. Perreault officially signed with the Seals in October 1963, at which point the accumulated dental damage—an occupational hazard for a maskless goaltending lifer—was referenced by San Francisco head coach Bud Poile.

"He's got the fastest glove in the west," Poile told Lippman, "and only two uppers and seven lowers."

Unfazed, as always, Perreault quipped: "Have plate, will travel."

And travel he did. After playing in 70 and 68 games in his two seasons with the Seals, he returned to Rochester—presumably without experiencing a flat tire—for four more years in New York state. Then, in 1969, it was off to the International League and a three-year residency with the Des Moines Oak Leafs.

To begin the 1969–70 season, the 38-year-old Perreault was appointed a player-coach. The double duty created this challenge: How does one coach a hockey team while dressing the part of a backup goalie?

Buck Turnbull reported in the October 29, 1969, *The Des Moines Register* that "Bob Perreault, by directive of new International Hockey League commissioner Bill Beagan, will coach the Leafs from behind the team box in his goalie uniform."

It was, by all accounts, another milestone in a nomadic netminding career.

"This is the first time to my knowledge that a goaltender has ever coached a team while dressed and ready to play," Oak Leafs GM Terry Slater told Turnbull as an October 29 home date with the Port Huron Flags drew closer. "But we have received word from the commissioner that every team must have two goalies dressed at all games from now on to avoid any long delays because of injuries. There are plenty of forwards and defencemen who both play and coach, but I've never heard of a goalie doing it."

So it came to be. With Gaye Cooley in goal, the Oak Leafs and Flags played to a 5–5 tie before a record crowd of 4,655 at the Des Moines Ice Arena.

Perreault played in 27 games as a first-year Oak Leaf. That total decreased to 19 the following season, during which his cousin (slick centre Gilbert Perreault) began what would be a Hall of Fame career with the Buffalo Sabres.

Then, in 1971–72, Bob Perreault—no longer a coach—appeared in an eye-popping 51 games despite turning 41 near mid-season.

Although backup goalies were in vogue by then, Perreault was loath to leave the ice. In late December 1971, for example, he experienced a win (4–1 over the Fort Wayne Komets) and a loss (of another tooth) on the same night.

"Perreault played the final eight minutes of the first period and the balance of the game with only the roots of a front tooth in his mouth," the *Register* reported on January 1, 1972. "The tooth, anchored by a partial plate, was knocked loose by one of his own players—defenceman Gerry Lecomte. It happened around 12:48 in the first period and Perreault was off the ice for about five minutes."

Even so, the indomitable Perreault was back in the net for the Oak Leafs' next game—a 6–1 loss to the Muskegon Lumberjacks. The showstopper was a 42-save performance by the Lumberjacks' Glenn (Chico) Resch, a future NHL star.

Then the unthinkable happened following the 1971–72 season. The venerable Perreault retired as a player.

Slater had just been appointed the Los Angeles Sharks' head coach. One of his first moves was to enlist Perreault as a scout.

Before season's end, he was back in goal—albeit for a cameo appearance. George Gardner was struggling in goal for the Sharks, so Slater decided to turn to an experienced hand and an unprotected head. It mattered not, in the head coach's appraisal, that Perreault had just turned 41.

The Sharks ended up celebrating a victory for the ages—the aged, anyway. Perreault backstopped Los Angeles to the aforementioned 4–2 win over Quebec before 7,114 eyewitnesses at the Los Angeles Sports Arena.

"Slater should have provided his maskless goalie with a rocking chair," read an excerpt from a game story from the *Long Beach Press-Telegram* on February 25, 1973. "The Nordiques only took 17 shots on goal."

A story in the *Pomona Progress Bulletin* noted that Nordiques goalie Richard Brodeur wasn't even alive in 1951 when his opposite number, Perreault, played his first game of professional hockey. Brodeur, who would play 305 games in the WHA and another 385 in the NHL, was born in 1952.

Brodeur and the Nordiques had been staked to a 1–0 lead when the game's first shot, by Yves Bergeron, eluded Perreault just 52 seconds into the first period. He allowed only one more goal the rest of the way, despite some conditioning issues.

"I've got to run a half-mile when I get home," Perreault told the *Press-Telegram*. "If I'm going to continue to play, I've got to try and get in shape."

Perreault's luck took a turn for the worse in January 1974, when he was called up to the Sharks from the Southern Hockey League's Greensboro Generals. He had spent the earlier part of the 1973–74 season mentoring younger players—there weren't many older ones—and making periodic starts.

With the Sharks mired in a losing streak that had swelled to five games, plans were made for Perreault to start his second game in the WHA, nearly 10 months after his introductory appearance in the new circuit.

"The remarkable Perreault remains active in a position many consider the toughest in sports," Dan Hafner wrote in the *Los Angeles Times* on January 4, 1974. "Disdaining the mask, now standard equipment for goaltenders, he retains the quick reflexes which enable him to ward off shots travelling at speeds of 120 mph. He began his career shortly after World War II."

The starting assignment was suddenly scrapped after Perreault suffered a fractured finger during the morning skate. Ergo, Ian Wilkie started in goal, with Russ Gillow backing up, and helped the Sharks defeat the visiting Edmonton Oilers 4–3.

Very soon, it was back to North Carolina for Perreault. He made 16 appearances in goal for the 1973–74 Greensboro Generals before being named the team's head coach on May 10, 1974. He was fired seven months later after the Generals' record dropped to 5–18 but, long after his hockey career, the garrulous goalie was remembered with affection and respect.

Perreault was only 49, sadly, when he was killed in a September 10, 1980, car accident in Saint-Étienne-des-Grès, Quebec. He was thrown from the vehicle and died instantly on impact.

He was posthumously inducted into the AHL Hall of Fame in 2014.

14

"You Can't Hurt Cement"

Russ Gillow's one shot at the NHL

Russ Gillow was a big-league Flyer—and a flier—for one memorable day: February 9, 1972.

At the time, the Philadelphia Flyers were experiencing a goaltending crisis that was born of misfortune.

On February 8 against the Vancouver Canucks, veteran Bruce Gamble had experienced discomfort during the game, but nonetheless remained in goal for the full 60 minutes as the Flyers won 3–1.

The following day, after the team flew to Oakland for a game against the California Golden Seals, the 33-year-old Gamble was admitted to hospital. It was soon determined that he had suffered a heart attack, which may very well have occurred during the first period against Vancouver. He was subsequently diagnosed with a congenital heart condition and advised to discontinue his hockey career.

It was eerily coincidental that on the very day when Gamble played his final NHL game, a generally flattering profile of the once-maskless goalie had appeared in the *Philadelphia Daily News*.

"Next to Gump Worsley, Bruce Gamble is the unlikeliest-looking pro athlete alive," Bill Fleischman wrote of a quiet goalie who was noted for long sideburns and short sentences. "Next to Gump Worsley, Bruce Gamble looks like Superman."

Gamble was playing at that level while making eight starts in a nine-game span for a Flyers team that was enjoying a sudden spasm of prosperity. Impressed and enlivened by the spectacle, fans at The Spectrum in Philadelphia had begun chanting his name.

"Yeah, I hear it," he told Chuck Newman of the *Philadelphia Inquirer* in early February. "It makes you feel good."

That being said, "he forced what Bruce Gamble uses for a smile," Newman wrote of a stoic goalie "who may be the most humble fan idol in all of hockey."

There were additional reasons to applaud Gamble after his one final standout performance—a 30-save effort in Vancouver. His spirited shutout bid lasted until the Canucks' Wayne Connelly scored with just 1:58 remaining in the game.

"If anybody on this team prays, they should say thank you for Bruce tonight," Bobby Clarke told reporters after scoring two of the three goals for the Flyers.

Gamble, meanwhile, had little time for conversation following a performance that was as courageous as it was sensational.

"I've never been sick after a game before," he told Fleischman before boarding the team's flight to California. "I was throwing up nothing."

Gamble, who had fallen to the ice early in the contest, later told the media that he thought he had been hit by a puck.

"Near the end of the game, Gamble told defenceman Barry Ashbee he didn't feel well and doubted he could make it to the final buzzer," the Associated Press reported. "The other team members thought it was due to fatigue from the extreme heat at Pacific Coliseum."

The reasons for Gamble's illness would soon become clear, making what turned out to be his farewell performance even more of a marvel.

"I don't think I've seen a better goaltending effort than Gamble's in a long, long time," Flyers general manager Keith Allen said to Fleischman the day after the Vancouver game. "He looked so confident in there. His reflexes were great."

Allen also had to act reflexively after learning of Gamble's diagnosis. The Flyers were left with one goalie—Doug Favell, who had been supplanted as the starter by Gamble—on their road trip.

With the Flyers' minor league reinforcements on the other side of the continent, Allen placed an emergency call to Spokane, Washington, where the 32-year-old Gillow was employed by the Jets of the Western International Hockey League.

"Keith Allen said, 'We've acquired you and we want you to go and play,'" Gillow recalled 50 years later. "I said, 'OK, fine.' I was working at a Ford garage at the time. My boss said, 'Sure, you can have the time off.'"

The Jets' moniker was supremely suited to the circumstances. Gillow hurriedly packed his bags, rushed to the Spokane airport, and boarded the next flight to northern California.

"After I landed in San Francisco, I flew on a helicopter to Oakland so I'd be on time for the game," recounted Gillow, who arrived at the Oakland-Alameda County Coliseum Arena with mere minutes to spare before the warmup. Talk about a Hollywood-type entrance!

"Yeah," Gillow agreed, "but I didn't play."

But he did have a preferred vantage point—from the Flyers' bench—as the Golden Seals posted a rare victory, prevailing 3–2 on the strength of a 38-save gem by Gilles Meloche.

Gillow had been under the impression that there was a greater likelihood of playing. It had been intimated that Favell was under the weather and therefore might not be able to answer the bell against the Seals. But, as it turned out, Gillow was essentially among the spectators—on a night when there were only 3,422 of them—for the one game in which he donned a big-league uniform.

"Well, that's just the way it is," Gillow reflected, matter-of-factly. "It was cool, sitting there and watching."

The following day, he headed back to the San Francisco airport—no helicopter this time—and was soon destined for Spokane. The NHL stay was abbreviated, yet memorable, because Allen had recalled goaltender Don (Smokey) McLeod from Philadelphia's AHL affiliate, the Providence Flyers.

Did Gillow leave the Oakland arena with a souvenir such as, say, the No. 30 jersey he wore for Philadelphia on February 8, 1972?

"No such luck," he said with a chuckle. "Just a 'thank you for coming.'"

Gillow's short, sedentary NHL stint was over, but there had been and would continue to be more eventful chapters to add to a puck-stopping profile that dated back to the mid-1940s.

"I always wanted to be a goalie, even when I was six," Gillow, who grew up in Hespeler, Ontario, said from his home in St. George, Utah. "When we were kids, we had a wading pool right below us and, in the wintertime, we'd have 20 kids in there. It was only 10 or 12 feet wide and about 20 feet long. We'd be in there with sticks, beating the hell out of each other—and I was the goalie. We'd use a tennis ball and it just went from there.

"We used to play under a streetlight, every night, and then they built an arena. Hespeler had never had an arena."

Once he played underneath a roof, his ceiling became even higher.

"I played on midget teams, juvenile teams and bantam teams, and I played in an industrial league at the same time, when I was 12 or 14, I guess," Gillow said. "I had about a mile and a half to go, so I put my equipment on a sled and took it down to the arena every night I could.

"The guy who was looking after the arena let in three or four of us kids when there was nobody else in there. We'd turn on three or four lights and we'd practise."

For Gillow, the light went on—in terms of aspiring to be a goaltender—at an early juncture.

"It was mostly from listening on the radio," he recalled. "Gump Worsley was a favourite—and Johnny Bower—and I just wanted to do that. That's all I really ever wanted to do."

The risks, documented so expansively for several chapters now, were not a deterrent.

"There's an old saying—for myself, anyway," Gillow said. "Somebody would say, 'Geez, you got hit in the head. Didn't that hurt?' And I'd say, 'Ahh, you can't hurt cement.'"

Gillow soon cemented his status as a goaltender of considerable ability and promise, to the extent that he was invited to the Detroit Red Wings' training camp.

"It was OK, but I was so overwhelmed just because I was so young," he said. "I didn't really play or practise with Detroit, because I was so young, but they were all there, too—all the stars.

"Terry Sawchuk was there, and I tried to ask him a few questions. It was, 'Get the hell out of here, kid.'"

Another Red Wings superstar was considerably more congenial.

"What impressed me the most was being able to talk with Gordie Howe," Gillow said.

"I got to go as a spare goalie to a Detroit game when they were playing in another town. I got on the bus from training camp and I'm sitting there all by myself, and who comes and sits beside me? Gordie. He just spent the whole time sitting there and talking to me. I was just going, 'Wow.'"

There were also some "ow" moments.

Most notably, there was what Ron Glover of the *Edmonton Journal* described as "a severe eye injury" Gillow suffered while playing for the Edmonton Oil Kings against the host St. Catharines Teepees in Game 1 of the 1960 Memorial Cup—which was then a two-team, best-of-seven series, with Canadian junior hockey supremacy at stake.

A shot by Chico Maki opened up a cut over Gillow's right eye. Although the wound would require 10 stitches, he remained in the game and ultimately shared in a 5–3 victory.

"They don't seem to hurt as much when you win," Gillow told the *Journal*.

More than 60 years later, he still referred to the ghastly-looking injury in a matter-of-fact manner.

"I stopped a shot and my eyes swelled up," Gillow recalled of that April 27, 1960, game. "It was fine as far as I was concerned. I went right back out and finished the game.

"The next morning in *The Toronto Globe and Mail*, there was my picture on the front page of the paper, with blood running down my face."

By the time *The Globe and Mail* hit the newsstands, Gillow's injury was beginning to worsen.

"The day after the game, I couldn't see anything," he continued. "My eye was swollen shut, so there was no way I could see to play."

Therefore, Dale Gaume got the call to start in goal for Edmonton in Game 2, won 6–2 by St. Catharines on April 29 at Maple Leaf Gardens (the site of all but one game in the 1960 Final).

Game 3 was played on May 1, when Gillow returned to action—still without a mask—and St. Catharines prevailed 9–1.

"My vision wasn't the best," he said, "but I could see OK."

Gillow wasn't his sharpest, which was understandable. He had missed Game 2 with what Glover referred to as "a black-and-purple mess of flesh laughingly called an eye."

The Oil Kings rebounded for a 9–7 victory that knotted the series at 2–2, whereupon St. Catharines won 9–6 and 7–3 to capture the Memorial Cup.

The following season, 1960–61, was a busy one for Gillow. Having graduated from the junior ranks, he had stints with the Edmonton Flyers (Western League), Milwaukee Falcons (International League), and Lacombe Rockets (of the Central Alberta loop).

He was comparably mobile in 1961–62, spending time in the Central Alberta circuit with both the Rockets and Oil Kings, in addition to suiting up for Edmonton's Flyers.

The return to Lacombe was noteworthy from the standpoint that Gillow became the first masked goalie in Central Alberta league history, according to Dwanye Erickson of the *Journal*.

"A dentist in Lacombe made the mask for me," Gillow said. "It was kind of a replica of Jacques Plante's mask.

"You still felt everything because it was still tight to your face so, really, I didn't like the thing."

Gillow was a mainstay in goal for Lacombe through the 1965–66 season, after which he was named the Central Alberta league's most valuable player.

That sensational season propelled Gillow to the pros. He spent 1966–67 with the IHL's Des Moines Oak Leafs, for whom he played in all 72 regular season games—at one point registering a team-record shutout streak of 168 minutes 57 seconds—and returned to his old ways of going maskless, with some exceptions.

Gillow had required 12 stitches above an eye following a 2–1 loss to the Dayton Gems on December 13, 1966. The next night, he did wear a mask as the Oak Leafs fell 4–3 to the Columbus Checkers. He soon ditched the mask, despite concerns expressed by his wife.

"We've talked about it a lot of times and I wish he would [wear a mask]," Diana Gillow told Buck Turnbull of the *Des Moines Tribune* in late February 1967. "I don't relish the idea of him getting cut up and having stitches in his face. But he says he can't see as well out of the corners of his eyes with a mask on, so I wouldn't want him to do anything that would hinder his play as a goalie."

Gillow's excellence in Des Moines was such that the Boston Bruins took an interest. He played for the Oklahoma City Blazers—the Bruins' chief minor league affiliate—in 1967–68 and 1968–69.

He boasted a league-high eight shutouts in '67–68 while playing primarily without a mask.

"I started the season with one, but it was not made especially for me," Gillow told *The Oklahoma City Times*. "It didn't fit perfect so I decided to continue playing without one. [Blazers trainer] Frank Gleeson has another one ordered and maybe I'll wear it."

So much for "maybe." Gillow soon gave in and wore a mask for good. During his stay with the 1969–70 Salt Lake Golden Eagles, an International League team that had purchased his rights from Boston, he posed for a close-up newspaper photo of his mask—a variation of Plante's porous, yet popular, "pretzel" model.

"The mask is designed to fit tightly around his face and is intended to secure protection from stray pucks," Steve Rudman wrote of Gillow in *The Salt Lake Tribune*. "If Gillow didn't wear the mask, his teeth would get scattered all over the ice.

"Maybe you think the most demanding position [in sports] is in the waning moments of a heavyweight prize fight. Your kidney is swollen and feels like it will burst, your nose is wall-to-wall, and you can't find your opponent because your stomach is hemorrhaging. True. But you can always try to hit back."

Gillow hit the road following one season in Salt Lake, joining a rival Western League franchise, the Seattle Totems. Then it was off to Spokane, where he was playing when the Flyers came calling.

Only three days after Gillow savoured the shortest of stints as an NHLer, there was another momentous development in his professional hockey career.

On February 12, 1972, he was selected by the Los Angeles Sharks during one of the 70 rounds that composed the WHA's general draft. That was a prelude to an invitation to the team's inaugural training camp.

"The Sharks called me up one day, out of the blue, and said, 'You come down here and we're going to sign you,'" Gillow recalled. "And I said, 'Yeah, really...'

"They said, 'We'll have a ticket for you at your airport and we'll fly you in. We'll pay for everything and it'll be first class. We're going to sign you.' Yeah, sure. I thought somebody was pulling my leg.

"I told my wife about it, and we were laughing about it and everything. The time came and I said, 'Well, OK. Let's go see. I can't lose anything. If I go to the airport and there's no ticket, fine. We'll come home.'

"So I went to the airport and, of course, there was a ticket to Los Angeles. It was first class and all the rest, and they signed me, just like that."

One had to like the remuneration, especially after so many years of slogging it out in the minors.

"That was where the division [in compensation] started," Gillow said. "When I first went to training camp in Detroit, the average salary in the National Hockey League was $7,500 a year. When I went to the World Hockey Association, there was money—like, 50 grand.

"Oh, wow! Yeah, I'll be there."

He was there, all right. In the WHA's maiden season, he boasted the league's second-best goals against average (2.88). Only the Cleveland Crusaders' Gerry Cheevers, who had been wooed away from the Stanley Cup-winning Bruins by a seven-year, $1.2-million contract, had a superior GAA (2.83).

"I did have a really good year," Gillow recalled, "so after the year was over—and I didn't ask for it—they said, 'OK, we want to renegotiate your contract.' I more than doubled my salary and got a four-year contract, no-cut."

The Sharks, however, could not guarantee that there wouldn't be any cuts as a result of flying pucks, so he took a serious look at an enhancement of his facial protection.

Good idea. After all, the ranks of the WHA's shooters included none other than Bobby Hull, who had been suitably enticed by the Winnipeg Jets and their offer of a landmark 10-year, $2.5-million contract.

"George Gardner was our main goalie," said Gillow, whose 38 appearances for the 1972–73 Sharks put him 11 behind Gardner. "I remember when we played Winnipeg, as soon as Bobby Hull hit the red line, George was standing on his tiptoes, he was so afraid of Bobby's shot.

"It was funny to us—we laughed about it—but it wasn't funny to George. He was just terrified of Bobby Hull. Who wouldn't be?"

Hence the need for an upgrade.

"We did have masks, but I decided to get another mask made," Gillow said. "I took the mask before I wore it and put a towel inside it, taped it to the goal post, and had the guys shoot at it. I wanted to see how strong it was and whether it was going to take the punishment, and it did.

"It was still tight to your face, and the reason I didn't like it was because I couldn't see well enough. That was my feeling, always.

"But here's the thing: It was 'either you wear a mask or you don't play.' It was one of the two. It was the same thing when I went to Edmonton to play junior. It was, 'What do you want to do? Do you want to go to school or do you want to play hockey? Make up your mind now.' I was, 'Well, I want to play hockey.'

"In the WHA, it was better hockey, but our equipment was still not good. There really wasn't much of anything.

"Our shoulder pads and arm pads were all like a one-piece unit that you slid your arms into. They were felt-filled and maybe a half-inch thick on your arms and your shoulders.

"Your belly pad was cut to fit in your belly so that it covered the middle, but there was nothing on the side of the ribs. I got hit in the ribs a few times and ended up with cracked ribs and everything else.

"It was basically that we were tougher. At that time, everybody was tougher. We played hurt. You were afraid that somebody was going to take your job.

"Now it's so much different. It's faster. More is expected of everybody. There's a coach for every player, I think.

"Back then, nobody taught us anything. There weren't any goalie coaches. Nobody ever said, 'You know, you should try this,' or, 'Do this and it'll work out for you.' Nobody ever said anything. It was, 'Do your best.'"

It is open to debate whether the goaltenders or the planes on which the Sharks flew made more stops.

Direct flights were rare. Commercial flights were the rule.

"We'd play in Chicago and, right after the game, get something to eat, get on a plane, and fly to Vancouver to play," Gillow said. "You'd get there two hours before game time and you'd be tired, but you'd get something to eat and you'd go play.

"I'm happy that I don't fly much anymore. There are so many restrictions and it's just a hassle. I thought at one time, 'I've been really lucky,' because we flew so much to so many different places and never had a problem. All it takes is one time…"

Hold on. Isn't flying considerably safer than, say, playing goal without a mask?

"Oh, heavens, no," a chuckling Gillow responded. "You have some control. When you're flying, you have no control."

Some events in the hockey world are also beyond a player's control—such as being traded, for example.

Gillow rang in 1974 in unceremonious fashion when he was traded on New Year's Day, along with left-winger Earl Heiskala, to the Jersey Knights for 36-year-old goaltender Jim McLeod.

The Knights were known as the New York Raiders during the WHA's introductory season, after which they were rebranded as the New York Golden Blades. The Golden Blades were such a smashing success that the league took over the team's operations just 24 games into the 1973–74 season.

Next stop: Cherry Hill, New Jersey, where the team was known as the Jersey Knights. Gillow, as it turned out, never wore a jersey for Jersey, although his rights technically belonged to the team for the second half of '73–74.

"The radio announcer called to tell me that I was traded," Gillow said. "I got ahold of the [Knights] team and they said, 'OK, here's the deal: We want you next year, not to finish this year or anything with us. We want to send you to Syracuse of the International league. If you finish the season there, we are moving to San Diego, so you would move to San Diego.' I said, 'OK, that sounds good. I'll go for that.'

"So they sent me to Syracuse. We won the championship. We had the toughest team, so we beat everybody. As soon as the last game was over and we won, I went to the airport.

"The guys were all celebrating and everything, and I went to the airport and slept there. I didn't want to miss a 7:00 flight to get back to L.A. and to my family. Then we could pack up and move to San Diego."

Gillow spent two seasons with the San Diego Mariners and established a home in the scenic southern California burg. Post-WHA, he played with the San Diego Sharks (an independent team) and San Diego Hawks (Pacific Hockey League).

Nearing 40 by the time he last suited up with the Hawks, he nonetheless continued to play hockey. At 43, he appeared in 16 games with the Western International Hockey League's Spokane Chiefs and remained between the pipes for several subsequent seasons.

"I played until I was 50—and this was with the old-timers," Gillow said, proudly. "I played because I enjoyed it, and it was just fun.

"There were guys my age and they were running at each other. They wanted to fight and all this stuff. I was thinking, 'Really? You're not going anywhere. Why the hell are you doing this?'

"I'd had enough, so I brought my equipment home and I said, 'That's it.' I stored it in the garage for six months, and then my wife said, 'Get rid of that stuff. It stinks,' so I did. And the only things I have are the two masks I wore.

"About five years ago, the dentist who made that first mask for me in Lacombe said, 'I still have the mold that we took to make your mask. Would you like to have it?' I said, 'Oh, OK,' so he shipped it to me. I have that mask and the other one."

Gillow's original mask is outdated, to put it mildly, but it is nonetheless a cornerstone of his plans for the future.

"Before I go, I'm going to put the mold on the side of the house," he concluded, "so that you'll know that I was always there."

15

The Daley Show

Joe Daley: From minding the net to minding the store

At long last, nobody did a double take when Joe Daley wore a mask at work.

The personable proprietor of the eponymous Joe Daley's Sports & Framing took all the necessary precautions when welcoming customers to his Winnipeg-based business during the COVID-19 pandemic period.

An expansive list of visitors included Craig Heisinger—senior vice-president and director, hockey operations/assistant general manager, with the NHL's Winnipeg Jets. A barefaced Daley had played for the first incarnation of the Jets when they debuted in the WHA in 1972.

"Craig said, 'Joe, I always thought you were crazy for not wearing a mask, and now I think you're smart for wearing one,'" Daley said with a laugh.

Always quick with a quip and a hello, Daley loves to entertain and engage with all customers.

"I have a wonderful son who pretty much runs the business," Travis Daley's proud father noted. "I call myself the Walmart greeter. I sit in my chair and say hi to pretty much everyone who comes in the door."

Heavy traffic on the doorstep of his goal crease did not compel Daley to don facial protection until the 1973–74 season—his second with the Jets and his 11th in professional hockey. By that time, the Jets goaltending tandem consisted of Daley and fellow veteran Ernie Wakely.

"We had decided right from the get-go that we were going to alternate every other game, and Ernie and I were quite comfortable alternating," Daley recalled. "Bobby Hull was our playing coach and he said, 'I know nothing about goaltending, so you guys figure out how you want to play.'

"One night, Ernie just said jokingly, 'I think you'd better start to figure out how to wear a mask because, when it's my night off, I want a night off.' I said, 'OK, let's try and get one made up.' That was really the first time I got a real good, comfortable mask and became comfortable wearing one."

Wakely had begun wearing a mask during the 1962–63 season, although the change did not become permanent until 1969. He spent most of '62–63 with the Eastern Professional Hockey League's Ottawa-Hull Canadiens, with whom everything was proceeding nicely until a defect in the mask was discovered.

Because of that, Wakely decided to revert back to a maskless state when the Canadiens opposed the Syracuse Braves on November 2, 1962.

"At the 13:58 mark of the third period with the Canadiens leading 5–1, Merve Kuryluk broke in on the left side and his shot hit Wakely squarely in the mouth," Gerry Redmond reported in the *Ottawa Journal* after Ottawa-Hull won 5–2. "For the first time in several games, Wakely wasn't wearing a mask and the shot caught him dead on in the mouth. It split his upper lip and the side of his face and he was taken to hospital for plastic surgery to repair the damage.

"His mask had a slight split and last night he decided to go without it. He won't again. And that is an order from Canadiens general manager Sam Pollock."

(The order didn't stick. There is irrefutable photographic evidence of Wakely playing maskless in 1967 and 1968. By the time he joined the St. Louis Blues in 1969, he had switched back to a mask—permanently.)

Pollock's immediate priority during the game against Syracuse was to find someone to replace a woozy Wakely. On that occasion, a standby netminder was not on the premises.

"Usually they have one, but with Jacques Plante out, Cesare Maniago has taken over [with the parent club in Montreal] and their handyman Claude Dufour has had to replace him in Spokane," Redmond wrote in the November 3, 1962, edition of the *Journal*. "So when disaster struck in the third period last night, Pollock walked into the dressing room and asked for volunteers. He got six from the ranks of the Canadiens, but Sam narrowed down the field by asking if anyone had played the position before. And young Norm Beaudin, a scoring standout with the Habs with six goals so far in the EPHL campaign, including the first last night, volunteered on the strength of a couple of games in goal as a midget six years ago.

"Canadiens checked Braves dizzy over the final six minutes and only two shots were on the net. One of them went in but that was deflected so no one will ever know how good Beaudin would be as a goalie."

Beaudin's offensive talent was beyond debate. Witness the 103 points he amassed for Winnipeg during the WHA's inaugural season, 1972–73. Also on-board with the original Jets was—talk about a small world!—Ernie Wakely, whom Beaudin had momentarily replaced in goal 10 years earlier.

Beaudin spent four seasons with the Jets and was therefore on the team when Daley finally committed to wearing a mask, thereby acceding to Wakely's wishes.

"I always felt there were going to be some issues with wearing masks, such as vision," said Daley, who also cited the possibility of overheating as a factor.

"Even with the mask I ended up wearing, it was very hot and sweaty, but I found that I adapted to it. I thought it was a well-made one and it certainly protected me well."

To that point, Daley had played in 106 NHL regular season games—suiting up for the Detroit Red Wings, Pittsburgh Penguins, and Buffalo Sabres from 1967 to 1972—and made another 70 appearances for the

Jets over their first two seasons. He had also logged 371 games' worth of minor league duty, dating back to 1961.

But who knows what the actual game count might be? After all, Daley—who was born in 1943—began playing goalie way back in the 1950s on a rink near the Bronx Park Community Centre in the Winnipeg suburb of East Kildonan.

"I went to the community club to play hockey and something just told me to sign up as a goalie," he remembered, "so I did and, as they say, the rest is history."

That history was celebrated in 2019 when a mural, celebrating Daley, was unveiled at the community centre where he took his first significant steps on skates and decided to become a goaltender.

"There was really no outside influence," he said. "Something just triggered me to put my name down there, and away I went."

The sparseness of what passed for goaltending equipment at the time, and for a few decades to follow, was neither an impediment nor a concern.

"Starting off as a youngster and having to use the equipment that was provided by the community club, it was primitive—and I mean *very* primitive," Daley said. "It was to the point that, on some weekends, if you didn't get the first choice of equipment, you might have been tying it on with skate laces and things like that.

"I saw that as being the norm and nothing was unusual about it. I guess I hoped that as I advanced, some of that stuff would get better. But, no, I never gave much thought to it and certainly wasn't discouraged by the fact that I didn't have the nicest of stuff to wear."

The equipment, in those days, was restricted to below the neck. Little thought was given to mask usage across the hockey universe until the late 1950s. Even then, goaltenders routinely disregarded the option of facial protection, such as it was.

"It didn't seem to be an issue, really," Daley said. "I never gave it much thought for quite some time. The blows that I took were pretty minimal over the course of time. There wasn't one startling moment like, for instance, when Jacques Plante got hit and decided, 'OK, that's enough.'"

That said, the Plante "moment," if you will, did provide pause for thought over the years.

"There have been a number of cases—maybe not as dramatic as that," Daley said. "I think that was a big one because it did change people's thinking and maybe that of some of the goalies as well.

"You see an incident like that and you start thinking that if a shot got away on a player and you took it in an area that was not very nice, you literally could get killed.

"That's not something to just shrug off and not think about. There's probably been a few cases over the years where you look back and think, 'My goodness, that was close to being life-threatening.'"

At the time, Daley attached more importance to developing his skills as a goaltender and moving up the chain. His talents attracted the attention of the NHL, to the extent that he became the property of the Boston Bruins, New York Rangers and, eventually, the Red Wings. The latter association was especially meaningful to Daley, because his idol was Detroit's No. 1 goalie at the time.

"Terry Sawchuk grew up in Winnipeg in the same area as I did," Daley said. "There was that connection, and I just liked the way he played the game. I loved his stance, his stature and, of course, his effectiveness. I always considered him one of the greatest of all-time, and still do.

"I never got to know Terry, and that's one thing that I regret. When I was in Detroit at the same time he was, I was a kid on my way up and he was obviously an established star, so we never connected.

"I think it's different today with organizations, and I know it is with players. There's not that separation. It has always been said that Terry considered anybody vying for his job to be a threat or whatever. Even though he was one of the greatest, he always felt like somebody was after his job if they were in camp, so you never got to socialize with somebody like that.

"I just wish I would have been able to have a chat with him and talk about the fact that we were from the same city, and the same area of the city, and talk a little bit about his youth and coming up through the system. It would have been interesting for me, but I never got that chance."

Daley did get a chance to wear a Red Wings jersey at the junior level during the 1961–62 and 1962–63 seasons, most of which were spent in Weyburn, Saskatchewan. At the time, Detroit sponsored the Saskatchewan Junior Hockey League's Weyburn Red Wings.

From Weyburn, Daley proceeded to Johnstown, Pennsylvania, where he was a workhorse for an earlier Jets team—the Eastern Hockey League version—in 1963–64 and 1964–65.

The Johnstown Jets and the city in which they were based later became the inspiration for the cinematic classic *Slap Slot*, which focused on the goonery of the semi-fictional Hanson brothers.

"I remember when the movie was made," Daley reminisced. "People said to me, 'Have you seen it?' I said, 'I really don't need to see it. I lived it.'

"By that, I mean that there were some nights when things got pretty scary and crazy while I was playing with Johnstown. Obviously, the movie was carried to an extreme, but I thought, 'Yeah, some of those things, I could relate to.'

"At the time, you think, 'I know that part of what's going on is really not pertaining to the game of hockey,' but it was what it was. Luckily, I was in a position that I was only concerned about my development and I didn't have to really get out there and participate in all the shenanigans.

"I looked at it as another stepping stone. It was an opportunity to play and that's all I really cared about."

In what respect, Daley was asked, did *Slap Shot* most closely resemble the reality he experienced at Johnstown's Cambria County War Memorial Arena?

"There were stick-swinging brawls," he responded. "There were fans getting involved either with support or with angst against you.

"There weren't necessarily the fights in the warmup but, once the puck was dropped, it got pretty ugly some nights."

There weren't many ugly goals against Daley, who was named the Eastern loop's rookie of the year for 1963–64. He made 66 appearances that season before playing in all 72 of Johnstown's games the following winter.

Next stop: Tennessee, where Daley toiled for the Central League's Memphis Wings for the better part of two seasons.

During the 1966–67 campaign, the Wings were wending their way northward, making stops in St. Louis and St. Paul, Minnesota as a prelude to playing an exhibition game against the Canadian national team in Winnipeg.

"We're having this morning practice and Lou Marcon couldn't raise the puck if you placed a bet on it," Daley began. "He comes down the ice and hits me right between the eyes. My head splits like an upside-down Y. Now I'm done.

"By the time we got to Winnipeg, I couldn't see out of one eye because it was swollen, so I never did play, and I was looking forward to it, with Winnipeg being my hometown."

He was especially looking forward to playing in the NHL, someday, and that chance finally arrived after the doubling of the league's ranks from six to 12 teams.

At 24, Daley was claimed from Detroit by Pittsburgh in the expansion draft of June 6, 1967. That was his ticket to the AHL and the Baltimore Clippers, who at the time were the Penguins' chief minor league affiliate.

"When I got drafted by Pittsburgh in 1967 and Red Kelly came in [as head coach], he was pretty adamant about me wearing a mask," Daley said. "In fact, you can find footage of me wearing one with the Penguins. But, that particular year, I got sent to Baltimore in the American league and, as soon as I got there, I certainly wasn't going to wear a mask."

Nor did he wear a mask in his NHL debut, on November 13, 1968, in Chicago. The Black Hawks won 6–5 on the strength of a tie-breaking goal by future Jets teammate Bobby Hull with 17 seconds remaining in the third period.

Daley faced 41 shots, 23 of which were fired—and stopped—during a scoreless first period.

The excellence of his goaltending was noted by Bill Heufelder, who mentioned in his *Pittsburgh Press* story that Chicago star Stan Mikita approached Daley before the second period and said: "You've done a night's work already."

Daley ended up playing in 29 games—all in the NHL—during the 1968–69 season. He made nine more appearances with Pittsburgh in 1969–70, with the bulk of his work that winter being done on behalf of Baltimore.

Although Daley was only an occasional big-leaguer in 1969–70, that season is significant because he and Les Binkley formed the NHL's last barefaced goalie tandem.

As a Penguin, Daley paid a painful price for being steadfastly maskless.

During a preseason game against the Minnesota North Stars, he was beaned by a Wayne Connelly shot and spent the night in hospital.

On another occasion with Pittsburgh, Daley faced a Philadelphia Flyers team that included a future Buffalo teammate, Gerry Meehan.

"Gerry fired a shot out of the corner and I thought, 'OK, I'm going to play this one off my chest,'" Daley remembered. "Well, as the puck's approaching me, I realize it's going higher than my chest, so I get up on my toes. Finally, I just turned my face and it hit me in the jaw and broke my jaw. I ended up on the other side of the net.

"I went to put my mouth together and I couldn't, because my broken jaw was in the middle of my mouth. Luckily, there was an orthodontist at the game. He came down to the dressing room and snapped my jaw back into place and, of course, off to the hospital I went."

Off to Buffalo he went on June 9, 1970. The Penguins' brass, expecting to lose him in the expansion draft, put him on waivers for monetary reasons.

When the Sabres snapped up Daley—making him the first player to join the new team—the Penguins were able to collect the $30,000 waiver price, as opposed to losing him for nothing. Sabres head coach and general manager Punch Imlach made the move shortly before an expansion draft stocked not only the Sabres, but also the Vancouver Canucks.

It was as a Sabre that Daley experienced the busiest game of his career. He faced 72—yes, 72—shots on December 10, 1970, in an 8–2 loss to a Boston powerhouse that included Phil Esposito (who was in the midst of a record-shattering, 76-goal season) and Bobby Orr (who finished 1970–71 with 139 points, still the most by an NHL defenceman).

"The Bruins had 72 shots on the Buffalo net, but they were talking to themselves about the manner in which they were frustrated by a black-haired and unmasked goaltender named Thomas Joseph Daley," Tom Fitzgerald wrote in the *Boston Globe*, adding that Daley "practically stood on his head in blocking off Boston shots, and for the first two periods kept out 40 of them."

Cue a third period in which Boston added 30 shots on goal—four more than Buffalo managed over the course of the 60-minute contest.

"The game was in Boston and my wife sat at home and watched it on TV," Daley said. "She was thinking, 'Oh my God! When is this going to end?'

"It was probably one of the more emotional games that I played in, only because after two periods we were tied 2–2. I had played really well up to that point, and then gave up six in the third period.

"We were playing arguably the best team in the league at that time, in their own building. It was just one of those nights that happened and a memory that I'll carry until I die."

Another one to remember: Later that season, Daley made 51 saves as Buffalo bounced Boston 7–5 on March 21, 1971, snapping the Bruins' winning streak at 13 games. But the 72-shot barrage is the one that is referenced more often.

"It's something that somebody brings up every once in a while in discussion with me," Daley noted. "I was pretty exhausted and emotionally whipped at the end of that one."

Daley's time in Buffalo was exhausted following just one season. After being traded to Detroit, he spent one more season in the NHL before joining the hometown Jets. Subsequently, Winnipeg signed a big-money deal with Hull, who had scored the winning goal in Daley's first NHL game.

Although Daley welcomed the new reality of not having to contend with Hull's howitzer during games, the Jets' goalie wasn't entirely home free.

"You faced the guy with probably the hardest shot in hockey every day in practice," Daley noted. "I enjoyed the challenge of trying to stop Bobby, so I was never scared of him. But that shot was something.

"I'd go home and say to my wife, 'Look at this one.' She'd say, 'Bobby?' And I'd go, 'Yup!' There were a few welts on my upper body that I took from him.

"It was a challenge, but it was enjoyable—and I'm certainly glad he was on my side."

So was good fortune, for the most part. Daley emerged from 16 years of professional hockey without any lingering injuries, and with most of his omnipresent smile intact, despite having suffered the broken jaw.

"People say, 'Did you ever get a tooth knocked out?' I say, 'Yeah, I did,'" he recounted.

"I went back to Weyburn to play in a benefit game for the junior team. I played the game without a mask. Darwin Mott's skate came up in a scramble and chipped two of my teeth. That was the first time in my life I had any damage to my teeth...and it was in a benefit game!

"Those were the things, I think, that were as scary as the direct shots—situations where you were trying to find a loose puck or something and a guy's stick caught you.

"I think most of us were probably concerned about our eyes more than anything, because it wouldn't take much to take a stick to your eye area and, bingo, you've got a problem for life."

Daley understood the occupational hazards during his playing days, but accepted the risks—ones that he wouldn't dare assume if, magically, he was able to return to the NHL.

"I certainly wouldn't ever consider playing a game of hockey today without a mask on," he conceded. "First of all, the sticks are a weapon. Back in the day, you had to look out for a guy or two on each team, but now almost everybody can shoot the puck with authority. I feel that some of them don't necessarily have total control of where it's going, so it would be life-threatening today to go out and try to play without a mask."

Life in hockey has been good to Daley. Approaching his 80th birthday, he reflected on the good fortune that allowed him to enjoy a lengthy playing career that concluded in his hometown. In fact, he was the only player who suited up for the WHA's Jets in each of their seven seasons.

Along the way, he helped Winnipeg win the Avco Cup—the league's championship trophy—in 1976, 1978, and 1979. He was a WHA first-team All-Star in 1975–76, his second season with a mask, and twice made the second team.

Daley will forever lead WHA goaltenders in regular season victories (167), playoff wins (30), and games played (308).

Oft-enshrined, he eventually entered the WHA Hall of Fame, Manitoba Hockey Hall of Fame, and Manitoba Sports Hall of Fame.

He is also eminently qualified for the Hall of Frame.

Time spent at his long-standing framing and sports business is a mutual pleasure for the owner and his customers.

"Sport has been my life," Daley said. "As a kid, I participated in almost all the sports, and obviously pursued a dream in hockey.

"My boys played sports and they played it to the level that they wanted to. They enjoyed it and I enjoyed watching them play. When my grandson played hockey, I enjoyed watching him.

"Now I feel it's important for me to be able to tell a story, so to speak. By that, I mean that there's a lot of people and a lot of kids who I encounter now who just enjoy coming in and having me talk about my past and what it was like."

Having registered an untold number of saves, Daley now ensures that the customers enjoy every stop.

16

Cooley's Head Prevailed

Minor league life and a major movie star

Gaye Cooley may come across as your typical Hollywood movie sidekick but, were it not for his years as a proudly unmasked goalie, he could have been a leading man.

"I like to say that I used to look like Rock Hudson," he reflected, "but I might look like Rock Pile now."

Call him a rock star, for the purposes of this project, with battle scars that border on the incalculable.

"I'm not sure exactly how many stitches there were," Cooley, who was in his mid-70s at the time of the interview, mused from his home in Orillia, Ontario. "Through the years, it was, 'I got 39 there, I got 27 here,' and you just figure it out. Maybe it was 400 or maybe it was 550, I don't know. I'm just saying around 500 stitches that I've got on my face.

"Now, that's just on my face, because I got some in my head, too. I got lots of sticks on top of the head."

Cooley never got to be an NHL A-lister, but he did provide a decade's worth of stellar performances at the professional level. All but one game over that period was spent in the minor leagues.

That is quite a tale of endurance when you consider that Cooley did not wear a conventional mask until his final full season (1975–76).

Even then, the long-disregarded goaltending implement was apt to spend part of the game sitting on the top of the net.

So, inevitably, there were days when he ended up sitting in the infirmary, undergoing repairs and adding yet another series of stitches (and stories) to what would become an eye-popping lifetime tally.

"After you started getting stitches, it really was no big deal," said Cooley, who debuted in the pros in 1967 and played his final game in December 1976.

"The only time it was a problem—and this shows you how crude it was—was when I was playing for Des Moines. We were in the playoffs against Toledo. It was a good game and we were up 1–0 and I got a shot in the face. I ended up needing 30 stitches, so they held up the game. It was, 'OK, take him in and sew him up, and we'll add the time to the next period.'

"Well, I went into the dressing room and I'm lying there and the doctor comes in. This guy's got a cigarette in his mouth with an Andy Capp type of ash hanging off the end of it, and he's got a pint of liquor in his back pocket. The smell of his breath was totally of liquor.

"He's leaning over and talking to me, and I can remember seeing this cigarette hanging over my face. I looked at the trainer and said, 'No way! I want you to tape up this thing. To hell with it! We'll wait until after the game and, when we get on the bus, we'll stop at Emergency at the hospital and we'll get them to sew it up.' That's what we did. I wouldn't let this guy do it.

"The doctor said, 'I'm all right,' and I said, 'You're not all right for me, with that cigarette ash hanging. You're not sewing me up!'

"This guy was not Marcus Welby, I'll tell you that."

Cooley's well-being was not served especially well by being a goaltender, but this is a man without regrets—someone who rattles off a string of hockey injuries as if he is reciting a simple game summary.

"Well, I've had three skull fractures," he began. "I've had at least 500 stitches in my face. I've had eyebrows cut right off..."

Eyebrows. Cut. Right. Off.

"I thought I'd lost my eye," he said by way of elaboration. "I was in Knoxville, Tennessee, and it was game day. We were having our skate in the morning and a puck chipped up and caught me right above the eyebrow.

"When I went down, the skin was cut so bad that I put my hand up to my eye and I couldn't see anything. I thought, 'Oh my God, I've lost my eye!'

"What happened was that the flap of skin had flopped right down over my eye. That was the scariest time I ever had. Then, when my trainer came out to fix it, he lifted the skin up and then I saw light again. It was like, 'My God!'

"Yeah, I had quite a few of those..."

Same with uniforms.

As a professional goaltender, he suited up for eight different teams and played in six leagues. That was after two standout seasons with the Michigan State University Spartans.

As a first-year collegiate player, he backstopped Michigan State to the NCAA men's hockey title and, for good measure, was named the most valuable player of the championship tournament—the Frozen Four.

"I went to Michigan State on a scholarship," Cooley recalled. "By then, I'd been hit in the teeth so many times that my teeth were growing backward, and they were all busted.

"When I was a freshman, I was having terrible toothaches, so I went to the dentist. In those days, the freshmen didn't play, so you had a whole year just to practise, so the doctor said, 'This is a freshman year for you. Those teeth have got to come out. You can't do anything with them, so we'll take them all out.'

"I was young and I didn't know any different, so I said, 'If that's what you've got to do, let's do it.' They took them all out in one day—all 16 on the top row.

"I'll tell you right now—and this is going to make you think that I'm really stupid—that I went to practice when I got out of getting my teeth done. My mouth was numb, anyway, so what the hell's the difference?

"It was quite hilarious, because I couldn't talk. My mouth was full of cotton-batten and crap, and I was spitting blood all the time. I lasted the whole practice. They wanted to give me painkillers and I was afraid to take any for the practice, because I didn't know what they'd do to me. I'd never taken pills before.

"So as soon as I got out of the shower after practice, it was hurting so bad that I went and took some of these pills and it was, 'Oh boy...these are something!'"

Cooley still has his bottom teeth, which miraculously survived a quarter-century of fearless, maskless goalkeeping that began in the minor hockey system of North Bay, Ontario.

"When I started out, there were no masks, so we just played the game," said Cooley, who was born in 1946. "We played because of the love of the game, not like these kids nowadays. It's all dollars and cents. We really had a love for the game.

"Jacques Plante came along and started the first mask, but the NHL didn't even catch on that quick with it. For it to filter down into the other leagues, that stuff didn't happen like that."

Cooley eventually ascended to the junior ranks, with the Northern Ontario league's North Bay Trappers, before heading to Michigan State.

He turned pro during the 1967–68 season, playing in 48 games with the Eastern League's Knoxville Knights. He also made one appearance with the International League's Port Huron Flags.

He was Port Huron's workhorse in 1968–69 before spending the following two IHL seasons with the Des Moines Oak Leafs. The second season in Iowa was notable due to a league-imposed edict requiring all goalies to (no!) wear a mask. (One year before, the IHL had made helmets mandatory for forwards and defencemen.)

"[Cooley] has accepted the fact that he'll have to wear [a mask]," Buck Turnbull wrote in the *Des Moines Register* on October 14, 1970, "and already has a cut-down version ready to go."

Cooley's doctored mask adhered to the letter of the rule but did not extend beyond the barest of standards. The result was a "mask" that looked like something Batman would wear, albeit one with larger-than-usual eyeholes. After Cooley and his trusty hacksaw were finished, the result was a pseudo-mask that still left the chin and mouth exposed.

"You've gone all your hockey life and you didn't wear a mask and you don't want to wear a mask, because I didn't want that stuff on my face," he said.

"It's like today with computers and stuff. Kids learn all about computers when they're very young and they grow up with it. But, all of a sudden, if you take someone who is 50 years old and say, 'Here's a computer. Show me what you can do with it,' you can't do anything with it, or you don't want to do anything with it.

"The mask was no different than the computer thing. It was like, 'My God, I'm going to fight this.' [Cutting the bottom of the mask and widening the eye holes] was my way of fighting it."

Cooley made a career out of stopping drives while on the ice. Away from the rink, he could also facilitate them.

He often drove the team bus, beginning in Des Moines, and carrying over into an extended stay with the Charlotte Checkers.

"Our bus driver used to love playing poker," Cooley recalled. "When we got on the bus, we'd get a couple of beers going and, all of a sudden, they'd set up a table. The bussy used to just love playing cards with the players.

"When the cards came out, the guys would go, 'Hey, bussy! Come on! Cooley, get up there and drive!' The bus driver would just move out and I'd slide in and away we'd go.

"He'd go back and lose his money at the card table and I'd sit there and drive the rest of the way home. We changed on the fly. We didn't waste any time. We had it down to a science.

"In the summertime when I was living in Charlotte, I drove a bus for the same company that our hockey team used to rent the bus from, so I was qualified to drive for the team—no problem.

"When you play the game, your adrenaline is so high that it takes a long time for you to come down. Some guys would really talk a lot on the bus and other guys wouldn't say much.

"In my case, I didn't play cards, so I'd be sitting there, maybe shooting the baloney with somebody, and they'd say, 'Hey, bussy! Are you ready to play?' He'd say, 'OK,' and I'd drive the bus.

"I really enjoyed it. When I retired, I drove charters for different companies for about eight years. I loved to travel and drive, so that's what I did."

As someone who liked to travel, Cooley certainly chose the right profession—that of a nomadic hockey goalie.

After one year with Charlotte of the Eastern loop, Cooley moved to the American Hockey League and spent most of the 1972–73 season with the Rochester Americans.

Cue a period of stability, or as much as one could realistically hope for in the unpredictable world of hockey. By the fall of 1973, he had returned to the Checkers—who had since moved to the Southern League—as their primary goalkeeper.

Two years down the road, the Checkers' Cooley was a familiar face with a new look.

A headline in the October 17, 1975, edition of the *Charlotte Observer* said it all: "Masked Cooley Faces Gulls." Why the change?

"I've been lucky too long and there's no sense pushing it," Cooley told Ben Olson of the *Observer*. "I don't get paid enough in this game to make it worth losing an eye or something. The mask does make me feel better. It's something on my head and that makes me more confident. And it works. I already took a good shot on it in an exhibition game."

Better yet, the $29.95 mask—purchased by Cooley at a sporting goods store—survived the impact.

"I wore that for the first part of the year," he recalled. "It was a wire-frame mask. Basically, it was a catcher's mask. I have claustrophobia and I can't stand something that closes my face in.

"I'd last a game or maybe half a game and I'd throw the damn thing away again. I just wasn't happy with what I was using. Then I finally picked up just a mask that had a screen on it, so I just said, 'Well, I can wear this once in a while if you want me to stay in the lineup.'"

It would have been sheer folly to dislodge him during the 1976 playoffs, which he began by backstopping Charlotte to the Southern League title.

Ordinarily, a player's season would culminate in a championship-clinching victory, but Cooley's playoff run was just beginning.

The Philadelphia Firebirds of the North American Hockey League encountered a void in goal after future NHLer Rejean Lemelin was injured. The Firebirds' brass frantically put in a call for Cooley, who was preoccupied with celebrating the Checkers' second successive league title.

"I called Gaye at a quarter of nine this morning—and he was just getting home," Firebirds head coach Gregg Pilling told Bill Fleischman of the *Philadelphia Daily News* in late March 1976. "He's an emergency replacement for us."

The widespread expectation was that Cooley would be a backup, but he quickly supplanted Roger Kosar as the starter.

Cooley's courage was as impressive as his puck-stopping. During a semifinal series against the Johnstown Jets, he suffered a dislocated jaw, only to finish the game and emerge as the victorious goalie.

"Ordinarily, someone in Cooley's situation might surround his face with pillows and a mattress," Fleischman wrote. "That the emergency import from Charlotte's Southern League champions went maskless suggests the man lives up to goaltenders' daffy reputations."

As Cooley told Fleischman: "If you worry about getting hurt, you might as well hang it up. You can get hurt crossing the street in this town. I've just about been run over three times."

Three days later, Cooley was back in goal for a Philadelphia team that clinched the series with a 14–10 victory over the visitors from Johnstown, Pennsylvania.

"After Johnstown's sixth goal, which 'trimmed' the Firebirds' lead to 11–6, goalkeeper Gaye Cooley stashed his mask atop the goal cage," Fleischman wrote, adding this quip from Pilling: "His mask was the only thing that didn't go in."

It was a banner night for Pilling, who also provided this gem after being notified that the door to his team's dressing room was locked:

"Open it. We let everything else in."

The Jets–Firebirds series is of historical significance for reasons that don't even remotely pertain to both teams' pursuit of the NAHL's championship trophy, the long-forgotten Lockhart Cup.

While the Firebirds were visiting Johnstown, some very interested and influential observers were part of a Universal Studios crew that was filming Hollywood's first hockey movie, *Slap Shot*—starring Paul Newman.

"The Jets players who will be in the movie have split the last month of the season finishing their schedule and putting makeup on for the cameras," a *Philadelphia Inquirer* reporter noted.

As it turned out, members of the Firebirds also had a role to play.

"We were sitting in the dressing room before one of the games," Cooley remembered. "We didn't know anything about this movie thing. In walked this fellow, a little short guy, and he said, 'You guys have got to sign these waivers,' and he starts passing these pieces of paper around. I said, 'What's this about?' He said, 'We're making a movie and you've got to sign these waivers so we're not liable to pay you. Your face won't be in the movie or anything. We're just going for crowd shots.'

"The guys started signing, but I said, 'No, I'm not signing that!' He said, 'What?' I said, 'I'm not signing that. What's it worth to you? If you're making a movie, it's got to be worth something.'

"The guy said, 'No, we're not paying you anything,' so I said, 'Well, I'm not signing.'

"As soon as I said that, the rest of the guys said, 'Well, I'm not signing, either,' so this guy walked out.

"The next thing you know, in walked another little short guy—Paul Newman. The first guy was his brother. He was the manager or whatever he was doing.

"Paul Newman said, 'What's the problem, guys?' His brother pointed to me and said, 'That's the guy there!' I said, 'There's no problem. If we're going to sign these waivers, it should be worth something, shouldn't it?'

"Paul Newman said, 'Well, what do you want? We're on a low budget.' I said, 'That's fine. Is it worth a case of beer to you, for each guy?' He said,

'Is that all you want?' I said, 'Yeah, a case of beer. We're hockey players. We're not making any money. What the hell. Beer's good enough for us!'

"He said, 'Where do you want the beer?' I said, 'That bus outside is our bus,' so he ended up getting the bottom of the bus filled with beer. We hardly had enough room to put any equipment in. We had to put it in the back of the bus.

"Yeah, it worked out pretty good..."

You might say that Gaye had nothing in his hand, but he still bluffed Paul Newman into paying for beer. Talk about your Cool(ey) Hand Luke.

With Cooley reliably tending the twine, the Firebirds kept rolling all the way to the NAHL title. He thus became the first goalie to win a championship in two professional leagues in the same season.

Not satisfied with that landmark feat, Cooley pursued a hat trick. Soon after his stint with Philadelphia, he joined the New England Whalers of the World Hockey Association.

The Whalers had encountered a goaltending shortage after their backup, Bruce Landon, injured a knee. That left New England, which was in the midst of a playoff series against the Houston Aeros, without anyone to serve as insurance in case misfortune were to befall starter Cap Raeder.

Paging Gaye Cooley! (Repeat.)

Once again, he was off to a new team for the playoffs, with one difference. Whereas the NAHL didn't have any rules prohibiting a "ringer" goalie from being elevated into a primary role, WHA rules were more restrictive. He was to be used only in case of emergency.

You'll never guess what happened...

"Cap Raeder broke a piece of equipment during the game, so they had to put the other goalie in while his equipment was being fixed," Cooley said. "Because it was an emergency and he couldn't play, I could go in.

"I went in while they were fixing up his pad or whatever was wrong with him. While they're fixing him up, naturally we're trying to stall the game—but then they drop the puck. When the play got blown down again, his issue was fixed, and he came back in.

"I think I was in there for something like 33 seconds. I went down in history for the shortest playing time."

WHA stats rounded off the time to one minute, during which Cooley did not face a shot. It was such a whirlwind that the veteran goalie had precious little time in which to soak in the surroundings at The Summit in Houston, where the home team won 5–2 on May 7, 1976, to even a best-of-seven semifinal at one game apiece.

The entire episode was such a blur that Cooley doesn't know to this day whether his abbreviated appearance in the WHA coincided with a shift that featured 48-year-old Aeros legend Gordie Howe.

"I don't even remember," Cooley said with a laugh. "I was just so happy to be there."

For a while, it seemed that the 33-second cameo in the WHA playoffs would be Cooley's swan song as a professional goalie.

He began the 1976–77 season as the Checkers' assistant general manager, only to have a scenario arise that was reminiscent of the NAHL/WHA playoffs.

Charlotte goalie Dave Tataryn was feeling just fine, thank you, but backup Dan Brady had been shelved with an elbow injury. Bob Blanchet had also been part of the Checkers' goaltending equation before being released not long before Brady was hurt. The net result was that, once more, Cooley was asked to don goalie garb.

Cooley suited up, again, on December 17, 1976, when Charlotte played host to the Tidewater Sharks. After the visitors went ahead 5–0 at 8:33 of the second period, the decision was made to give Tataryn a respite for the remainder of the game. In came Cooley, who mopped up as Tidewater cruised to a 7–0 victory.

The following evening against the host Greensboro Generals, Checkers head coach Barry Burnett opted to start Cooley, who went the distance as the North Carolina-based home side won 4–2.

That turned out to be Cooley's 482nd and final game of professional hockey. The significance of that contest, however, extended far past December 18, 1976, as hockey historians and researchers eventually sought to determine whether Cooley was the slippery sport's last intentionally maskless goaltender.

Word of mouth proved to be unreliable, as one would expect after so many years, and media coverage at the time was hit-and-miss.

Cooley's comeback was mentioned only in passing in contemporaneous reports by the *Charlotte Daily News*. There was nary a reference to his mask—or lack thereof?—in stories pertaining to the games of December 17 and 18.

That created a quandary. After all, how can one conduct what aspires to be the definitive study of maskless goalies without conclusively determining the identity of The Last One.

The debate—was it Cooley or the star of Chapter 17, Andy Brown?—had persisted among hockey researchers for several decades, even though the answer proved to be Wayne Rutledge. (The very same Wayne Rutledge was in goal for Houston when Cooley made his WHA cameo.)

The Cooley–Brown mystery thriller was ultimately resolved by someone who did not have any connection to the sport: Danielle Pritchett of the Greensboro Public Library.

Pritchett was contacted via email in 2021 and asked if she could search the library's archive of stories from the *Greensboro Daily News*. The hope was that Cooley and his facial protection, or possible lack thereof, would be referenced somewhere in the newspaper's coverage of the Checkers–Generals game.

Pritchett was kind enough to find and forward the story and, crucially, an accompanying photo. The picture, taken by Joe Rodriguez of the *Daily News*, just happened to show Cooley—and his mask!

Therefore, it could be declared that Andy Brown had edged Gaye Cooley in the bare-face race—by a nose, if you will.

17

Andy Brown, Unmasked

Professional hockey's last resolute rebel

Andy Brown would rather bare his face than his soul.

Such was the snap conclusion after hockey's last full-time maskless goalie was contacted via telephone and asked to be interviewed for this project.

"I'm not interested," Brown, then a 77-year-old, Indiana-based horse breeder, said politely but firmly in 2021. "I'm so busy right now with horses and that. I'm just not interested, OK?"

At that point, it was time to resort to the fine art of bold-faced begging—asking if he could spare, say, five minutes...please?

"No," Brown reiterated. "I've been away from that stuff and I like to stay away from it, OK?"

Fair enough.

"Nice to talk to you, buddy," he concluded. "Good luck with your book."

It was the most cordial of rejections—Brown's disposition being consistent with the positive impression he left on erstwhile teammates such as Mickey Redmond.

"I remember him being a really, really good guy—a very friendly, easygoing guy," said Redmond, who got to know Brown during the colourful goalie's stints with the 1971–72 and 1972–73 Detroit Red Wings. "He wasn't one of those wound-up kind of guys. He had a wonderful personality.

"He was a real character."

Dennis Sobchuk can attest to that. He was a member of the World Hockey Association's Cincinnati Stingers when Brown suited up for the Indianapolis Racers in what would be his last game of professional hockey—a relief appearance on November 13, 1976.

"In those WHA days, you could have a two-inch curve on your stick," Sobchuk recalled. "The shots would be like a boomerang. One time, we were up 7–1 with a minute or two left and I let one go that grazed Andy's ear. I went in for the rebound and I could see him coming at me with his stick over his shoulders. I'm going in and he's coming out, so I do a 180 and I'm going the other way.

"How often do you see a goalie chasing a forward? There were a lot of goons in our league, but not many goalie goons."

The numbers are a testament to Brown's tempestuousness. As a member of the Eastern League's Johnstown Jets, Brown piled up 118 penalty minutes during the 1967–68 season.

Brown also boasted eyebrow-raising penalty-minute totals of 75 (with the 1974–75 Racers), 73 (Baltimore Clippers, AHL, 1970–71), and 60 (Pittsburgh Penguins, 1973–74).

The latter figure is notable for its historical significance. The 60 minutes' worth of infractions, accumulated over his final 36 NHL games, was then a league single-season record for a goaltender.

Brown applied the *coup de grace* in his farewell to the big leagues, registering a minor penalty (served by Wayne Bianchin) at 15:03 of the second period in a 6–3 loss to the host Atlanta Flames on April 7, 1974.

Not since then has an intentionally maskless goalie appeared in an NHL game.

(Six games earlier, Brown had recorded his first and only NHL shutout—the final goose-egg by a barefaced NHLer—as Pittsburgh dumped Detroit 8–0 on March 24, 1974. He made 23 saves, the most difficult of which were on two blasts by Redmond during his second successive 50-goal season.)

Also during the 1973–74 season, Brown obliterated the previous NHL record for penalty minutes by a goalie—42, set in 1972–73 by Billy Smith of the New York Islanders.

Brown's benchmark for belligerence endured until 1979–80, when the Boston Bruins' Gerry Cheevers was penalized 62 minutes. Cheevers and Brown were at 60 until the Bruins goaler added a minor penalty for shooting the puck into the stands.

"It was a 5–1 hockey game with half a minute to play, so I just couldn't allow the chance to pass," Cheevers said afterward. "Records are difficult to get, so you have to grab one when you can, even if isn't one of the most glittering ones in the book."

As of this writing, Brown had descended to seventh on the all-time list. The top three spots were monopolized by Ron Hextall, who as a member of the Philadelphia Flyers piled up penalty-minute totals of 113 (1988–89), 104 (1987–88), and 89 (1986–87).

Hextall's father, Bryan Jr., spent five of his eight NHL seasons as a forward with Pittsburgh and, in fact, was part of the Penguins when Brown joined the team in 1973. Hextall and Brown were also teammates with the 1973–74 Penguins until the 32-year-old forward was placed on waivers near mid-season.

And here's the kicker: Hextall was claimed by Atlanta on January 6, 1974. Three months later, he played for the Flames—against Brown—in the maskless goalie's NHL finale.

The following day, also in Atlanta, sporting history was made in a far more significant manner when the Braves' Hank Aaron belted his 715th home run to overtake Babe Ruth as Major League Baseball's all-time leader.

Home, for Andy Brown, was Hamilton, Ontario, where he played minor hockey and charted an unlikely and occasionally meandering path to the pros.

He endured the 1962–63 season as a member of the Ontario Hockey Association's Brampton Seven-Ups, an offensively fizzling team that was sorely lacking in pop.

It wasn't inconceivable for the opposition to be seven up on the Seven-Ups, who had a 12–24–4 record. Brown's 5.54 goals against average, compiled in 20 games, was more of an indictment of the supporting cast than it was of his goaltending.

By 1964, Brown had landed in Newfoundland's senior league with the Gander Flyers. A quick gander at his swollen goals against average—5.84—hardly signals an NHLer in the making.

But persistence paid off for Brown, who in 1965 began to wend his way through the minors, most often mired in the obscurity of the Eastern League. One season (1966–67) with the Long Island Ducks—it must have been a down year—was sandwiched between two years with Johnstown (1965–66 and 1967–68).

Brown was able to make 45 regular season appearances for Long Island despite not having two toes on his right foot. The toes were amputated following a welding accident that occurred as training camp approached in 1966.

After three seasons in the EHL, Brown was off to Baltimore, where he began a successful, three-year run in the American League. The location was a natural, in that his uncle—also named Andy Brown—played for and coached the Clippers in the mid-1950s.

Along with having that family connection, the presence of young Andy Brown on the Clippers garnered attention due to his appearance.

"The Clippers' Andy Brown was struck in the face by a puck the other day, making you wonder why hockey goalies don't wear masks," Doug Brown (no relation) wrote in the December 11, 1968, *Baltimore Sun*.

"Brown, an American Hockey League rookie, was hit on the left cheek by a puck that glanced up from his own stick. Knocked unconscious, Andy later came off the ice smiling, complaining only that 'you don't mind it so much in a game, but in practice....' It was the second time this season he has been hit in that spot. On another occasion he lost three front teeth and had a 12-stitch cut in his mouth. One year, he recalls, he had a black eye all season. He estimated he's had 100 stitches in his head and face. Yet, like many goalies, Brown won't wear a mask."

He did wear several hats. As a complement to making a living as a goaltender, he spent off-seasons indulging an accompanying passion for auto racing by driving sprint cars and super-modified vehicles on circuits that took him around Eastern Canada and into the northeastern United States.

In a 1969 interview with Ed Atwater of the *Baltimore Sun*, Brown made his auto-racing aspirations abundantly clear: "Indianapolis."

He had a head-start, in a sense, because one of his cars had been driven by racing legend Mario Andretti in the 1964 Indianapolis 500.

Whether Brown was racing at 100-plus miles per hour or facing pucks that travelled at a comparable velocity, he seemed to be happiest when speed and an accompanying element of risk were involved.

Back in the AHL with Baltimore, he suffered a facial injury before a 5–0 loss to the host Montreal Voyageurs on October 25, 1969.

"Brown was hit near the left eye by a puck in the warmup," Atwater reported. "Six stitches at the corner of an eye and an ugly bruise underneath make him a fit subject for a Halloween party."

Masks optional, of course.

Brown proceeded to play in 40 games with the 1969–70 Clippers, registering a 3.60 goals against average and one shutout. He was even busier—and better—while playing 50 games in 1970–71, boasting a 2.88 GAA and four shutouts.

In the spring of 1971, Brown was named an AHL first-team All-Star, having also made a concerted effort to become a brawl-star goalie (see: 73 penalty minutes).

The oft-sutured Brown was also capable of being a cut-up off the ice, as noted by *Sun* scribe Larry Hargrove on December 9, 1970.

"His two professions are a definite giveaway to the 26-year-old's personality," Hargrove wrote. "Care-free, loose and lively, Brown is one of those live-for-today-and-see-what-tomorrow-brings types."

Hargrove referred to Brown as a "settling influence" on the hockey team, lauding his ability to keep the mood light during a long and often-gruelling hockey season. Cited was an example of Brown with a shopping bag over his head inside a grocery store, "walking around like the monster that swallowed Cleveland."

Hargrove had an exclusive: Brown's face was covered.

"Even when he was injured during the playoffs last season, Andy couldn't contain his natural prankish ways," Hargrove continued, recounting a story in which "Andy grabbed a roll of tape, stole one of trainer Gump Embro's shoes, and completely mummified it. Brownie never passes up a chance to create a little laughter. And despite this, he has developed into one of the top goaltenders in the American league."

Albeit one who, in the caption of a photo that accompanied the story, was described as "Kooky Andy Brown."

One tough kooky, to be sure.

"He had no fear of anything," former Clippers goaltending cohort Joe Daley remembered.

In that spirit, Gordon Beard of the Associated Press wrote a profile that was picked up by the *Sun* for its March 26, 1971, edition and headlined: "Fast, Swinging Life is Andy Brown's Style."

"Andy Brown lives a dangerous life," Beard began. "He's an ice hockey goalie, a racing car driver...and a swinging bachelor."

Delving deeper into the goalie's personal life, Beard wrote: "As for his bachelorhood and dates, the handsome Canadian blocks questions about that phase of his life the way he turns aside shots at the nets. 'I'm the only unmarried player on the club,' he says with a smile, 'and that presents absolutely no problem. I phone my mother once a week.'"

Brown's big breakthrough arrived on June 7, 1971, when Detroit claimed him from Baltimore in the inter-league draft.

After beginning the ensuing season in the minors, Brown was promoted by Detroit and made his NHL debut on February 20, 1972, in a 4–3 loss to the host New York Rangers. Redmond scored one of the Red Wings' goals during a game in which Brown impressively made 39 saves. Five days later, however, he was dispatched to the Central League's Fort Worth Wings.

Brown soon winged his way back to Detroit and made 21 saves on March 12 when Chicago won 3–2 at The Olympia.

In a losing cause, Brown caught the eye of columnist Joe Falls.

"He has some age on him for being a rookie," Falls wrote in the *Detroit Free Press*. "He is 28. And he looks as if he has been through the wars. At least 10 of his teeth are missing, his face is bumped and scarred from looking at too many slap shots.

"And when he finally pulled off his socks in the dressing room, his right foot was exposed without the top of his big toe. 'Oh, that,' he shrugged, alluding to his days in construction. 'That came off in a pile-driving accident.'"

Mr. Hockey was honoured on the very same day Brown made his second NHL appearance.

"Brown is the son of the late Adam Brown, a former Red Wing forward," Falls noted. "It's a strange coincidence, but it was the elder Brown who set up Gordie Howe for his first major-league goal and now here is his son performing more than 25 years later on Gordie Howe Day."

There was a stretch of Andy Brown days to follow. He played in each of Detroit's final nine games of the 1971–72 season.

The momentum was interrupted when Brown began the 1972–73 campaign in Fort Worth. After another 22 games in the Central circuit, he was again summoned by Detroit, whereupon he played in seven NHL games within a month. His fortunes soon cooled, to the extent that he was peddled to Pittsburgh on February 25, 1973. As a Penguin, Brown played in nine games over the second half of the 1972–73 season. Then came 1973–74—his first (and last) full NHL season.

Appearing in 36 of the Penguins' 78 games, Brown posted a 3.54 goals against average. His 13–16–4 record was good for a .445 winning percentage, which exceeded the team's overall mark of .417.

Not long after reaching the peak of his short-lived NHL career, his interest was piqued by the World Hockey Association.

The Minnesota Fighting Saints, who two years earlier had selected Brown in the WHA's inaugural player draft, traded his rights to a team known as the Racers on July 1, 1974. Very soon, he would attain his earlier-stated goal: "Indianapolis."

The Penguins had hoped to retain Brown. In fact, Bob Whitley of the *Post-Gazette* reported that the team had offered the free-spirited goalie a two-year contract with a total value of $150,000. The Racers wheeled and dealed more successfully, wooing him with a reported five-year pact calling for a six-figure annual stipend.

"I rate him the second-best goalie in the league right now [behind the Cleveland Crusaders' Gerry Cheevers] and he has a chance to be the best," Racers director of player personnel Chuck Catto told Dave Overpeck of the *Indianapolis Star*. "I think he's the type of player we need on this team. He's a spirited guy who wants to win. I think he could be a leader for us on the ice and in the dressing room."

It was a full-circle transaction for Brown, whose father had played for the American League's Indianapolis Capitols in the early 1940s.

Brown felt right at home for other reasons. A member of the United States Auto Club since 1970, he was comfortably close to Indianapolis Motor Speedway—home of the Indy 500.

"I have a goal," Brown told Dick Mittman of the *Indianapolis News*, "and that is to win that sucker. I'll walk on my hands and knees from Market Square Arena out there if I could get a ride."

The Indianapolis team rode Brown's goaltending to most of its meagre successes in 1974–75. He played in 52 of the Racers' 78 games and was also the team's lone representative in the WHA's All-Star festivities.

The Racers were last-placers in the 14-team league, going 18–57–3. Brown's 15–35–0 slate (.300) actually borders on the exceptional when you consider that the Racers were 3–22–3 (.161) when he was not the goaltender of record.

With a .250 overall winning percentage, the Racers were only halfway to Indy .500.

Somehow, Brown recorded two shutouts for a sad-sack team. In so doing, he certainly lived up to his moniker: "Fearless."

"Feckless" was the best description of the '74–75 Racers, whose fortunes (or lack thereof) were exemplified by a 9–2 loss to the Toronto

Toros. Compounding the misery, Brown suffered an eight-stitch cut on the back of his head while allowing the Toros' eighth goal.

"Roger Cote's stick hit me," Brown, referencing an accident involving a Racers teammate, told Dick Denny of the *Indianapolis News*. "If we were winning, it wouldn't hurt a bit."

A little levity never hurt, given the plight of the Pacers. Brown delivered that, and more, while telling Susan Lennis of the *Indianapolis Star* about a beloved black poodle named Little Bit.

"He can answer the phone," Brown proudly told Lennis, "and he watches television each night so when I come home from a game he knows whether we won or lost."

A demonstration of distemper put Brown in the doghouse and the record book (again) on March 30, 1975. During a 5–3 loss to the Minnesota Fighting Saints, Brown was issued a misconduct that fattened his penalty-minutes total to 75—then the most in a season by a professional hockey goaltender.

The following evening, Brown's courage was on display during a 4–1 loss to the Winnipeg Jets. That night, 11-year-old Jim Shields—then of Saskatoon, Saskatchewan—visited the Winnipeg Arena to attend his first pro hockey game.

"It was very exciting to go to this big arena with a lot more fans than the old arena in Saskatoon," remembered Shields, whose team was in Winnipeg for a minor hockey tournament. "I don't recall much of the game, as the only big name I really knew—or saw on TV playing—was Bobby Hull.

"The biggest memory was when Andy Brown came out at the start of the game. I remember thinking to myself that he was crazy to be in there without a mask against Bobby Hull's big shot. I was a goalie, but I never played without a mask.

"Some time in the second period, Andy Brown went down on the ice after getting hit in the face with a puck."

Brown had been clocked by the Jets' Thommie Bergman with 6:50 left in the second stanza. The wounded goalie was rushed to the Racers' dressing room, where he underwent repairs. Meanwhile, Ed Dyck took Brown's place between the pipes—for a mere 2:37.

"Then Andy Brown was back in the net, without a mask," Shields marvelled. "We could see that he had a bandage on, so he must have gotten stitched up and gone back in the game without any further thought.

"Incredible courage."

Winnipeg went on to win 4–1, even though Hull—who entered the contest with 75 goals in 73 games that season—was limited to one official shot. Such picayune details are not what resonate with Shields to this day.

"My biggest memory is still seeing Andy Brown playing without a mask," he concluded. "Oh...and, to top it all off, we also won the tournament."

Winning became more frequent for the Racers in 1975–76. Although their 35–39–6 record radiated mediocrity, it was nonetheless good enough for first place in the East Division.

Brown's goals against average improved to 3.60, from 4.15 the previous season, but his playing time was greatly reduced due to injury. Michel Dion was the busiest of the Racers' netminders, registering a 2.74 GAA in 31 games. Brown was next in line at 24, followed by Leif Holmqvist (19), and Jim Park (11).

Holmqvist, by the way, had already carved out his niche in maskless-goalie history. While playing in Sweden and representing his home country internationally, he protected his head without actually wearing a mask. Neat trick, that.

The answer, for Holmqvist, was to wear a conventional player's helmet. A helmeted Holmqvist faced (literally) the United States, for example, in the world hockey championship on March 20, 1971.

By the time Holmqvist migrated to North America, where he spent a solitary season in the WHA, he was wearing a conventional, face-hugging fibreglass mask.

And Andy Brown was wearing...a smile—at least after notching the 1975–76 Racers' only shutout. The 4–0 victory, celebrated on October 23, 1975, was against the Houston Aeros and his father's former Detroit teammate, Gordie Howe.

The shutout of Houston, which had not been blanked in any of its previous 184 games, was the last whitewash of Brown's hockey career. Coincidence: He made 35 saves in each of his three WHA shutouts.

The second half of the 1975–76 season was beyond saving for Brown. He was pretty much a write-off after sustaining a pulled back muscle in practice on Boxing Day. The following summer, though, he was back on the track as part of the United States Auto Club's roster.

All of that was preamble to Brown's shortened season of 1976–77. Actually, the "77" part was not applicable to the 32-year-old goalie, who never saw a millisecond of action beyond November 13, 1976.

But, with Andy Brown being Andy Brown, the conclusion of his professional hockey career was bound to be quirky.

So figure this out.

In each of Brown's final two appearances, the masked starting goalie (Dion) was hit in the face and ironically would be forced to leave the game at some point. On both occasions, he was replaced by the unmasked Brown, who would emerge unscathed from mop-up duty.

Logically, would it not stand to reason that a maskless goalie was far more apt to be injured in the line of duty and therefore give way to a masked backup?

Anyway, here are the gory (at least for Dion) details....

November 10, 1976: As reported by the *Indianapolis Star*, Dion suffered a gash over his right eyebrow, courtesy of a high shot taken by the Phoenix Roadrunners' Robbie Ftorek. While arrangements were being made for Dion to be taken to hospital, Brown entered the game at 14:18 of the third period. The score, 3–3 at the time, held up through overtime.

November 13, 1976: Dion was back in goal, only to be dizzied once more. At 4:30 of the first period, the Cincinnati Stingers' Ron Plumb hit Dion plum in the face with a shot that was, in its own right, a stinger. This time, Dion was not immediately replaced. He continued to patrol the Racers' crease until 13:32 of the third period. The writing was on the wall when a Dave Inkpen goal gave Cincinnati a 7–2 lead, so Dion headed to the bench. In came Brown—one final time, as it turned out. His farewell to hockey consisted of 6:28 of shutout duty, albeit in a 7–3 loss at Cincinnati's Richfield Coliseum.

The next night, Brown injured his back, again, while warming up for a road game against the Quebec Nordiques. After being helped off the ice, he was taken to the hospital for X-rays. The diagnosis: a ruptured disc.

Brown underwent surgery on November 26, 1976. The following year, the Racers cancelled his contract—not long before the entire organization went completely off-track.

The Racers folded in mid-December 1978, shortly after the team had sold its primary asset—somebody named Wayne Gretzky—to the Edmonton Oilers.

Post-hockey, Brown continued to drive fast cars while branching off into horse racing. Well into his 70s, he was training horses and living in Trafalgar, Indiana, near Indianapolis.

In a profile of Brown that appeared in the February 27, 2020, edition of *Indianapolis Monthly*, writer Dave Seminara noted that the once-maskless goalie had not set foot inside a hockey arena since his time as a player.

"Hell, yes, I miss it," Brown told Seminara, "but I love my horses, and I'm happy with how my life turned out."

The outlook was unaffected by the accumulation of more than 300 stitches and the loss of every tooth—presumably a consequence of not wearing a mask.

"Everybody else made a big deal about it. I just played," Brown told Geoff Kirbyson for *The Hot Line*, a book about the Jets' terrific troika of Hull, Anders Hedberg, and Ulf Nilsson. "But nobody wanted me to make any Brad Pitt movies, that's for sure."

Maybe not, but should there be a sequel to *Scarface*…

18

The Dancing Bear

Wayne Rutledge and three minutes of making history

THE DANCING BEAR WAS BAREFACED FOR A FRACTION OF HIS FINAL season of professional hockey.

In that fragment of time, Wayne Rutledge made history—inadvertently, yet undeniably—by becoming the last maskless goalie in North American professional hockey.

He certainly didn't plan it that way. Honestly, though, how many things did unfold as designed in the often-unpredictable, always-colourful World Hockey Association?

Rutledge wasn't even supposed to play in a February 17, 1978, game between the Houston Aeros and the visiting Cincinnati Stingers. Aeros head coach Bill Dineen had opted to start Lynn Zimmerman in net, and there he stayed well into the third period. Then came an unanticipated twist.

"With four minutes left, Zimmerman skated to the Aeros' bench on a delayed penalty," John McClain wrote in the *Houston Chronicle*. "He stopped to get some water, and Houston was forced to use Rutledge, who did not wear a mask."

Why were the Aeros suddenly required to make a goaltending change on account of a what is conventionally a simple water break? That much remains unclear.

And why did Rutledge, who was otherwise masked for all six of his seasons in the WHA, enter the game without anything adorning his face?

"I didn't think I'd be in that long," Rutledge explained to McClain.

The cameo appearance in the cage turned out to be far more eventful than expected, from a short- and long-term perspective.

Rutledge was greeted by the Stingers' Rick Dudley, who was foiled on a breakaway by what McClain described as "a beautiful stop." The Aeros' temporary 'tender made one more important save, on an undisclosed shooter, before Zimmerman returned to the game with the score tied at 3–3 and one minute remaining in the third period.

Cincinnati ended up winning 4–3 when swift-skating Peter Marsh tallied at 4:02 of overtime. Beware the strides of Marsh…

Dudley, coincidentally, had scored two goals for Cincinnati in its 7–3 victory over the Indianapolis Racers on November 13, 1976, in the last game ever played by a full-time maskless goalie (Andy Brown).

The Racers' head coach on that occasion was Jacques Demers, who was also the Stingers' bench boss when they faced the momentarily maskless Rutledge on February 17, 1978.

The latter contest, played at The Summit in Houston, was witnessed by 7,487 spectators, including Bob Rennison and his nephew (Richard) and niece (Rachel). In a diary entry dated February 17, 1978, Rennison wrote: "Tonight me Rachel & Dickie went to the Aeros game. Cincy won 4–3. Rut played without a mask."

Rennison recalled 44 years later that the general reaction at The Summit to Rutledge's masklessness was that "nobody made a big deal of it."

But it was a big deal to Rennison, who went downstairs after the game to get autographs and meet the players.

"When Rutledge walked by us, I asked him, 'Why didn't you wear a mask?'" Rennison remembered. "He said, 'Well, I never used to wear a mask.'"

True enough. In the autumn of 1969, Rutledge—then of the Los Angeles Kings—was one of only seven NHL goaltenders who had yet to switch to facial protection.

Rutledge remained maskless for the duration of the 1969–70 campaign—his last of three seasons in the NHL. When the 1970–71 season began, he was a masked member of the Denver Spurs.

He remained in the Western league, with the 1971–72 Salt Lake Golden Eagles, before signing with the Aeros and playing in 175 games over the first six seasons of the WHA's seven-year existence.

As an Aero, Rutledge tended goal for 11,240 minutes, counting regular season and playoff competition. He was maskless for only three of those minutes—just 0.026 per cent of the time.

That was three minutes too many for Sharyn Rutledge, who recalled with a chuckle that she "was kind of annoyed" with her husband for appearing, albeit briefly, without a mask—despite the historical significance of that abbreviated relief stint.

The nickname? Nobody is quite sure who applied the "Dancing Bear" label, but it seems to be related to Rutledge's agility and size. At 6'2", he was atypically tall for a goalie of his era.

"He was a big bear," noted Jack Stanfield, a former Aeros teammate and broadcaster. "For a big guy, he was a strong skater and he could move around pretty well."

That he did, in the professional ranks, until finding stability and savouring sustained success in Houston.

Much earlier, back in 1959, the Ontario-born Rutledge had been introduced to junior hockey with the hometown Barrie Flyers. After he spent one Ontario Hockey Association season with Barrie, the team moved to Niagara Falls, where he played for two more years.

He subsequently became a netminding nomad, playing for seven teams in five different leagues over four seasons.

The 1962–63 campaign was especially memorable. With Rutledge sparkling in goal, the Windsor Bulldogs won the Allan Cup—which is awarded to the Canadian senior A hockey champion. The celebration was such that parades were held in Windsor, Ontario, and nearby Detroit.

"It was pretty exciting for people on both sides of the border," Sharyn Rutledge recalled.

Also of note was the 1965–66 campaign, in which Rutledge registered seven shutouts in 70 games with the Minnesota Rangers en route to being named the Central League's top goalie. He played in another 70 Central league games the following season, with the Omaha Knights.

Over those two seasons, Rutledge didn't miss as much as a millisecond of action, despite playing without a mask.

He had worn a mask for part of the 1964–65 Central League season, as a member of the St. Paul Rangers, but soon performed an about-face.

"I still wear it in practice, but it got to the point where I wasn't playing very well while wearing a mask in a match, so I discarded it," Rutledge told Hal Brown of the *Lincoln Star* in December 1966. "I think it made me lazy."

By that time, Rutledge had overcome a hankering for food that had resulted in his weight mushrooming to 240 pounds at one point in 1965.

"In two months I got down to 200," Rutledge told Bob Fowler of the *Minneapolis Tribune* in November 1965. "I just quit eating. I cut out starch foods, like potatoes, and I skipped breakfast and dinner.

"Hungry? Man, I was starving. But I want to get to the big-time. And if I make it, not eating for two months will have been a small price to pay."

Rutledge eventually reached the big-time. He may have stopped expanding, but NHL operatives weren't so inclined.

Plans were announced for the addition of six teams for the 1967–68 season, when the NHL would double in size.

On June 6, 1967, the 25-year-old Rutledge was claimed by Los Angeles from the New York Rangers to begin Round 2 of the expansion draft.

The first two rounds were used to stock teams with goalies. The proceedings had begun when Los Angeles picked living legend Terry Sawchuk first overall, barely two months after he had backstopped Toronto to a Stanley Cup-clinching victory.

Despite Sawchuk's King-sized stature in the game, it was Rutledge who became the first person to tend goal for the new Los Angeles franchise.

Sawchuk suffered an elbow injury in practice, a mere two days before Los Angeles was to play its inaugural regular season game. That created some leverage for Rutledge, who had not signed a contract with the Kings to that point.

"You got 'em now, kid," Rutledge, as quoted by Sawchuk biographer David Dupuis, recalled the grizzled goalie telling him. "They have to sign you now."

Rutledge signed for $12,000 just in time to tend goal during each of the Kings' first four games, beginning with a 4–2 victory over the Philadelphia Flyers on October 14, 1967, at a once-unlikely hockey venue, the Long Beach Arena.

"We practised on an ice pad in Burbank, north of L.A., and in Long Beach," Rutledge told Dupuis, who wrote *Sawchuk: The Troubles and Triumphs of the World's Greatest Goalie*. "We were 20 guys in five cars and nobody knew where the hell we were going. The dressing rooms were like large washrooms with no seats.

"Between practices, the trainers had to dry our equipment on the patio in the sun. We often practised in still-wet equipment. It was all very poorly organized."

The Kings were anything but poor over Rutledge's first four NHL starts, recording two victories and two ties. He continued to impress, even after Sawchuk's long-awaited coronation as a King, by enjoying an 11–4–2 start. Sawchuk, by contrast, had but two wins and a tie to show for his first nine games with Los Angeles.

"I gave myself until I was 25 to make it," Rutledge told Chuck Garrity of the *Los Angeles Times*. "The expansion gave me my chance and I'm finally making fair money. But I have to have a good year to make more money next year. If I don't, I'll still give it up."

The story in the *Times* was headlined: "Rutledge Makes NHL—Hard Way." The overline read: "Goalie Overcomes Handicaps."

"He's supposedly too big to be a goalie," Garrity began. "And he wears contact lenses. So, with two strikes on him, Wayne Rutledge has found his way to the major leagues with the Los Angeles Kings."

Rich Roberts of the *Independent*, based in Long Beach, also took note of Rutledge's story. Roberts' article, headlined "Rutledge Record Written on His Face," was also subtitled, "Wounds Reflect Medal Of Valor."

During the interview, Rutledge walked the writer through the sundry scars of battle.

"This one with the three stitches is the shot I stopped last Wednesday," he told Roberts in December 1967. "And this one over here is where a stick got me Friday. The one up here? Another stick, I guess."

Rutledge also noted that he had been cut more often in the early stages of the 1967–68 season than had been the case in 82 games, playoffs included, with Omaha in 1966–67.

"Already this season he has had his nose broken when a teammate slapped the puck into his puss, and Sunday at Boston he took a nine-count when a deflection hit him like a shot from a .45," Roberts reported. "Fortunately, the puck hit him 'flat.' If the frozen rubber disc had rotated to an edge, Rutledge's cheekbone could have been smashed. Instead, it is only swollen, red, and grotesque."

By that point, Rutledge had already been knocked out cold during a game in Boston. He regained consciousness with the assistance of seven ammonia caps. Once the cobwebs dissipated, he finished the game.

"It's only the second time I've been knocked out," Rutledge told Mike Lamey of the *Minneapolis Star*. "Last year I was hit in the face only twice. Now five already this year."

That includes the previously referenced broken nose, which was initially left untreated.

"I played three games before I went to the hospital," Rutledge told Lamey. "It didn't bother me but by the time I got to the doctor it had set itself. They had to rebreak it before they could set it."

Rutledge was nonetheless appreciative of his first big break—the long-awaited introduction to the NHL.

"There's no sense hanging around in the minors," he said in an interview with United Press International. "The major league is the only place to play."

Rutledge was the only NHL goalie without a shutout during the early months of the 1967–68 campaign before he got into the act by notching the first goose-egg in Kings history. He made 21 saves on December 23, 1967, as Los Angeles blanked the St. Louis Blues 4–0. Several of the stops, in the appraisal of an unidentified Associated Press correspondent, were "spectacular."

Rutledge went on to go 21–15–5 for a 1967–68 Kings team that was otherwise 10–18–5. His goals against average (2.88) was superior to that of Sawchuk (3.07), who played in nine fewer games than the younger goalie.

The 26-year-old NHL rookie's highlight reel also included a 2–0 victory over Toronto on February 12, 1968, when he made 31 saves before a home crowd at the newly opened Forum.

"It was Rutledge's second shutout," Roberts wrote in the *Independent*, "but first, as he put it, against 'guys you've heard about since you've been playing midget.'"

Rutledge was shut out in the shutout department over his next 47 NHL regular season games, extending through 1969–70. He made what would be his final big-league appearance on March 31, 1970, playing the final two periods after Kings starter Denis DeJordy allowed three Minnesota goals over the opening 20 minutes. The North Stars ended up winning 5–2.

So concluded a second successive injury-marred season for Rutledge. A pulled groin had limited him to 15 games as a second-year King. In an attempt to correct the problem, surgery was performed in the fall of 1969.

"He pulled his groin so badly that it got infected," recalled Todd Rutledge, Wayne's son.

The operation delayed the start of Rutledge's 1969–70 season until the Kings' 25th game.

Overall, he was limited to 20 appearances for a 14–52–10 Los Angeles team that would establish an ignominious, since-eclipsed NHL record for losses in a single season.

When Rutledge was the goaltender of record, he was 2–12–1, but it was a stretch to blame anyone who was placed in the unenviable position of defending the Kings' net.

For instance, Rutledge was one of the few Kings players who demonstrated any heart on Valentine's Day, 1970, when he faced 61 St. Louis shots and stopped all but two.

From St. Louis, it was on to Philadelphia, where the Flyers peppered Rutledge with 55 shots and won 7–2.

The overworked Rutledge emerged from the second successive barrage as the co-owner of an NHL regular season record for most shots faced by a goaltender in back-to-back games (116).

Chicago's Al Rollins faced 58 shots on October 9, 1955, versus Toronto and another 58 six nights later against Detroit. (As of 2022, there had been seven instances of a goalie being tested 116 or more times over two consecutive playoff games, which can include extended overtime sessions and, therefore, elevated shots-on-goal totals.)

It was quite the workload for Rutledge, but there was nary a word of complaint. He was simply delighted to be playing regularly once again.

"I'd become a forgotten man," Rutledge told Roberts. "When you're playing, everyone knows who you are. When you're hurt, you'd rather be dead."

Rutledge made that comment after his 15th appearance of the season, adding: "It's nice to be remembered."

Rutledge had hoped to spend a fourth season with Los Angeles, but the Kings sent him and 13 other players to Denver in September 1970. The change of scenery was accompanied by an adjustment in appearance.

He began the 1970–71 season by wearing a mask, the reasons being:

- The tragic tale of Minnesota forward Bill Masterton, who in 1968 became the first (and heretofore only) NHL player to die from injuries sustained in a game, created lingering unease. A helmetless Masterton cracked his head on the ice against the Oakland Seals on January 13, 1968. He quickly lost consciousness and died 30 hours later. (The NHL made helmets compulsory for all new players, effective with the 1979–80 season. Helmetless players were grandfathered. The last such skater was Craig MacTavish, who made his farewell appearance on April 20, 1997, when he suited up for St. Louis in a 3–2 playoff loss to Detroit. One of his teammates on that day was Brett Hull, whose father Bobby had played an integral role in the disappearance of the maskless goalie by virtue of his cannon-like blasts.)

- Concerns raised by Rutledge's wife. As Sharyn put it 50-plus years later: "I must admit he got a little prodding from me."
- Input from Wendy Rutledge (now Fraser), who was unsettled by one Kings' road trip in which her father ended up with two black eyes, a broken nose, and an assortment of stitches. "Our daughter was starting to worry about her dad," Sharyn recalled, "and she was only four."

Nerves were calmed when Rutledge joined the Spurs and the by-then-dominant ranks of the masked goaltenders. He spent one season with the Western League team before joining the Salt Lake Golden Eagles.

It was a career-enhancing move for Rutledge, who was named the Golden Eagles' MVP for the 1971–72 season in addition to being decorated as a second team WHL All-Star. With 3,517 minutes played, he was by far the league's busiest goaltender.

Concurrently, a slate of WHA teams was being pieced together. Rutledge was placed on the preferred list for a club that was to be based in Dayton, Ohio. When the Dayton franchise did not get off the ground, Houston became the next option. It was an enticing one, indeed, for Rutledge.

On May 29, 1972, he became one of the first two players signed by the Aeros. The other one was a former Los Angeles teammate, centre Gord Labossiere.

"Houston, we have liftoff" was the theme on October 12, 1972, when Don McLeod was in goal for the Aeros in their first game. The Aeros posted a 3–2 victory over the Chicago Cougars.

The next night, Rutledge returned to Los Angeles—where he had become the first starting goalie in Kings history—and made his WHA debut. He was the victorious netminder as the Aeros edged the Los Angeles Sharks 3–2.

Al Larson covered that game for the *Long Beach Press-Telegram*. Near the end of the story, Larson included a quote from WHA president Gary Davidson. Asked about the prevalence of pugilism and penalties in the league's first few games, Davidson replied: "Free-for-alls have no place in the WHA."

Somebody neglected to pass along that information to Bill Goldthorpe.

Goldy Goldthorpe is best known as the inspiration behind Ogie Oglethorpe—a classically cantankerous character in *Slap Shot*.

The living, breathing version of Ogie pulled off the mean feat of playing for six different WHA teams in only three seasons despite seeing duty in a mere 36 games. One of them was played on April 28, 1974, when Goldthorpe and the aptly named Minnesota Fighting Saints opposed the Aeros.

"Goldthorpe had this hair-do like Ronald McDonald—this big, red-headed Afro," former Aeros broadcaster Jerry Trupiano said.

The former McDonald's jingle, "You deserve a break today," was applicable to Rutledge on that evening at the St. Paul Civic Center. McLeod started in goal, meaning that Rutledge was seated near the end of the Aeros' bench.

"The teams' benches were beside each other," said Todd Rutledge, Wayne's son. "A brawl broke out and 'Ogie Oglethorpe' jumped over the boards. Dad reached out to give him a yank and ended up with a mitt full of red hair."

Goldthorpe, always a handful, soon became the only player to be thrown out of that game.

For Rutledge, in general, the mindset was more cordial than combative.

"He wasn't shy," Todd added. "He could go up and talk to anybody, even guys that he fought.

"I once met an ex-professional hockey player who told me, 'Your dad was the nicest man. He gave me the biggest beating I ever received in my entire life, but I loved him.'"

That sentiment was seemingly universal.

"You could talk to 20 people and I would be shocked if they didn't all come up with the same refrain," former Aeros broadcaster Barry Warner said. "He was just a good dude—the type of guy you would like to sit back and have a beer with.

"He was like Mr. Rogers. If you couldn't get along with Wayne Rutledge, you had serious personality defects."

Imbued with a fantastic sense of humour, Rutledge liked to keep things light. So did the family dog.

"Everybody knew about Bear," Todd Rutledge said of the aptly named pooch, chuckling. "He ate an entire set of Christmas lights, while they were plugged in. Another time, he ate the leather interior seats in the car."

Even then, Wayne Rutledge's cheerful exterior was unaffected. In fact, he made light of it.

"Rut was a damned good person from Barrie, Ontario," Warner said. "He never dwelled on 'woulda, coulda, shoulda.' That wasn't his persona. He looked on the bright side of things and loved being around people. He was just a prince of a guy."

Not to mention a King, for three years.

Instead of lamenting the end of his NHL career, Rutledge made the absolute best of his time in Houston.

Over six WHL seasons, he posted a 3.24 goals against average and six shutouts.

He helped Houston win a league title in 1974 and subsequently played in the 1975 and 1977 WHA All-Star Games.

Moreover, Rutledge was undefeated as a coach.

With head coach Bill Dineen battling exhaustion and the flu, Rutledge—resplendent in a lime-green suit—and left-winger Ted Taylor manned the bench for a February 22, 1978, game in Edmonton. Just five days after becoming professional hockey's final intentionally maskless goaltender, Rutledge helped to coach Houston to a 6–5 victory over the Oilers.

"Rutledge and I both decided on the lines, but Rut made most of the decisions on the bench," Taylor told Ray Turchansky of the *Edmonton Journal.*

That season, Rutledge made only four more appearances in goal. He saw duty in the Aeros' regular season finale and in three playoff contests, the last of which was on April 25, 1978. On that day, at Le Colisée in Quebec City, his 16-year pro career as a goaltender came to an end. He was 36 years old.

Post-hockey, Wayne and Sharyn Rutledge moved back to Ontario with their three children (Wendy, Todd, and Chet) and settled on a farm near Huntsville, north of Toronto.

"He was quite upset when all his hockey gear, including his mask, was stolen when we moved back to Canada," Todd said. "It was in a big, wooden crate and it was broken into while it was being transported."

Back in Ontario, Wayne raised cattle, pigs, and champion racing Quarter Horses. He also worked with glass and mirrors, which he cut and installed, in addition to operating a Western clothing, boot, and tack shop in Huntsville. And—whew!—he was also a restaurant owner and auctioneer, although family came first and foremost.

"He was always busy," remembered Sharyn, who married Wayne in 1962. "He loved being outside, because the bulk of his [hockey] career was spent inside. He loved being on the farm and was out in the field all day long."

Fielding correspondence from fans was another source of enjoyment.

"Mom and Dad used to get letters from all over the world," Todd said. "People would ask for his autograph, as they did when he played. He felt that it was a privilege.

"He always took pride in signing his autograph legibly. Now, when a player signs an autograph, it's just a scribble."

Rutledge left his signature on his hometown to the extent that, in 2000, he was inducted into the Barrie Sports Hall of Fame.

Just four years later, Rutledge was diagnosed with melanoma, which metastasized extensively. He died on October 2, 2004, at 62, the same age at which his father had passed away.

A few days later, Wayne Rutledge was remembered when friends and loved ones gathered at the Bracebridge fairgrounds in the largest building on the property—one that Wayne had used consistently for his auctions. A venue of that dimension was required to accommodate 500 people.

"Everybody got up and told stories," Sharyn Rutledge remembered. "It was a true celebration of life."

One that was fit for a King.

PART FOUR: MODERN TIMES

19

Dave Dryden's Influence and Innovation

Modified mask ushers in new age

DAVE DRYDEN, AN INTEGRAL FIGURE IN THE EVOLUTION OF GOALTENDERS' equipment and the enhancement of player safety, is often mentioned as part of a tandem.

In his 20s, he was among the earliest examples of the two-goalie system at work. Whereas the likes of Glenn Hall once played in every game, every season, understudies such as Dryden entered (and altered) the equation in the mid-1960s.

Dryden is also routinely referenced in conjunction with his younger sibling, Ken. They made history on March 20, 1971, becoming the principals in the NHL's first brother-versus-brother goaltending matchup.

With less fanfare, but with an undeniable impact that has been visible for nearly a half-century, the elder Dryden collaborated with a fellow visionary named Greg Harrison.

"Dave Dryden was responsible for the cage combination mask—the idea—and Greg Harrison was the one who developed it for him," stated

Sportmask's Tony Priolo, whose company has long produced customized facial protection for goaltenders.

"When Jacques Plante first donned the mask in '59, it was just another layer of skin. Logically, it was, 'I don't want to get my skin cut, so I'll just put the molded piece of fibreglass, made off a plaster face mold, on my face and use that as a second skin so I won't get some superficial cuts.'

"It evolved from there, but the materials haven't. It's like using a product wrong all your life, and then using the same product with a different application. It's, 'Oh my God, I had no idea!'

"They used the fibreglass mask and they figured it was too close to the face, so what are we going to do? You get hit in the face and you break your orbital bone or your brow bone because of the dispersion, so someone figured it out."

That someone was Dave Dryden.

"The cage combination mask evolved from that man's mind," Priolo continued. "He decided to cut out all the crucial parts that were touching the face on the fibreglass mask and put a cage there.

"It's kind of like a buffer now—which was brilliant—and it hasn't really changed since then, except for thicker padding."

But so much has changed in other ways since Dryden first strapped on the pads, 70 years ago.

"I never even thought of masks at all when I was growing up," said Dryden, who was born in 1941—six years before Ken, a future Hockey Hall of Famer, arrived on the scene in Hamilton, Ontario.

"Probably the first inkling of a mask was one that we used to play ball hockey. In 1953, we moved into a new house and I was 12 years old. Dad had the backyard paved and put out a couple of hockey nets.

"Ken would have been six years old and I remember my mom saying, 'Well, there's no way he's going to play with the older boys unless he's got something on his face.' So Ken, when he was playing ball hockey as a little kid with kids who were almost teenagers, had a baseball mask on.

"We acknowledged that he needed something like that, but nobody else was really thinking about masks."

A mask did become topical during the 1960–61 season, when 19-year-old Dave Dryden was injured while playing for the Toronto-based St. Michael's Majors.

"I got hit in the eye," he recalled in 2021, during an interview for this book. "It hemorrhaged and I was sandbagged in the hospital for a couple of weeks. It was a serious sort of thing. I nearly lost my eye. Prior to that, I'd been hit in the face, but I'd never been hit right in the eye.

"I was out for a long time. When I came back, they had a mask for me. It was the biggest, heaviest, ugliest thing ever, but I had to wear it. I only wore it in practice and didn't like it at all.

"The next year, St. Mike's [left the major A division]. I went to the [Toronto] Marlies junior A team and Turk Broda was my coach. I had been thinking, 'Well, maybe I should wear a mask of some kind—just a store-bought one that's really basic,' but Turk had said that no goalie of his was going to wear a mask. That was the way it was, so I didn't wear a mask."

Dryden's 1961–62 campaign, spent primarily with the Marlies, included one game that unfolded while he was comfortably seated high above the hallowed ice at Maple Leaf Gardens.

"Dave had been employed, on and off, for three years as the stand-by goalie at the Gardens," his father, Murray, wrote in *Playing the Shots at Both Ends: The Story of Ken and Dave Dryden*. "It was quite a good deal. He got a good seat in the press box to watch the game and also was paid $10. And for three years he never once had to go into the nets."

That all changed on February 3, 1962, when the New York Rangers were in Toronto to face the Maple Leafs. Early in the second period, Rangers goalie Gump Worsley suffered an elbow injury that necessitated his removal from the game.

A call was promptly put out for Dryden, who scurried downstairs and reported to the Rangers' dressing room.

Welcome to the big leagues, kid.

A story by the Associated Press noted that the emergency goalie did "a fine job" during a 23-save effort, even though the Rangers lost 4–1.

"I didn't wear a mask for that one," Dryden noted, "but after that I wore a mask all the time."

At the time, Dryden and his future wife, Sandra, were engaged. Dave's regular job was as an elementary school teacher. His plan was not to play professional hockey, but instead to combine teaching with tending goal at the senior level. Accordingly, he played for the OHA's Senior A Galt Hornets from 1962 to 1964.

"Knowing that it was not pro, I just decided that, 'Well, if I am going to play, and I'd like to, I'm just going to make my own mask and wear it,'" he said. "That satisfied my wife and everybody else, so that's when I started sort of wearing it."

Dave Dryden, inventor, was born.

Initially, Dryden wore a store-bought mask while playing for Galt.

"But I just figured that I could do better," he said. "I liked to tinker around with things. A lot of goalies were like that with their equipment.

"The store-bought mask that I started with was a little bit away from the face. I could see why people could say that it impacted your vision a little bit, so I just thought, 'Well, I'll make one for myself.'

"My wife helped me. We made a mold of my face with plaster of Paris. Then I started messing around with it and just made my own, and it worked just fine.

"Then, after you've worn it for a while, you realize there are ways you can improve it, so I just kept on upgrading and upgrading and upgrading."

Dryden himself was being upgraded, in terms of the tier at which he played. He turned pro in 1964 with the AHL's Buffalo Bisons, as a short-term substitute for the injured Ed Chadwick, and by 1965 was a member of the Chicago Black Hawks.

Dryden was a beneficiary of a rule, introduced midway through the 1964–65 NHL season, mandating that each of the six teams carry two goaltenders.

Whereas Hall had been Chicago's workhouse in 1963–64, he ceded some of his time in the crease to Denis DeJordy in 1964–65. The following season, Mr. Goalie played in 64 games, with Dryden—whom the Black Hawks had signed as a free agent on March 12, 1965—making 11 appearances.

Dryden spent the following season with the Central League's St. Louis Braves. Then it was back to the Windy City, where he played in 57 games over a period that spanned 1967 to 1969.

The trade winds soon started blowing, with Dryden being involved in two cash deals. First came the Black Hawks' June 10, 1970, trade with the Pittsburgh Penguins, who dispatched him to the Buffalo Sabres just four months later.

So began a precedent-setting, four-season stay with the Sabres.

Landmark No. 1: Ken Dryden made his NHL debut on March 14, 1971, backstopping Montreal to a 5–1 victory in Pittsburgh. Meanwhile, Ken's elder brother was in the process of shutting out the host Minnesota North Stars, 5–0. It was believed to be the first time in NHL history that two brothers had tended goal on the same night. Asked about Ken, Dave told Mike Lamey of the *Minneapolis Star*: "I'm going to call him first thing in the morning—collect."

Landmark No. 2: Six days later, the Drydens opposed one another... eventually.

As for how hockey history unfolded in this instance, well, it's complicated.

Dave started in goal for Buffalo at the Montreal Forum. Well aware of the possible significance of the occasion, Sabres head coach and general manager Punch Imlach had hoped to play a role in facilitating an eagerly anticipated Dryden-versus-Dryden goaltending duel.

Snag: Canadiens head coach Al MacNeil opted to start Rogatien Vachon in goal. Lamenting an opportunity that was seemingly lost, Imlach replaced Dave Dryden with (barefaced) Joe Daley just two minutes into the game, following the first whistle.

Hold on! Vachon was injured at 13:07 of the second period. Ken took over in net. Seizing the moment, Imlach sent Dave back into the game, which ended with Montreal winning 4–2.

"When the final whistle blew the brothers skated to centre ice and shook hands," Murray Dryden, who attended the game, wrote in *Playing the Shots at Both Ends*. "The picture appears on the back cover of this book and we used it on our Christmas cards that year."

Ken Dryden's face lacked a cover, save for the aforementioned catcher's mask, until he was a freshman at Cornell University in Ithaca, New York.

"I was the same as everybody at that time," Ken said.

"There were two explanations about not wearing a mask and they were ones that every top-level goalie would say who didn't wear one. It was what all the rest of us would read about and hear about and believe and repeat back.

"The first explanation was that they're too hot—so hot that you just sweat like crazy underneath a mask. The more important reason, and the standard one, was that you can't see the puck at your feet.

"Those were the two insurmountable barriers. They made sense in the way in which when you want something to be, you decide that something is the explanation, whether it's a good explanation or it isn't."

Because of those barriers, the younger Dryden emerged with the usual medley of stitches and shiners, and without consideration of wearing a mask as he progressed through the junior ranks.

"I don't remember that there was an alternative," he said. "I don't remember that there was a mask to be worn.

"Then again, so much of it is, 'I'm a goalie. Goalies don't wear masks. It's what we do. It's how we do it.'"

Then he arrived at Cornell and quickly discovered that masks were mandatory. Therefore, a plaster of Paris facial mold was made and sent away to Montreal. From that, a Plante-style "pretzel mask" was tailored to fit someone who would become the next in a series of Canadiens goaltending greats.

Ken Dryden and his barely-there mask exploded into prominence during the 1971 Stanley Cup playoffs. After playing in only six regular season games with the 1970–71 Canadiens, the 23-year-old rookie became a workhorse in the spring and helped Montreal win the first of six titles he would celebrate in only eight seasons as an NHLer.

In fact, Dryden inadvertently went maskless for a fraction of a game on May 14, 1977, when the Canadiens completed a sweep of the championship series by defeating Boston 2–1 in overtime.

The Bruins' only goal was scored by Bobby Schmautz, 23 seconds after Dryden's mask had been knocked off during a goal-mouth collision.

"The ending of a very strange play, in which Ken Dryden was playing without his mask," Dick Irvin said during *Hockey Night in Canada*'s telecast, adding: "I can't recall ever seeing a goaltender lose his mask in the middle of a play, the way Dryden did that time."

The mask preceded the puck into the net after Schmautz and Canadiens defenceman Serge Savard collided with Dryden near the crease.

After Schmautz opened the scoring at 11:38 of the first period, Dryden used his stick to fish the puck *and* the mask out of the net.

(Such things do happen periodically. On November 25, 2022, for example, the Dallas Stars' Jason Robertson scored a goal after his team's captain, Jamie Benn, was pushed into Winnipeg Jets goaltender Connor Hellebuyck by defenceman Josh Morrissey. The collision knocked off Hellebuyck's mask, but play continued for a few seconds until Robertson scored.)

Dryden stymied the Bruins for the remainder of the contest, which ended with Jacques Lemaire's Stanley Cup–winning goal 4:32 into sudden-death overtime.

Two more championship-clinching victories ensued before Dryden announced his retirement on July 9, 1979, just shy of his 32nd birthday. He went on to become a successful lawyer, author, politician, and hockey executive.

At the time of his retirement, Dryden was the owner of a fibreglass mask that covered all of his face and part of his neck. The mask looks archaic by today's standards, but it was nonetheless a significant improvement, protection-wise, from the porous "pretzel" model that had previously been worn.

"You're looking at it out of time," Dryden said. "At the time, we thought we were unbelievably well-protected, because the alternative was no mask at all.

"We knew the limitations of the mask, or one like it. If you got hit, it hurt. If you got hit, you may well get cut underneath it, much more with your skin splitting rather than it being carved from the force of the shot.

"But what it seemed to us was that it helped you avoid the worst and, by doing that, it was a lot better than anything we had had before.

"So, sure, you look at it out of time and it looks as if it's hardly anything. It may be historically hardly anything, but it was a whole lot in its time."

By the time Ken Dryden concluded a brilliant goaltending career, his brother was preparing for one final season as a player and a concurrent return to the NHL.

Like many players of his era, Dave Dryden had been enticed by the WHA, to which he migrated after playing in 120 games for Buffalo.

The first stop had been Chicago—one of his former big-league homes—when he signed with the Cougars and provided an instant injection of credibility and class.

"Dave Dryden is a rarity among goaltenders," Robert Markus wrote in the *Chicago Tribune* on June 7, 1974. "He is totally sane. He does not require frequent trips to a spa or Miami Beach to settle his nerves. He does not snap at post-game questioners or withdraw in sullen silence. He does not even turn his back to the room after a defeat and dress with his nose in his locker stall.

"Dryden, in fact, is such a nice, sane guy that for a while his friends despaired of his ever becoming a first-rate goalie."

This much wasn't a rarity in the WHA: There was a financial crisis.

The Cougars were in such dire financial straits that Dryden, teammates Pat Stapleton (who moonlighted as the team's head coach) and Ralph Backstrom, and attorney Jeff Rosen purchased the debt-ridden club in December 1974.

It was a noble, but ultimately futile, effort. The Cougars continued to average roughly 3,000 spectators per game before the league pulled the plug on the troubled team in May 1975.

Dryden was soon snapped up in a dispersal draft by the Edmonton Oilers, for whom he would make the final 229 appearances of his playing career.

Included was one contest in which the most revered Edmonton player of all was *not* an Oiler.

An 18-year-old Wayne Gretzky, fresh out of the Ontario Hockey League and the Sault Ste. Marie Greyhounds, played his first eight games as a professional with the 1978–79 Indianapolis Racers under owner Nelson Skalbania.

The Great One, as Gretzky would soon come to be known, was held without a point in his first two WHA games before erupting for an assist—on a goal by Richie LeDuc—in a 4–0 victory over the host Quebec Nordiques on October 18, 1978.

Two nights later, a goal-less Gretzky and his Indianapolis teammates were at home to Dave Dryden and the Oilers. The Racers' head coach at the time was none other than Stapleton, with whom Dryden had played—and even partnered in ownership—during his time suiting up for the Cougars. Behold one of the least-prophetic conversations in hockey history.

"I never used to talk to the opposition when we went into town, but Pat was such a good friend that when I was with the Oilers and we went in there to Indianapolis, I did give him a call and ask how he was doing," Dryden remembered.

"He said, 'I'm doing fine, but this kid that Skalbania got me, he's turning out to be a washout. He hasn't got any [goals] so far and I'm really worried about what's going to happen with him.'

"That night, he got two goals on me—and they were the crappiest goals. One of them was a dribbler that went right through my legs. It was absolutely a bad goal."

No. 99's first two goals as a pro came 34 seconds apart—at 6:07 and 6:41 of the second period—before 6,386 spectators and 9,607 vacant seats at Market Square Arena.

Trivia time: An assist on Gretzky's second goal was awarded to Don Larway, who nearly two years earlier had become the last person to score on an intentionally maskless netminder.

Larway, then of the Houston Aeros, had beaten the Racers' Andy Brown at 18:13 of the third period on November 9, 1976, to complete the scoring in a 7–2 Houston victory. That was the final start by Brown, who made two subsequent relief appearances before a back injury ended his hockey career.

Everything was just getting started in the autumn of 1978 for Gretzky, whose scoring spasm versus Dryden ignited a 46-goal, 110-point, two-team rookie year. Over the subsequent 20 seasons, Gretzky established 61 NHL records, including all-time standards for goals (894) and points (2,857).

Worth noting, though, is the fact that Dave Dryden and associates enjoyed the last laugh on Gretzky's breakout evening. After his second goal staked Indianapolis to a 3–1 lead, the Oilers rallied to win 4–3. It helped considerably that Dryden stoned Kevin Nugent on a penalty shot.

Gretzky scored one more goal over his following four games. Then, on November 2, 1978, he was traded to Edmonton, where he received a lighthearted welcome from Dryden.

"I kept you in the league," Dave jokingly told Gretzky after the trade, "because otherwise you were going back to Sault Ste. Marie."

Following Gretzky's inaugural season, the Oilers and three other WHA teams—the Nordiques, Hartford Whalers, and Winnipeg Jets—were absorbed by the NHL.

Dryden was the starting goaltender in the Oilers' first NHL game, a 4–2 loss in Chicago on October 10, 1979.

Four days later, he was on the ice to witness yet another early-career milestone by Gretzky. At 18:51 of the third period against the Vancouver Canucks, Gretzky notched his first NHL goal. He concluded the scoring in a 4–4 tie.

Dryden played in 14 games over the Oilers' first two months as an NHL entity before announcing his retirement as a player on December 22, 1979.

"For the first time in my career, I just wasn't enjoying the things I had to do to get ready for a game," he told a group of reporters that included Cam Cole of the *Edmonton Journal*, "and I always said when I stopped enjoying the game or any part of it, I'd get out."

His influence, however, would endure.

Dryden had worn a fibreglass mask—one that was typically his own handiwork—for the vast majority of his time in professional hockey.

Like all goalies of his day, he dealt with the usual assortment of nicks to the face. His philosophy was suitably cutting-edge.

"What I was finding with the masks that I made was that they prevented cuts and all of that stuff, but realistically when you looked at it, if a puck hit in the wrong way it could still damage your eye," Dryden said. "And, when you took a shot off one of those fibreglass masks, it really shook you."

Hence the decision to take a shot at a new concept. Having taken note of European-born WHA goaltenders who had worn a regular player's helmet, plus a cage that covered the face, he was once again in a tinkering mood.

"I still liked the feeling of the fibreglass mask and the way it encased your head and everything else," he said. "I figured that I didn't need a helmet, so I just started messing around and thinking, 'Geez, I can come up with something here.'

"I got a whole bunch of solder wire and chopped up an old mask and came up with some things. I knew what I wanted and how I wanted the wires around the eyes."

It helped that he was wired into Greg Harrison, who was then working for Cooper, a Canadian-based sporting-equipment manufacturer.

"I had been working with Cooper at that time with all my equipment," Dryden said. "I'd go in in May, after the season, and say, 'OK, guys, I want to redesign this. I want to redesign that…' and they were really good.

"I talked to Greg and he said, 'I'm making some masks. I can make this one up for you,' so I worked with him and we came up with a mask that I used in '77 in the WHA, and I loved it."

The revolutionary cage combination—consisting of wires in front of the face, forehead and chin, and a fibreglass shell surrounding the head—was born. Then came the testing process.

"The first year that I had the mask, the Oilers actually went to Finland and Sweden during training camp," Dryden recalled. "I can still remember the first game, which was in Finland. There was a rolling puck going out from behind the net, right out into the slot. The Finnish player wound up for a slap shot and, as soon as it hit me in the face, I thought, 'I'm friggin' dead.'

"Then I'm standing there and I'm thinking, 'I didn't even feel a thing.' It was like, 'Wow! This actually is going to work.' Then I was totally sold on it."

So was Glenn (Chico) Resch, who ditched his full-face fibreglass mask and sported a cage combination with the 1977–78 New York Islanders. The transformation took place not long after training camp, at which a Swedish goalie named Göran Högosta—whose NHL career would consist of only 22 games—left a lasting impression.

"I remember him getting hit in the shoulders, in the head, in the face, and he just goes and shakes his head," Resch marvelled. "He just took a shot right in the face, and it was no big deal.

"I thought, 'I've got this stupid old fibreglass mask on that I was wearing when Bobby Nystrom broke my nose in practice, and I'm wearing *this*?'

"I said to Greg Harrison, 'Greg, I'm going to go to a cage,' and then he came back to me and said, 'Chico, I've figured out a way to do this. I do the same mold, cut out the inside, and put the cage over the frontal part of the mask.' I said, 'That's good for me,' and I still have that mask."

Resch wore the Dryden/Harrison-inspired model for the remainder of his fine NHL career, one that lasted from 1973 to 1987 and also included stints with the Colorado Rockies (now New Jersey Devils) and Philadelphia Flyers.

Harrison, for his part, ended up making a business out of mask manufacturing. An early step was a partnership with Dryden that related solely to the pioneering of a hybrid mask that, with a few alterations, is still a tool of the trade.

"Where I find the satisfaction is just from the fact that I've always wanted to be part of things evolving," Dryden reflected. "Lots of people like things the same as they've always been traditionally. I love tradition, but I love to see it when people use creativity to solve a problem that way.

"We did have a problem as goalies. Here we were getting hurt and we didn't really need to get hurt."

Step 1 was taken on November 1, 1959, when Jacques Plante's unsightly mask was unveiled at Madison Square Garden.

"It was advanced back then," Sportmask's Tony Priolo noted. "It was space-age."

The rest of the blank spaces were ultimately filled in thanks in large part to Dave Dryden.

"I give hockey credit," he said from Oakville, Ontario. "Hockey has kept up pretty well with our knowledge and our understanding of things, with all of the concussion protocols and everything that there is now.

"I always thought the league was slow with visors but, like we were saying with masks, it takes a while for the culture to change. I always figured that it shouldn't be the culture that changed. It should be your employers that change the rules because they can do that. The players, even if they don't like it, have to go along with it.

"The team has to be like a parent in all of this and say, 'I know you guys want to leave it the way it is, but we know what's better for you, so this is what the rule is going to be.'

"The guys will bitch and moan, but they'll end up doing it and then end up realizing, 'Hey, that was a good idea.'"

Dave Dryden embraced the idea of a book about maskless goalies, to the extent that he was kind enough to take and transmit some selfies that included his old masks. He also proofread the manuscript in the summer of 2022.

Sadly, one final email to him—sent on August 31 of that year—was not answered. It was completely unlike him not to respond.

The reasoning became all too clear a few weeks later, when the hockey world was saddened to learn that Dave Dryden had died on October 4, 2022, of complications from chronic thromboembolic pulmonary hypertension surgery. He was 81 years old.

The NHL quickly released a statement, in which Dryden was lauded as a former goaltender, equipment innovator, educator, and philanthropist.

"Respected and liked by all who were lucky enough to know him, Dryden made contributions to our game beyond his 14 seasons tending goal as a pro in the NHL and WHA—including a memorable game when he and brother, Ken, became the first siblings to play goal against each other in the NHL," commissioner Gary Bettman said.

"In the mid-1970s, he reimagined the goalie mask, designing the combination fibreglass helmet and birdcage front that greatly increased protection, transformed the way the position could be played and remains the most popular in use today.

"After retirement, he worked with the league on refinements to equipment, always focused on better protecting athletes. He also pursued a lengthy post-playing career as an elementary school principal and ran the bed-providing charity that his parents founded, Sleeping Children Around the World.

"We send our deepest condolences to Dave's wife, Sandra, their two children, and six grandchildren, and all whose lives and careers were improved by his work. And, in his name, the NHL will be making a donation to Sleeping Children Around the World."

20

Today's Tender Moments

Life between the pipes in the 21st century

Robin Lehner survived Capital punishment—in the form of an Alexander Ovechkin howitzer to the head during a January 24, 2022, NHL game between the Washington Capitals and Vegas Golden Knights.

One shudders at the thought of how a grizzled maskless goalie would have fared if faced with Ovechkin's 99-miles-per-hour blast, which damaged Lehner's mask.

"That shot actually cracked the cage," the Vegas goaltender said a few weeks later, during his 12th NHL season, in an interview for this book. "Some of the welding snapped off. I hadn't seen that before.

"It could have gone all the way in if it was a little bit harder. You kind of think you got lucky a little bit."

Lehner acknowledged that he felt "a little out of it" for a second or two as the consequence of a searing shot that also "hurt a bit."

No wonder. The blast left a U-shaped indentation in some of the bars that, while proving to be pliable, nonetheless served the purpose of protecting his face.

Lehner remained in the game, albeit with a backup mask. However, the primary mask, to which Ovechkin had added a puck-mark, was soon back in service.

All in a day's work for Lehner, who has largely become inured to shots that fly around or into his head.

"I think the majority of the time that it actually hits the mask, it leaves your ears ringing a bit," he said.

"It depends on where they hit the cage. If it hits the skinny parts of your cage, it helps a little bit because it cushions it. You don't get the ringing in the ears that you do if it hits the metal bar or if it actually hits the helmet. Then you black out for a little bit—for a second.

"It was a hard shot [by Ovechkin]. Instincts kind of take over and you can still find the puck, but that was a hard one."

Former junior goalie Carl Stankowski has been there, done that, dating back to his time in the British Columbia Hockey League.

"When I was in Penticton [during the 2019–20 season], I caught this one-timer at the start of practice," he recalled. "It smoked me in the head—right on the cage—and my cage was dented in.

"It was one of those times when you realize, 'Thank God I have a mask on.'"

A similar sentiment occurred to the Minnesota Wild's Cam Talbot on March 25, 2021, while he was in the process of blanking the Blues 2–0.

"Justin Faulk of St. Louis blasted an absolute bomb from the point," Talbot recalled "He stepped into a one-timer and it got stuck in my cat-eye [cage].

"I'd never seen a puck get stuck in the cage before. I didn't even know it was possible. It came at me so hard and kind of came in on an angle, like a knuckle-puck, and it literally got stuck.

"It was coming right toward me, so I kind of blinked for a second. When I opened my eyes, the puck was like an inch from my eyeball. "It was actually kind of scary."

The scary precedent was set on May 24, 2000, when the New Jersey Devils' Scott Gomez took aim during Game 6 of a playoff series against the Philadelphia Flyers.

"Brian Boucher got the puck stuck in his cage," goaltender-turned-broadcaster Martin Biron said, "and it could have been really dangerous."

And it was...for the mask, anyway. Boucher, whose cheekbone was nicked by the intrusive puck, completed the game protected by a cage he had originally worn in the minors with the Philadelphia Phantoms.

"You get hit in the mask, usually you get your bell rung," Boucher told Jay Greenberg of the *New York Post* after New Jersey won 2–1, "but all I saw was black until I realized it was just the puck I was seeing, not darkness."

The attention soon shifted from the Flyers to pliers, which were required to extricate the puck from the cage.

And then there are times when a cleaning solution comes in handy.

March 30, 2021, was one of those days—unexpectedly eventful as it was.

"Thought you would like this," Stankowski wrote in a Twitter direct message while attaching a photo of his freshly marked-up mask—an image that left an imprint in more ways than one. "Got a shot in practice today and the puck left the WHL logo on my bucket."

A maskless goalie may have kicked the bucket as a consequence of such a blow. But Stankowski—who was just fine, thank you—was bemused by the whole thing.

In casual fashion, he also discussed the occasional aftermath of a puck to the head.

"Sometimes you can be smelling rubber off your cage," he said. "I've had that happen a couple of times. It's just right on the cage when it hits hard. For a good 10 seconds, you can smell burning rubber or hot rubber."

In this case, "you" is used in the general sense—or scents, as the case may be.

"You get that smell even if you make saves with your pads," Lehner noted. "You can definitely smell it when it hits the side of your mask and leaves a mark."

A marked improvement in goaltenders' protection allows them to shrug off such experiences as quickly as the burnt-rubber smell dissipates.

"It maybe lasts a couple of seconds—five or 10 seconds, tops," veteran NHL goalie James Reimer observed. "When you get hit in the head, you're obviously going to take a couple of whiffs of burnt rubber. It's like, 'Oh, that's odd,' and then you don't smell it after that.

"You're just thankful that you've got the mask on in that case."

The gratitude is not limited to goalies who have ascended to hockey's highest echelon.

"My son's 17 and he's a goalie," Biron said in 2021, "so I asked him one time, 'Have you ever smelled burnt rubber when the puck hits you in the face?' He said, 'Yeah.'

"Guys are shooting a lot harder now at 17."

Stankowski had just turned 17 when, as a rookie, he backstopped the Seattle Thunderbirds to the 2016–17 WHL championship. That season, he became a second-generation major-junior goalie, following in the footsteps of his father, Brent (Medicine Hat Tigers, 1981–82).

"My dad played with one of those wood masks," Calgary-born Carl Stankowski joked. "It's at the house. Sometimes I put it on and think, 'Wow...I don't know if I could take a shot to the head with this thing.'"

A shake of the head is the reflexive response when Stankowski tries to comprehend the professional lives of his puck-stopping predecessors.

"I think that's where the goalies' stereotype comes in," he mused. "Back in the day, playing with no mask, you've got to be a little bit crazy to do that."

"Crazy" would be one word for it.

"Those guys were absolutely insane," marvelled Cam Talbot, whose lengthy NHL goaltending career began in 2013.

"They were warriors. There was no padding—no protection there whatsoever. I would never be a goalie if it was still like that. I will tell you that much right now.

"You couldn't pay me to stand in front of a puck wearing the kind of masks that those guys used to wear, or wearing no mask at all."

He is more inclined to pay homage to them.

"I know that sticks weren't like they are now, and they weren't even curved," Talbot continued. "The puck didn't get up high all that often.

But if you take a puck in the face, you take a puck in the face. It doesn't matter if it's coming at you 50 miles per hour or 90. It's still going to hurt.

"Yeah, I'll go stand in front of it with no helmet on...no chance."

But nobody thought twice about that, once upon a time—for the longest time.

"They were glorified back-catchers," Talbot said of his early predecessors. "The pads were pillows taped to their legs, essentially. What they wore to stop a piece of vulcanized rubber is just insane to me."

Reimer is comparably incredulous.

"I'm just stunned, really," he said. "They're way tougher than I am, that's for sure. I can't even imagine standing in front of a shot without a mask. I'm just so impressed by Jacques Plante and those guys and how tough they were. Honestly, I can't even think about it. "I'm usually a pretty nice guy about getting hit in the head. Most of the guys will come up to me and go, 'Sorry, sorry, sorry, sorry!" I just kind of laugh it off and go, 'Well, obviously, you weren't aiming at the middle of the net, so no big deal.'

"But I can't imagine not wearing a mask. That's just bizarre to me. I'm in awe of those guys. I have all the respect in the world for them. If you can give them some more props, that's awesome."

Commendation should not be reserved solely for the grizzled goalies of yesteryear. Anyone who stands in front of a net—regardless of the level of protection—is blessed with rare courage.

Maskless goalies may be long gone, but the same cannot be said for shots to the noggin.

"The ones where you get hit square are the ones that can ring your bell a little bit," Reimer said. "For me, the worst part of getting hit in the head—and only goalies can attest to this—is that it stuns you.

"A lot of people go, 'It's so loud.' I've had times when I've been hit in the head and it feels like my eardrums are going to pop. It's such a concussive bang, with the puck hitting your mask, that it stuns you.

"It's like if you hold a pot over your head and smash it with some metal. It rattles your cage—literally. It's not so much that the force of the puck actually hurts you. It's just that it stuns you. That's the worst part of being hit in the head, I think—just that it rattles your cage."

Being hit, period, is hardly a picnic if a shot finds the wrong place at the wrong time.

"I'm sure you've seen the [thick] chest pad and the stuff that we wear now and I still get stingers through them," Talbot observed. "There are some spots where it's not doubled up or something like that.

"If you get it in the wrong spot, your arm goes numb. A shot hits my forearm sometimes and I can't even hold on to my stick. My hand just goes numb. It still hurts—and that's with the protection that we have now.

"Those [maskless] guys must have had ice bags all over their bodies 24 hours a day. It's crazy to think how much it would have hurt back then."

There's that word again: crazy.

Continuing with that theme, we bring you Max Paddock—another modern-day minder of the net who struggles to relate to the maskless mentality of long ago.

"It really is unthinkable," said Paddock, who excelled in the major-junior Western Hockey League for the Regina Pats and Prince Albert Raiders before enrolling at Acadia University in Wolfville, Nova Scotia.

"You've got to have some screws loose in your mind to want to do that, but the masks have allowed the game to change. Now goalies are going down in the butterfly. They're on their knees whereas, back then, they stood up and made the kick saves. The masks have completely changed how goalie is being played."

The mask not only protects the face, which was once its primary purpose, but also the net.

The alteration in style, leading to the disappearance of the once-stalwart stand-up goalie, has put the last line of defence in the path of the puck far more frequently than once was the case.

"You're pretty lucky if you come out of practice without getting one in the head," Paddock said. "The ones that come at you and hit you square in the forehead or even right in the face area are the ones that sting the most, because there's nowhere for the puck to go, other than your head and your neck taking the full-on force of it.

"If it hits you off the shell and grazes off, you almost don't even feel those ones. Sometimes pucks hit you in the chin. We even wear these plastic danglers that cover your throat. I can't even imagine getting a puck to the throat, either. It's almost more than just the face that the helmet protects. It's the neck and even a little bit of the collarbone area, too."

It would seem, on the surface, that engaging in the live combat of a game would put the goaltenders in the greatest danger. Not necessarily.

"Honestly, in a game it doesn't happen too much, because you're only getting 30 shots on average in a game," Paddock noted. "In practice, you're getting 200 or 250 shots, so there's just that much more time to get those stingers. Plus, guys are trying to score in practice and they can just walk in and shoot, whereas maybe 10 of the 30 shots are coming from the outside in a game.

"In practice, guys just get a pass, skate in, and take a shot. Some drills are three-shot drills and everybody on the team has got to go through the drill at least twice, so that's 50 or 75 shots in one drill."

Not that the games are a safe haven by any means, especially when it seems that every player, regardless of age and experience, can fire the puck.

Case in point: Connor Bedard, who made his much anticipated juniors debut on March 12, 2021. Paddock was the opposing goaltender during that game, which had barely begun when Bedard ensured that his first shift would be memorable by ringing an NHL-calibre shot off the Raiders' goalie's mask.

"That one definitely caught me by surprise, because you don't think of a 15-year-old kid doing that," said Paddock, who allowed two goals by Bedard while helping Prince Albert win 6–3. "I've skated with 15-year-olds. Being older than them, you don't expect a shot to come at you as quickly as his does.

"That one got me right on the chin, so my ears were ringing for a little bit."

By the end of that game, Bedard had already seen half as much WHL duty as Al MacInnis, who dressed for two contests with the 1979–80 Regina team. He went on to excel in the Ontario league, with the

Kitchener Rangers, before starring in the NHL with the Calgary Flames and St. Louis Blues.

"Black and blue" was often an apt description for a rival netminder after facing MacInnis, considering the terrifying velocity of a slap shot that helped him amass 340 goals and 1,274 points and become a mortal lock for admission into the Hockey Hall of Fame.

"When Al was winding up, you were on high alert," goalie-turned-broadcaster Kelly Hrudey said. "Facing him was a real intense challenge.

"When I was with Los Angeles and we were in Calgary, the Flames were on a five-on-three power play and MacInnis had a one-timer in the high slot. The puck ricocheted off the very top of my mask, hit the glass behind it, and absolutely shattered the glass."

Better that than a cheekbone—a fate that could have befallen a goalie in the good ol' days.

"I felt fortunate that it didn't get me straight on," Hrudey continued. "That it shattered the glass didn't surprise me whatsoever. That's the hardest shot in the game, although Brett Hull eventually was at that point.

"Al MacInnis was the first guy who I felt had that sort of velocity on the shot, and then it was Brett Hull. For both guys, it was, 'I know I've got to get a piece of this. I know it probably won't feel very good, but it's all in the line of duty.'

"I think my worst injury from a direct shot was from one taken by Brett Hull. It was a one-timer from about 15 feet out. It got me in the groin and I had to go to the hospital after the game. It was not pleasant."

Not just from the perspective of a goaltender.

"I got it right in the testicles," Hrudey said. "There was no actual damage other than a bruise, but you can imagine how bad that was. When you get it in the groin and you have to go to the hospital, you know it's bad."

Yet, Hrudey was back in the lineup within a week.

The King could certainly use his crown.

"I played in New York with Henrik Lundqvist," Cam Talbot recalled, referencing Rangers goaltending royalty. "If the puck was coming at his head, he would actually use his head to make the save and direct the puck out of play. It was incredible.

"He wouldn't put his glove in front of his face because, I think it was Tommy Salo back in the Olympics for Sweden, he put his hand in front of his face, missed the puck, it hit him on the top of his head, rolled over, and went in. Sweden ended up losing that game, so now no Swedish goalie puts their hand in front of their face. They'll use their helmet as a tool to block it.

"Henrik was unbelievable at it. He would actually knock it out of the way. He had rebound control with his head. I've never seen anything like it.

"It was like a soccer move. He would just snap his neck and deflect it out of play. It blew my mind every time I saw it. I saw it the first time and I was like, 'Did he do that on purpose?' Then the more I got to know him, I realized, 'Yeah, that's actually a tactic.'

"I'm going to try to catch that 10 times out of 10 if I have a chance to, but he just liked using his head. I don't know what it was. He was really freaking good at it."

Not to mention every other aspect of goaltending, for that matter—to the point where the John Tortorella-led Rangers coaching staff mandated special protection for the team's meal ticket.

"We had a practice one day and Brian Boyle came down on Henrik Lundqvist and took a shot and hit him right in the neck area," said Martin Biron, who played for the Rangers from 2010 to 2014. "Hank went down. Right then, Torts blew the whistle. Jim Schoenfeld, who was an assistant coach and assistant general manager with us at the time, called everybody to centre ice and just ripped the guys a new one: 'You are taking headshots on the guy who's going to win you a Stanley Cup?! Are you crazy?! You keep the shots low on Lundqvist! With Lundqvist, everything's low. If you want to hit a goalie in the head, do it on Marty's side!'

"I'm like, 'Thanks. You just put a bull's-eye on my face.' That was funny, but it just shows that I got hit in the head quite often."

Irrespective of the era, do goalies need their heads examined for other reasons?

"For the longest time, I thought, 'How stupid can you be to want to be a goalie?'" Biron reflected. "But now, the equipment is so state-of-the-art. They're so well-protected. I say, 'How stupid can you be to be a forward or a defenceman and lay out and block shots?' They're the crazy ones.

"It helps the goalies. Don't get me wrong. It's great that guys block shots, but they have about 20 per cent of the protection that goalies do, and they still get in front of shots. I would be a goalie 100 times over being a defenceman because of that aspect of trying to block shots as a defenceman."

Hrudey is quick to concur.

"Totally," he stated. "Whenever I'm broadcasting a game, sometimes I'm terrified when the guys get in front of the shots because, as Marty said, they don't have the same protection that the goaltender has. I don't think any goalies play with fear anymore, because they're so well-protected.

"Now, on occasion, you might get dinged up a little bit, but they're not playing with fear. And if I were a defenceman or a skater and I'm in the line of fire, I have to think that I would have some fear, because the potential that I am going to break a bone is real."

James Reimer seconds—or thirds—the notion.

"Those guys are crazy," he said while a member of the San Jose Sharks. "We've got a bunch of guys on our team that sacrifice. Landon Ferraro, he always stands in there and takes a beating.

"I can't fathom stepping in front of a one-timer with whatever these guys wear. They always look at us like we're the ones who are crazy, but the guys who block shots, they're nuts."

Right, Gumper?

"People always say goalies are different," Gump Worsley told Dick Irvin Jr. "We all have our little idiosyncrasies, but so do the guys who play forward and defence.

"They say we're nuts because we go in there and try to stop the puck. At least we've got the equipment. What about the defencemen who stand there and try to block the same shots? They don't have the kind of equipment a goalie does. So who's the dopiest—the goalies or the defencemen?"

Good question.

"It's not everyone who can be a goalie but, in this day and age, just look at how our team in Vegas plays," Robin Lehner concluded. "I'm almost more afraid for our defencemen. At least we have padding. Our defencemen are expected to block all the shots that they can as well. I think they take way more of a beating than we do.

"It's insane. I don't even want them to do it. I feel bad, because they don't have all the padding, and they get hit in bad spots quite often. We've had a lot of broken bones on the team. It sucks when you see them take one in front of you, but it's part of our game, part of our system.

"It takes more courage for them to step in front with their pads than it does for us."

The pads? Well, that's another story entirely…

21

Taking It on the Shin

No pain, no game, for brave blockers of shots

Craig Ludwig, shot-blocker supreme, padded a resume like nobody else in National Hockey League history.

His pair of shin pads, worn for the entirety of a 1,256-game big-league career, looked more like tree trunks. Suitably, they did seem to get a little wider each year.

As they grew, so did his legend.

"Remember Craig Ludwig and those extra-wide shin pads?" former NHL forward Trent McCleary said. "Those were ridiculous!"

They were also a calling card.

"I played college hockey with Craig Ludwig, and those shin pads of his just kept getting bigger and bigger," marvelled former University of North Dakota defence cohort James Patrick, himself a veteran of more than 1,000 NHL games. "Every year, I think he taped a bigger piece of foam to the back and they just spread out.

"He would be a stand-up goalie in front of the goalie, with his big shin pads."

And without a mask, or any hesitation.

Ludwig was so courageous, and so proficient at what he did, that a tattered piece of equipment became part of his story.

"One time, I got an email from the Hall of Fame," the former Montreal Canadiens, New York Islanders, Minnesota North Stars, and Dallas Stars rearguard mused. "I didn't know if they were playing tricks on me or what, but they asked if they could have my shin pads.

"At the time, my twins were about 14 years old, and they were saying, 'No, Dad. I want to wear them!' I'm like, 'Dude, nobody's wearing these things. They're all moldy and stuff inside,' so I didn't respond to the email.

"Then I got another email, asking the same thing. I did respond to that one, but ultimately, I got a phone call, saying, 'Mr. Ludwig, we've been trying to get a hold of you, blah blah blah.' I just said to them, 'I'll make you a deal. You can have my shin pads if you take me.'

"There's never been an email or a phone call since then."

Nonetheless, there has been an enshrinement. Ludwig entered the Wisconsin Hockey Hall of Fame in 2002.

The induction was a tribute to an honest worker whose contributions cannot be measured by a reliance upon the sport's traditional markers.

The offensive totals—38 goals and 184 assists in 17 seasons—are as modest as the self-deprecating Ludwig. He enjoyed a lengthy and successful career by performing an unglamorous but invaluable role, even at the considerable risk of his well-being.

The fine art of habitually and effectively falling or sliding in front of shots taken by some of the game's most dangerous gunners is not for everybody.

But it was part of the package for Ludwig—an old-school player with suitably antiquated equipment, at least as far as his lower legs were concerned.

The shin pads were actually relics from 1979–80—his first of three seasons at North Dakota.

"When I was a freshman, I walked on to UND and I made the team," recalled Ludwig, a product of Rhinelander, Wisconsin. "I ended up getting a pair of used shin pads and a pair of used shoulder pads—and there was nothing to the shoulder pads at the time—and I wore the same ones my whole career. I had our trainer fix them all the time."

Plastic and duct tape were essential ingredients. Ahhh, the glamorous life of a big-league defenceman...

"The shin pads were so cracked that my socks would end up being all full of blood at the end of a game," Ludwig recalled. "I still don't have much feeling in my legs and my feet anymore from being hit with pucks.

"People would say, 'Man, just wear new pads.' I'd say, 'Nope.'"

That was a rote response when any sort of equipment upgrade was suggested or offered.

"I probably wore four pairs of skates, max, my whole career," Ludwig noted. "Now they go through a pair a week.

"I just never liked the new equipment. I always liked old, raggedy stuff, so there wasn't a lot of padding."

But there were plenty of cuts and bruises.

"I blame it all on Rick Wilson," Ludwig said, jokingly, in reference to someone who coached him with UND, Minnesota, and Dallas. "After practices, he would always grab a bunch of pucks. He would stand at the blue line and we'd stand near the faceoff dot. He would tee off and we were always working on going down and blocking shots.

"Once you get the timing down, you don't even think about it. I think the whole key is 'don't get hit and don't get hurt early' when you first start doing it.

"I was pretty lucky, for the most part, where I never really got injured while blocking a shot. I know I broke my foot a couple of times. They'd stick a needle in it and say, 'You're good to go.' There's nothing you can do.

"It's just like anything else. It's confidence."

That mind frame was buoyed by plenty of homework, with an emphasis on opposing shooters, from Wayne Gretzky to the most anonymous fourth-line worker ant.

"I would go over every game and I would pick out their tendencies," Ludwig said. "It would be, 'This guy does that. He likes to go to his backhand. This guy is a one-timer guy. He'll try to fake a shot, get you to go down, and go around you.'

"I would go through all 20 names on the roster and try to find things to remember about those guys. It's just to give yourself a bit of an edge.

"So I kind of had an idea of where guys would shoot and which guys would fake it and want to go around you. There were all those little things.

"I'm sure it's more important for goal scorers to think about that kind of stuff when they're trying to score goals, as opposed to some dummy trying to block a shot. But you'd have to know where to have your head when you go down, and you had to know how to go down.

"Gretz did it to me a couple of times. You'd go down to take a passing lane away on a two-on-one. The smart ones would wait and then they'd shoot at your legs and it would ricochet into the net. It would come off your legs and go in, so you've got to change the angle at which you'd go down."

The scouting being done, the savviest shot-blockers would welcome the impact of a vulcanized-rubber projectile that was travelling at a dangerous speed. (Do not try this yourself.)

"It feels great when you get hit, and you get hit in the right spot," Ludwig noted. "When it hits your pad in the pants, or when it hits your glove and it doesn't break your hand, it feels great. I guess it feels great because you know you didn't break something.

"Everybody's got a role. You have to bring something to the table and I guess that was part of what I could bring."

The medical examination table was the destination at times but, all things considered, Ludwig emerged from the rigours of yeoman duty without too many battle scars.

"There was a New Year's Eve game here in Dallas," said Ludwig, who remained in Texas after concluding his playing career with the Stanley Cup–winning Stars in 1999. "Gary Suter was on the point [preparing to shoot]. I went down and he kind of hesitated. After he took a shot, I slid out of the lane that I needed to be in, but I stuck my arm out on the ice. The shot hit me in the hand and broke my hand.

"I was in surgery that night. I didn't miss any games. They just put a couple of pins in and you were fine. But there was nothing major for me. You got hit a couple of times in the head but, at the time, we didn't even know what concussions were, so that wasn't a problem.

"It became part of my identity because, like anything else, your confidence allows you to get better at it. You kind of know the whens and wheres.

"The distance that somebody is away from you is important, obviously, because there are guys who go down on both knees as opposed to laying down, and the guy's 10 feet away from them—and I'm thinking, 'Boy, you're an idiot,' because the puck has got a chance to elevate and hit you right between the eyes.

"You can go down in front of a guy who is two feet away from you and you don't have to worry about anything. It hits you in the stomach at the highest."

Failing that, it might hit the goalie...you know, the person whose *occupation* it is to get hit by the puck—or find another vocation.

So what about the barefaced goalies, way back when, who were the last line of defence? Is a comparatively unprotected shot-blocker the closest equivalent to the maskless versions of Johnny Bower, Gump Worsley, Terry Sawchuk, et al?

"I look at that differently because, if somebody's going down to block a shot and his head is toward the guy who is shooting, he's an idiot," Ludwig opined.

"Our heads were always turned the other way. I was never really worried about getting hit in the face, because you'd go down in a way that your face is behind you. You'd get hit in the back of the head, maybe, but that's part of the learning thing.

"But I think of those goaltenders who didn't wear a mask when they first started. They can't turn their heads. They've got to know where the puck is. They've got to get their blocker on it or stop it somehow.

"The other thing is, let's hope that it hits me if I'm trying to block it. And if it doesn't, the goalie had better stop it. Those guys can't turn their back or turn away from a shot. If they do that, it's going in the net and they probably won't start anymore."

James Patrick was hit by shots more often than he cares to remember—even though the impact was an indication of a job well done.

"I remember taking a Mats Sundin slap shot on a power play," Patrick recalled. "He hit me in the pants and, even though I was wearing padding, I had a charleyhorse.

"It was one of those things. I wasn't close enough to him and he wound up. At that point, you're in no-man's land. You have to stand in there. As that D-man, you have to stay there when your mind's going, 'Oh my God! This is going to hurt!' That one stands out for me.

"I never got hit by Al Iafrate or Al MacInnis, but I remember seeing them hit guys and seeing guys laying on the ice and then they could barely get off, or guys getting out of the way.

"Those were my two images of some real brave, dumb forward."

Not that there is an absence of courage among the often-bruised blue-liners.

"Defencemen in the NHL now are way better protected than they were 30 years ago, 40 years ago," said Patrick, who played in the NHL from 1983 to 2004. "Defencemen have way more padding. Every defenceman in the league wears skate guards. Well, no one wore those 30 years ago. I think everyone wears a [face] shield now. No one wore a shield 40 years ago.

"Everyone shoots the puck harder now, but no one shoots the puck harder than Al MacInnis or Al Iafrate did. They could shoot it 110 miles per hour. Shea Weber and Zdeno Chára shoot it around 110 miles per hour now. I'd say the only difference is that the average guy on a team now fires the puck pretty hard.

"The game is so fast now. Because of that, things happen and players don't have time to defend themselves. You can get a puck in the face. You can get a puck in the mouth. You can get a puck in the neck. It can happen so quickly that you can't defend yourself, so I do think that is a fact in today's game, compared to when we played.

"There's better protection, but you can still get hurt, believe me, with what you're wearing now."

The expectations and exhortations of today's coaches, who view shot-blocking as an essential part of the defensive strategy, are a factor.

"Younger kids at our level are so harped on," Patrick said during his fifth season as head coach of the WHL's Winnipeg Ice. "It never ends. They just keep hearing about 'compete' and 'battle.' I'm as bad as any other coach. So it's not optional. You have to do it.

"Some guys are unbelievable at it. I do think there are some players who have found their niche and they think, 'This is my way to succeed. I love playing this game, so I will do whatever it takes.'

"There are the elite players who are so skilled. They're going to play in the NHL for 15 years and we're going to love watching them, but there are some guys who realize very quickly, 'How do I differentiate myself? I'm an average player. I'm not a great skater. I'm an average puck-handler, puck-mover. What can I do to keep me here?'

"And there are guys who go above and beyond. Those are the guys who love playing the game, and they say, 'I'll block everything. I'll do whatever it takes.' They get their foot in the door and then they keep doing that. A number of guys have made a career out of playing that way.

"The other thing is the way the game is coached. I talk about a guy like [John] Tortorella. His teams play so hard defensively and are in shot lanes more than any team, and that rubs off on other teams. It's a copy-cat league, so I think that's a big part of it."

Some players, though, are virtually impossible to duplicate. Consider the case of Andrei Markov, who patrolled the Montreal Canadiens' blue line from 2000 to 2017.

"Man, could that guy block shots," Patrick said, admiringly. "He was incredible. I would see him block a shot and go, 'OK, he's done,' and he would be back five minutes later."

Markov's fine career consisted of 990 regular season games (plus 89 playoff contests) and an untold number of bruises. Patrick, who topped Markov's games-played total by 290, was 22nd all-time in regular season appearances by a defenceman—four spots ahead of Ludwig—as of this writing. MacInnis was 11th, with 1,416 games.

The careers of MacInnis and Patrick merged when they were teammates with the 1993–94 Calgary Flames. They were also opponents for 19 seasons. Therefore, Patrick is ideally qualified to describe instances of opposing forwards and, to a lesser extent, defencemen scattering as MacInnis prepared to unleash the most lethal of slap shots.

"When he wound up," Patrick said, "it was like the parting of the Red Sea."

Would that be comparable, then, to the commotion surrounding a Trent McCleary howitzer?

"Yeah, sure!" McCleary, who was known for agitating opponents during the 192 games he played in The Show, said with a laugh. "I don't think I took a slap shot in my NHL career. I never had time. Guys wanted to kill me. I was never on the ice long enough to wind up."

When Patrick discussed players who would do anything possible to "differentiate" themselves and stick around in the NHL, he could have been referring to McCleary—an undrafted forward who never scored more than 23 goals in a season with the WHL's Swift Current Broncos, whom he captained at the 1993 Memorial Cup.

Honest workers such as McCleary scratched and clawed to get to the NHL, and to remain at that level. To do so, there was an unspoken obligation to perform unglamorous tasks such as blocking shots.

"There's kind of an insanity to it, but it's maybe a controlled insanity," McCleary said. "You don't even think about it, though. That's the funny thing. Can you get hurt? Absolutely. But do we worry about it? No. I don't think you can play this game if you're worried about accidents or injuries.

"It's almost a badge of honour, because you see the guys who eat pucks. When they get back to the bench, they're the heroes. As much as the goalies get the credit—and they definitely deserve it—with the defencemen and the forwards who block shots, you know there are ice packs on a lot of body parts after a game."

In McCleary's case, the aftermath of one game was infinitely worse.

On January 29, 2000, while playing for Montreal against the visiting Philadelphia Flyers, McCleary went all out to block a shot by defenceman Chris Therien.

The blast hit McCleary square in the throat, shattering his larynx and leading to a collapsed lung.

He rushed to the Canadiens' bench and, unable to breathe, crumpled to the ground. Prompt medical attention at the arena restored an airway, but the situation remained critical.

Still clad in his hockey equipment, McCleary was rushed to hospital, where an emergency tracheotomy was performed and his life was saved.

All because of a blocked shot that was "screwed up royally," in the recollection of McCleary.

"I just slid too far," he said. "My timing was off and the puck kind of bounced off the [boards] slower than I thought it was going to. I slid way past where I thought I was going to get it.

"[Therien] was kind of waiting for the puck to move before he shot, and I slid too far. It was 100 per cent my fault. It shouldn't have been up there. It should have been in my shin pads. That's what I was planning for."

Could any form of equipment have prevented such a life-threatening injury?

"Not really," McCleary responded. "Somebody did a study. To break the impact of that shot, the neck protector would have had to be two inches thick. Well, you're not going to be able to skate around with a two-inch-thick neck guard.

"It's a round puck hitting a round bone perfectly. An ear-nose-throat surgeon I know saw me go down and thought, 'He'll be fine. It'll scare the shit out of him, because you don't break that bone. It's cartilage.' It's round bone, round puck. You're not going to break it.

"When he found out that it shattered, he thought, 'Holy smokes!'

"I should have bought a lottery ticket. That's the chance of that happening."

At least within the context of hockey.

"[The surgeon] said that they mostly saw those injuries back in the days when they had the big protruding dashes on cars," McCleary continued. "There would be an accident and you'd go flying into the dashboard and your throat would hit the protruding dash.

"Of course, everybody would be dead. You can't breathe because you fracture your larynx. You die in two or three minutes. People rarely see that extent of a fracture. That's where the odds of that happening with a puck are just minute, just so small.

"That was just a freak injury. There's way more likelihood of getting cut by a skate. That's why the neck protectors are made of Kevlar and stuff like that—the good ones are, anyway. They're meant to be cut-proof, not to stop a puck."

It is long been common for goaltenders to wear neck protection. But that was not the case when Clint Malarchuk suffered a lacerated jugular vein while tending goal for the Buffalo Sabres on March 22, 1989. As the result of a collision near the net, one of St. Louis Blues forward Steve Tuttle's skates made contact with the front of Malarchuk's neck and sliced open his jugular vein.

If not for prompt medical attention, Malarchuk would have bled to death. Remarkably, he was back on the ice 10 days later, wearing a neck guard.

McCleary also made a comeback attempt, albeit an abbreviated one. He announced his retirement on September 20, 2000, just 12 days after turning 28.

"Believe me, I do not feel sorry for myself—not a bit," McCleary, who was retained by the Canadiens in a scouting capacity, said in 2022. "I was incredibly fortunate to have a career and incredibly fortunate to have something bad happen and survive and incredibly fortunate the way Montreal took care of me, getting me into their organization with scouting and all that stuff. I still accept some of their offers to come down [from Swift Current] and watch some games and things like that. Everything worked out.

"Would I block that shot again? Absolutely—hopefully with a different outcome. I would have done it in a heartbeat. That was the one thing that I never got a chance to do in my exhibition game when I tried to come back. I wanted to prove to myself and everybody else that I wasn't scared to do it.

"It's easy for me to talk about it now. I don't get teary-eyed or anything. It gives me something to celebrate.

"Hey, I've been here for 22 years [since the injury]. I take it pretty loosely, just because you live by the sword and you die by the sword.

"You go about your business. Life's too short."

So was McCleary's NHL career—although it lasted 192 more games than that of a vast majority of undrafted players.

One of the keys, in retrospect, was an unblinking willingness to perform, and even embrace, "crazy" tasks such as blocking shots or going out of one's way to irritate a 6'5", 245-pound opponent.

"I was crazy to take runs at Derian Hatcher," McCleary said with a laugh. "I was crazy to take runs at everybody. That's the only reason why I was here, because I would do what nobody else really wanted to do.

"Everybody said, 'You are flippin' crazy!' Yeah, but you do what you have to do. That's why when you ask if I would block it again, yeah, 100 per cent. No question. That's what got me there in the first place."

Lasting evidence of his time there is not difficult to uncover.

"My voice is a little raspier," McCleary concluded. "I do have a scar, but it's a badge of honour. Honestly, for a career-ending injury, it couldn't be any better, because the only thing I can't do is high-end athletics.

"That's a great excuse when my wife yells at me to go to the gym. I say, 'I've got this injury, honey. It's terrible!'

"I feel way worse for these guys who get concussions and who hurt shoulders and knees. When you're dealing with those injuries, they're somewhat like life sentences."

Epilogue: Closing the Book

The lives, lumps, and lasting legacy of the maskless goaltenders

WHEREAS GOALTENDERS WERE ONCE INVARIABLY BAREFACED, THE pendulum has swung to the point where a mask can now display a mask.

Such was the case on February 20, 2011, when Carey Price paid homage to an earlier Montreal Canadiens goaltending great by donning a modern cage combination mask that had been specially painted to commemorate the manner in which Jacques Plante had changed the face of the game on November 1, 1959.

On that long-ago evening at Madison Square Garden, Plante introduced a mask that quickly became a standard component of his equipment. One by one, goaltenders at all levels emulated Plante—occasionally against their will—and by November 1976 the maskless marvels had all but vanished from professional hockey.

The iconic image of Plante slipping a primitive-looking, cream-coloured fibreglass shield over his bloodied, bandaged beak served as a template for artist David Arrigo, who had been commissioned by Price to create the mask-terpiece.

The finished product was presented to Price one day before the Canadiens faced off against the host Calgary Flames in an outdoor game, the 2011 Heritage Classic, at McMahon Stadium.

On display only once in an NHL game before being retired by Price, the retro mask became hockey's version of "David"—as in Arrigo, a multifaceted artist whose trademark murals have been showcased at marquee events such as the Super Bowl and the Olympics.

One of his sidelights has become the customization of goalie masks, such as the one that had been painstakingly painted for Price.

"Carey and I were brainstorming some ideas to tie it in with the old feel, the old look," Arrigo recalled. "We thought it would be fun to create that mask. I started doing the research and then started creating some imagery. In a fun way, it was called 'the ugly mask.'"

Ugly has seldom looked so sensational.

"Carey was very, very pleased with the mask," said Arrigo, whose client wasn't nearly as satisfied with the Canadiens' 4–0 loss to Calgary in the outdoor game. "Unfortunately, he didn't pull out a win with it, but it got a lot of great reaction, especially through the media.

"One of the funnier things that came out of it was that it made it all the way to England. On a British [television] show, they had a picture of a kid who had tattooed his face with a skull, and then they had a picture of [Price's] mask. They put out a survey: 'What was uglier?' The kid with the skull ended up winning."

It doubled as a resounding win for Arrigo, who had also designed the program cover for the 2011 Heritage Classic.

"It was a huge challenge, trying to figure out how to wrap [the images of Plante] literally around Carey's mask without it becoming too cartoonish, if you would, so we tried to keep it as simple as possible," Arrigo said. "Those eyes that we put on the top of the mask are actually Jacques Plante's eyes, and then the ears on the side are Carey's. The mouth is Jacques Plante's."

Arrigo is a Hall of Famer in his own right, even without formally being enshrined. He has long had dealings with the Hockey Hall of Fame, as evidenced by the inductees' murals he has painted.

As well, he has continued to work closely with NHL goaltenders such as Price, Brian Elliott, Brent Johnson, and Mike Smith.

"The masks," Arrigo noted, "have become such a billboard to their soul."

That even applies to goalies who seldom, if ever, receive top billing.

Arrigo has designed masks for goalies as young as 10, and for others who will never get anywhere near an NHL game without paying for admission...and parking, lest we forget.

In fact, a recreational goalie enlisted Arrigo to paint the image of a pained Plante, from 1959, on the side of a modern-day face shield.

Arrigo was happy to comply, for reasons that transcended artistic or commercial reasons. He is, after all, a kindred spirit—someone who, once upon a time, was a member of the goaltending fraternity.

"Then, when I got to 16, I realized I wasn't growing," he said with a chuckle. "I was about 5'8" and I was a crappy goalie, so I had to get to the Hockey Hall of Fame a different way. I did it through my artwork.

"Saying that, I remember seeing the pictures of the ferociousness of the cuts on the goalies' faces. It's just incredible that these guys would go through that without a mask."

The limited-use Price mask is but one of myriad examples of the degree to which goaltenders of all eras regard Plante with reverence.

"Throughout history, it has been said that 'necessity has been the mother of invention,'" erstwhile NHL goalie Ed Staniowski said. "Nowhere is that statement truer than when one considers the need for and development of the goalie mask in the game of ice hockey.

"Considering the speed of the shots goalies historically faced and the force generated by today's shooters, it would not be a stretch to suggest that someone would have been killed playing goal were it not for Clint Benedict briefly donning the first mask, followed by Jacques Plante in 1959."

Benedict was 84 when he passed away on November 12, 1976—only one day before hockey's last full-time maskless goalie, Andy Brown, played in what would be his final game. Benedict had entered the Hockey Hall of Fame 11 years earlier.

Plante was enshrined in 1978, as soon as he became eligible, and remained involved in the game for the rest of a life that ended all too soon.

For much of his retirement, he lived in Switzerland, but routinely returned to North America to mentor goalies. He had been working part-time with the St. Louis Blues when he died of stomach cancer in Geneva on February 27, 1986. He was only 57 years old.

Tributes poured in from across the hockey world. All these years later, the greats of the goaltending game still seize every opportunity to offer appreciation and thanks.

"Jacques Plante changed the whole game as far as goaltending is concerned," said one of his proteges, Bernie Parent.

Parent is an example of how the old fibreglass masks, while incontestably an improvement over the no-mask era, were not infallible.

He was wearing a Plante-style mask, as had been the custom since the two goalies were teammates with Toronto in the early 1970s, on February 17, 1979, when Philadelphia faced the New York Rangers.

"[Flyers defenceman] Jimmy Watson was trying to shove Don Maloney of the Rangers out of the crease and his stick came up and poked through my mask and slashed my right eye," Parent wrote in his 2012 book, *Unmasked*. "Bam! In an instant, my career was over.

"They led me off the ice with blood gushing down my face. The tendons had been slashed. They couldn't save the vision in that eye. The next morning, I was completely blind, because the shock had caused me to lose vision in the other eye. I officially retired on June 1, 1979."

Five years later, Parent became the first Flyer to enter the Hall of Fame.

Like Parent, Bruce Gamble was only 33 when his NHL career ended suddenly, prematurely, and unexpectedly while tending goal for Philadelphia.

Wearing what was then a state-of-the-art Plante-designed mask, Gamble suffered a career-ending heart attack during a February 8, 1972, game against the Vancouver Canucks.

He soon became a scout for the Flyers, but it was a role that he hardly relished and eventually relinquished. A relative told the *Philadelphia Inquirer* that Gamble had become "very depressed" after the heart attack, to the point where he was sometimes characterized as a recluse.

But he was actually someone who loved being a teammate and delighted in the accompanying camaraderie, to the extent that he was drawn back to the game. When an old-timers team—the Keystone Kellys—was formed, he could not return to the crease quickly enough.

Games with the Kellys were, according to teammate Richard Dekker, "one of the biggest things in his life." In an interview with United Press International, Dekker said Gamble had been approached about playing for one of the original six (pre-expansion) teams in an exhibition series that was to be televised.

"He was really happy about that," Dekker added, "and he had been looking forward to doing the show for a long time."

With that event drawing closer, Gamble suited up for the Keystone club—consisting of players aged 35 and over—on the evening of December 29, 1982. He was in good spirits and appeared to be in excellent health, by all accounts.

Early the following morning, the 44-year-old Gamble collapsed at his home in Niagara Falls, Ontario. He was rushed to hospital, where he was pronounced dead after a massive heart attack.

"After the December 29 game, he was supposed to meet friends at his favourite bar...but his friends knew something was wrong when Bruce never showed," Sam McManis wrote in the January 16, 1983, edition of the *Los Angeles Times*.

The story from the *Times* revealed that Gamble had actually suffered a previous heart attack, in 1979, but "had recovered completely." The same could be said of his state of mind, thanks in large part to his friends and his return to the crease.

"For the first time in a long time, Bruce was excited," Terri Olsson, with whom Gamble had resided in Niagara Falls after separating from his wife, told McManis. "When the guys would come and pick him up for the games, he'd be waiting on the porch for them to come. That's all he cared about.

"He didn't check with doctors about playing. In fact, he hadn't seen a doctor in two years. He told me that hockey was his life. He said, 'If I can't play hockey, I don't know what else to do.'"

Roger Crozier's life also ended at an early age. He was only 53 when he died of cancer on January 11, 1996, in Newark, Delaware.

Beginning in 1963, Crozier spent seven seasons with Detroit before becoming an original member of the Buffalo Sabres in the fall of 1970. He was a Sabre for six seasons before winding up his playing career with the 1976–77 Washington Capitals.

Also with Washington, he was the team's interim general manager in 1981–82, in addition to coaching the team for one game that season.

Post-hockey, Crozier joined the MBNA America Bank in 1983 and became the head of construction—the formal titles being executive vice-president and director of facility management.

"Roger built buildings from the inside out and for the people inside them," read a portion of a full-page newspaper advertisement MBNA purchased in the *Detroit Free Press* after Crozier passed away. "He built buildings that are spotless all the time; where people are treated like Customers. He built buildings that always look pleasant; buildings that are a pleasure to enter every morning.

"MBNA's physical surroundings reveal something about Roger's character. We hope when people look at MNBA buildings, they see Roger. Not obtrusive, but very strong. Not glamorous, but very classy.

"Everywhere MBNA people serve their Customers, they do it better because of his energy and his love of life—because of Roger. You're our hero, Roger; we're exceedingly proud of you. We'll miss you always."

Crozier was in his first season of junior hockey, with the 1959–60 St. Catharines Teepees, when Don Simmons became the NHL's second masked goaltender—following Jacques Plante.

All totaled, Simmons played 248 games in the NHL and another 487 in the minors. John McGourty provided some other numbers during a flashback that was posted on nhl.com.

"Don Simmons suffered 15 broken noses, had an eye knocked out of its socket, and was a candidate for a tracheotomy after getting hit in the throat during a game," McGourty wrote in 2009. "Thankfully, he resumed breathing before being rushed to the hospital."

As one of hockey's mask-wearing pioneers, it was only fitting that he would become the founder of Don Simmons Sports Inc., the specialty of which was goalie equipment.

"Our first job as goaltenders was to stay alive and then stop the puck," Simmons told McGourty. "The owners frowned on [masks]. They wanted that macho thing. They liked it when a guy came out with his nose hanging down his face."

Simmons added: "Putting on a mask was just sensible, common sense. If I can protect my face, I can play more games and help my team."

He did precisely that in the spring of 1962, as a member of the Toronto Maple Leafs.

After a blast by Chicago's Bobby Hull injured Leafs legend Johnny Bower in Game 4 of the Stanley Cup Final, Simmons took over and was the victorious goaltender in the subsequent two contests—including Toronto's Cup-clinching 2–1 victory on April 22, 1962.

That was the first of three consecutive titles for the Maple Leafs. Simmons, a member of the team from 1961 to 1964, shared in each of those championships.

He was 79 when he died on September 24, 2010.

Simmons was the first NHL goaltender to certifiably wear a mask that had been designed by Gene Long.

Long, a trainer and track coach at Hamilton College in Clinton, New York, had made masks for NCAA goalies—one of whom was Hamilton's Don Spencer.

Spencer and Long were featured in a *USA TODAY* article that Kevin Allen filed on the weekend of the 50th anniversary of Plante's first game with a mask. Allen's article speculated that the design of Plante's mask was influenced by Long.

Bill Burchmore of Montreal is conventionally credited with the unofficial patent, but prominent hockey researcher Fred Addis expressed some doubts.

"If you want to say that an American invented the technology that allowed Plante to pioneer his innovation, I think you can make that case," Addis told Allen in October 2009.

The *USA TODAY* story noted that Long had manufactured a fibreglass mask for Spencer late in the 1958–59 season after he had sustained numerous facial injuries.

In the spring of 1959, Spencer spotted an article in *The New York Times* in which Plante had expressed an interest in protecting his face. Reading that, Spencer wrote to Plante and referenced Long and the manner in which the fibreglass mask had been constructed.

"I was thinking I might even get a couple of tickets to the Stanley Cup playoffs," Spencer told Allen. "I never heard back from him."

Plante eventually unveiled a fibreglass mask that was said to be the brainchild of Burchmore, who had worked for Fibreglass Canada.

But is it that cut and dried? In an attempt to resolve that question, an email was sent to Addis. The response in July 2022 was as quick as it was detailed:

> In February 1959, Gene Long built the first form-fitting fibreglass mask for Hamilton College goalie Don Spencer. This is well-documented and Spencer is still alive in Morgantown, West Virginia.
>
> During the NHL playoffs that spring, Spencer read in *The New York Times* that Plante was looking for or trying to perfect a face mask. Spencer sent him a letter telling him about his Long fibreglass mask in April 1959.
>
> At the time Plante's experiments only ever involved trying to bend or modify the traditional plexiglass visor, then popular. He tried bending it to better fit his face and he cut out a section for his eyes to mitigate the glare normally associated with plexi visors. There are photos of Plante with his modified visors.
>
> I can only assume that upon receiving Spencer's letter, Bill Burchmore at Fibreglass Canada was contacted by Plante.
>
> We know that neither Gene Long [nor] Don Spencer ever heard from Plante.
>
> The recipe for constructing a fibreglass mask would have been easily deduced by Burchmore, as the use of fibreglass cloth

and liquid resin had been in wide use in post-war, non-military applications.

It is unclear whether Long's mask-building recipe was shared by one of Long's Clinton, New York, associates—a sporting-goods salesman named Murray who purported to be Long's business partner.

Burchmore's experiments were not known prior to August/September 1959. The first we hear of a new approach to mask-making is in early September when Plante has an appointment with a doctor to make a plaster impression of his face.

And then of course, we see Plante's new mask at Montreal's training camp in September.

I believe Burchmore's timeline for inventing Plante's mask is backdated to protect himself and eventually Plante's business from possible legal action.

Even if we assume that Long and Burchmore were working coincidentally, there is no Burchmore prototype that pre-dates Long's February 1959 first mask built for Don Spencer.

Long was always very clear that no one would ever have heard of his Hamilton College mask innovations had it not been for Plante pioneering his mask at MSG on November 1, 1959.

There was never any controversy surrounding Johnny Bower—an unfailingly amiable sort who looked like everyone's favourite uncle.

As beloved a figure as anyone who has ever played the game, Bower kept his age a mystery for the duration of an illustrious playing career.

In retirement, he also proved to be ageless and inexhaustible, representing the Maple Leafs—and hockey in general—modestly and with distinction into his 90s.

"He was the nicest person you'll ever meet, and he didn't know how to say no to anybody," John Bower III said. "One of the reasons why grandpa was so popular was because Johnny Bower wasn't a brand. Johnny Bower was somebody who genuinely cared about people.

"Whether he was signing an autograph for somebody or listening to somebody tell a story about why they were a fan or somebody who was downtrodden asking for some help, he'd listen. He made them feel like they were the most important person that he knew. It's a gift that very few people have."

Johnny Bower gave people the gift of his time and attention into his final weeks. After a short battle with pneumonia, he died on December 26, 2017, at age 93.

"Johnny was beloved by so many for much more than his Hall of Fame credentials as a player," Maple Leafs president and alternate governor Brendan Shanahan said in a media release. "It was his generosity of spirit, kindness and passion for people that made him a legend at life."

One of hockey's all-time Hall of Fame people was honoured yet again on a face shield that was unveiled in 2019 by then-Toronto goaltender Frederik Andersen. Mask artist David Gunnarsson wrote on Instagram (@daveart) that Andersen "wanted a tribute to the legendary Leafs goalie Johnny Bower in the design."

There was a time, back in the 1950s, when the Rangers could not decide between Bower or Gump Worsley as their starting goalie.

It was a coin-flip, as it turned out, as both goalies ended up in the Hall of Fame. Bower was inducted in 1976, four years before Worsley.

After scouting for the Minnesota North Stars for 14 years, Worsley stepped away from the game and lived a quiet life in his hometown of Montreal.

The Gumper died at Honoré-Mercier Hospital in Saint-Hyacinthe, Quebec, on January 26, 2007, four days after suffering a heart attack. He was 77.

He was remembered in the *Minneapolis Star Tribune* as "a goalie who was human, heroic, and often hilarious."

"He was the most unlikely-looking athlete ever," former North Stars teammate Lou Nanne told columnist Jim Souhan. "But if you wanted to win a big game, he was the guy."

True, but there can only be one Mr. Goalie.

His stature is such that Glenn Hall Drive and Glenn Hall Park can be found in his hometown of Humboldt, Saskatchewan.

Let's not forget Glenn Hall Centennial Arena in Stony Plain, Alberta, which is about 25 miles west of Edmonton.

Comfortably into his 90s, the ultimate goaltending iron man enjoys the haven that is his 155-acre farm. The visitors often include his children, grandchildren, and great-grandchildren, who are more of a priority than the sport he played so well for so long.

"I don't really watch much hockey," Hall said in 2021, during an interview for this book. "I watch it the next day [on the highlight packages] and see the goals that are scored, and I question some of the moves the goalkeepers make."

For years, Hall has kept in close touch with his great friend, nhl.com scribe Dave Stubbs. In 2022, Stubbs turned to his must-follow Twitter account (@Dave_Stubbs) to offer a medley of his favourite quotes from Hall.

On the routine after allowing a goal: "No, I don't fish the puck out of the net. Why would I? I didn't put it there."

On an outcome that, at least from one perspective, was not picture-perfect: "A photographer once told me he'd have had a great picture if I hadn't stopped the puck. I didn't apologize."

Nor does Hall apologize for his leisurely lifestyle: "I do nothing better than anybody you ever knew. I can go out and do nothing all day. And it takes me a long time do it."

Gerry Cheevers was wearing his distinctive mask—you know, the one with the painted-on stitches—when he backstopped the Boston Bruins to a 1970 Stanley Cup victory over Hall and the St. Louis Blues.

With Cheevers in goal, the Bruins celebrated another Cup-clinching victory in 1972, blanking the Rangers to close out the series.

On the strength of those triumphs, Cheevers is known as one of hockey's all-time great money goaltenders.

Even so, he is not someone who can be swayed by the almighty buck.

His iconic mask is not for sale.

"I've turned down a lot of money for that mask—an awful lot of money," Cheevers said.

How much has he been offered?

"Plenty," he replied. "Not recently, but plenty.

"And I'll be truthful. A person out of Toronto who collects vintage masks, evidently through an agent, offered me serious money—I thought it was a couple of hundred thousand—and I wouldn't take it."

Was it tempting?

"No," Cheevers responded. "I gave the mask to my grandson."

That would be Jon DeBonis—the son of Cheevers' daughter, Sherril.

"The mask is at Northwestern University in Chicago in my grandson's room," the proud grandfather of Jon, Julianna, Laura, and Cate said in 2021 during an interview for this book.

"It's where it's supposed to be—in my family."

Another big save for Gerry Cheevers.

Acknowledgments

NOW THAT I AM NEARLY FINISHED, WHERE TO BEGIN? THERE ARE SO many people to thank…

Let's start at home. Profuse thanks to my dream wife for so patiently putting up with my dream project.

I met Chryssoula Filippakopoulos in a hockey arena, appropriately, on November 19, 1994. It took me only two and a half years to manufacture enough courage to ask her out. Our first date—a suppertime chat—preceded (what else?) a hockey game.

She grew up in Toronto, cheering for the Maple Leafs. As of this writing, the Leafs' Stanley Cup drought was even longer than my wife's name. (If this one doesn't get me divorced, nothing will.)

Please indulge me as I regale you with the quintessential Chryssoula "book moment."

The phone rang one fine day in 2021. It was a former NHL and WHA goalie, responding to my interview request.

We spent a couple of minutes setting up a day and time for a formal chat. Once the call concluded, there was the following exchange:

Chryssoula: "Who was that?"

Me: "Dave Dryden."

Chryssoula: "Didn't he used to play for Buffalo?"

Bingo! (I married well, didn't I?)

Chryssoula and our rescue dog, Candy, inspire me to keep breathing on a regular basis. I would be lost without "my girls," as I call them.

Candy is so lovable, and such a craver of attention, that I had to find a neutral site at which to write—the alternative being to cuddle up next to her for the next, oh, eight hours. As one who will never require a muzzle, sweet Candy will always be maskless.

Due to my genial growler, my writing refuge became the grounds of the Good Earth Coffeehouse (Golden Mile location; Regina, Saskatchewan), where approximately 96.3428 per cent of this book was composed. Sincere thanks to Anne Warawa, Chris Petry, Ainsley Remple, Diya Sharma, Sof Sidorenko Sperling, Ceiligh Dodds, Emily Paul, Neesa Hintz, Amaret Porter, Amy Brandt, Charlie McNeil, Mila Carleton, and Rayna Little for all the coffee and cheerful conversation. I hope I was deemed to have tipped in a thoughtful manner.

(*Breaking news:* Amy also has a dog named Candy.)

What an honour it was to solicit the thoughts and input of several preeminent hockey historians, all of whom were endlessly helpful. Dick Irvin Jr., Dave Stubbs, Geoff Kirbyson, Todd Denault, and The Maven himself, Stan Fischler, could not have been kinder or more co-operative. Their names appeared on, or in, many of the books that are listed in a voluminous bibliography. Of course, the cherished copy of Gerry Cheevers' *Goaltender* is in there, too.

Speaking of the printed word, which is rather crucial to this process: thank you times infinity to the wonderful people at Triumph Books. I am so grateful to Michelle Bruton, Clarissa Young, Noah Amstadter, and everyone else who makes the Chicago-based publisher a great gift to writers and readers alike.

Before I submitted the manuscript, I was aided by the finest crew of (uncompensated) proofreaders I could imagine.

Chryssoula came through, as always, putting her English and journalism degrees to excellent use.

Dr. Mark Anderson—the recently retired principal at Luther College High School—is the best friend anyone could ever have. The way Mark and his wife, Roxanne, changed my life is also worth a book, albeit a self-obsessed volume.

Profuse thanks as well to Luther art teacher extraordinaire Drew Hunter, whose remarkable talent is on display on the cover of this book.

A prolific author named Russell Wangersky was also of invaluable assistance. Russell, the former editor in chief of the *Regina Leader-Post* and *The StarPhoenix* and now a valued employee of the *Winnipeg Free Press*, is equally gifted as a person and a professional. The version of this book that I sent to Russell for perusal included what I presume to be an autocorrect error (excuses, excuses) that magically transformed "bleeding profusely" into "blessing profusely" in Chapter 4. Russell, bleed (oops) his heart, spotted the gaffe. Profuse (!) thanks to Russell and to former managing editor Tim Switzer, managing editor at the *Leader-Post*, for allowing me the time to address a maskless obsession.

Todd Denault, who wrote the definitive biography of Jacques Plante, was kind enough to fact-check the portions of the book that pertained to the goalie-mask pioneer. Todd was a remarkable resource from so many standpoints. And all of his hockey books are must-read material.

Doug Norris, goaltending historian nonpareil, was endlessly helpful.

His Twitter account (@GoalieHistory) is a must-follow. He, too, consented to peruse the manuscript, thereby providing me with peace of mind, along with details that I simply could not have dreamed of finding anywhere else. He also went to considerable lengths to confirm fundamental dates, statistics, you name it. I am beyond indebted to him.

Dave Dryden—yes, he used to play for Buffalo—was an amazing resource from several perspectives. He was as kind and helpful as he was knowledgeable. It was absolutely crushing to discover, not even a month before the manuscript was due, that he had died.

One of the real eye-openers, from this perspective, pertained to Dryden's enduring and invaluable influence on goaltending and player safety.

Think about it: the no-frills fibreglass mask, introduced by Jacques Plante in 1959, was virtually obsolete by the mid-1980s. Even a primitive form of protection was a monumental step forward for Plante and all goaltenders, but that style of mask had a shelf life of roughly a quarter-century.

Now, how about the cage combination mask that Dave pioneered in collaboration with Greg Harrison? The 50th anniversary of that mask is drawing ever closer.

Only three months before he died, Dave was kind enough to proofread the book for me. I had never touched base with him for any reason until early in 2021. Very quickly, he felt like a long-time friend.

That description applies to Glenn (Chico) Resch, whom I first had the privilege of interviewing on the family farm near Lajord, Saskatchewan, in the summer of 1986. Chico is one of hockey's all-time nice guys, in addition to being an accomplished goaltender and a student of hockey history. He was thoughtful enough to write the foreword after taking the time to peruse the manuscript.

The illustrious list of (uncompensated) proofreaders also included Murray Mandryk, Cyndi Cherney, Destiny Kaus, Shadia Ismail, and Jim Hopson. I am more grateful than words can express.

Kudos as well to the mighty Duck—Glen Duck—whose comprehensive library of hockey books was rather liberally accessed by this writer. Some long-out-of-print editions, such as Gump Worsley's autobiography, would have cost me a small fortune to purchase or even duplicate. Glen, as it turned out, had four copies of *They Call Me Gump*.

I called Glen a godsend at various stages in the research process. And I passed along to him this friendly advice: sell the three extra copies and make $$$!

I am also indebted to countless columnists and correspondents, whose fine work and lasting excellence allowed me to include contemporaneous accounts of the often dangerous life of a goaltender.

The wonder that is newspapers.com has allowed me ridiculously easy, once-unthinkable access to dispatches that date back to the 1920s. A scroll-like enumeration of the newspapers that served as resources, along with a parenthetical list of the writers whose work is incorporated into my own, appears below.

Another shout-out must be extended to the brains behind the Society of International Hockey Research. Well into the process of writing this book, I was introduced to the SIHR. The Society's chairman, Aubrey

Ferguson, referred me to an article entitled "The Year of the Mask" by Fred Addis. Fred's painstaking and precise timeline of goalies' facial injuries and mask innovators was a tremendous resource. I am now an SIHR member for life—or for as long as they will have me, anyway.

Thanks as well to Fred for shedding some light on the manufacture of fibreglass masks by Gene Long in the late 1950s.

Words of gratitude must also be extended to Stuart McComish, the NHL's manager of statistics and research. He answered innumerable emails over nearly two years and invariably came through with the obscure, yet invaluable, facts I was craving. The man is a genial genius.

As was the case with my previous three books—all about my current employer, the Saskatchewan Roughriders—I wrote much of the text while listening to jazz. Once again, I must applaud the brilliance of the peerless pianist, the late Oscar Peterson. Oscar's treasury of recordings always put me in a good mood—even when I realized that I had, oh, only 68,000 words to go. His widow, Kelly Peterson, is a dear friend and one of the warmest, most supportive people I have ever had the privilege of meeting.

Thank you, additionally, to the Roughriders for hiring me as the senior journalist and team historian in February 2023. Just like that, the football team added a writer who was applying the finishing touches to a hockey book. I am deeply indebted to Craig Reynolds (president/CEO), Anthony Partipilo (chief brand officer), Arielle Zerr (director, communications), and everyone with the Roughriders for being so welcoming, so supportive, and so amazing at their jobs. It is an honour to be part of this beloved team.

My gratitude also extends, of course, to everyone who agreed to be interviewed, typically at length and sometimes repeatedly: David Arrigo, Red Berenson, Martin Biron, John Bower III, Gerry Cheevers, Gaye Cooley, Joe Daley, Dave Dryden, Ken Dryden, Stan Fischler, Norm Fong, Russ Gillow, Marc Habscheid, Glenn Hall, Bill Hay, Kelly Hrudey, Dennis Hull, Dick Irvin Jr., Ed Johnston, Marshall Johnston, Robin Lehner, Craig Ludwig, Trent McCleary, Max Paddock, Bernie Parent, James Patrick, Tony Priolo, Mickey Redmond, James Reimer, Bob Rennison, Glenn (Chico) Resch, Sharyn Rutledge, Todd Rutledge, Jerry

Sawchuk, Jim Shields, Dennis Sobchuk, Jack Stanfield, Ed Staniowski, Carl Stankowski, Cam Talbot, Jerry Trupiano, Cliff Walker, Barry Warner, and Ian Young.

Yet another legion of people provided invaluable assistance in various forms. Here's to the good nature of Jeffrey Barnes, Trevor Bjergso, Jeffrey Byle, Craig Campbell, Vincent F. Cimini, John Dellapina, Gregg Drinnan, Annie Fu, Carter Haroldson, Lila Haroldson, Mack Heisinger, Dennis Hendricksen, Zack Hill, Les Holmlund, Cindy Kimes, Kelly Masse, John McClain, Kelly McCrimmon, Brian McNair, Kevin Mitchell, Brian Munz, Gini Parent, Norm Park, Rich Preston, Danielle Pritchett, Daryl Reaugh, Dr. Tom Robinson, Kevin Shaw, Aaron Sickman, Brett Smith, Matt Stephens, Kyle Stuetzel, Matthew Vachon, Curtis Walker, Dick White, Eddie Wooten, and Jenny Young.

Thank you, especially, to my parents—Alan Vanstone (1920–82) and G. Helen Vanstone-Mather (1934–2019). For the first time, Mom will not be the first recipient of my book. But this fourth-time author will take her a copy, with flowers, and leave it at her grave. Dad, a voracious reader who instilled in me a passion for the written word, will always be right beside her at Riverside Memorial Park Cemetery in Regina.

Thanks as well to you for investing time and money in my book. I hope that it is something that you enjoyed and will recommend. If not, well, blame the author.

One final thank-you—to all the maskless goalies, whose courage, competitiveness and, yes, cuts made this all possible. I wish it were possible to acknowledge every one of them, in every league, but space and time constraints do not make that feasible.

That said, here is one final shout-out to every member of the NHL's barefaced brethren, dating back to the league's inception in 1917:

George Abbott, Don Aiken, Andy Aitkenhead, Red Almas, Lorne Anderson, Hank Bassen, Baz Bastien, Gordie Bell, Clint Benedict, Harvey Bennett, Bill Beveridge, Paul Bibeault, André Binette, Les Binkley, Richard Bittner, Gilles Boisvert, Claude Bourque, Lionel Bouvrette, Johnny Bower, Frank Brimsek, Turk Broda, Len Broderick, Art Brooks, Frank Brophy, Andy Brown, Steve Buzinski, Lorne Chabot, Ed

Chadwick, Gerry Cheevers, Les Colvin, Alec Connell, Maurice Courteau, Roger Crozier, Abbie Cox, Wilf Cude, Claude Cyr, Joe Daley, Nick Damore, Bob DeCourcy, Norm Defelice, Denis DeJordy, Bill Dickie, Connie Dion, Clarence (Dolly) Dolson, Bill Durnan, Dave Dryden, Roy Edwards, Claude Evans, Jake Forbes, Hec Fowler, Emile Francis, Jim Franks, Ray Frederick, Bruce Gamble, Bert Gardiner, Chuck Gardiner, George Gardner, Dave Gatherum, Paul Gauthier, Jack Gélineau, Ed Giacomin, Paul Goodman, Benny Grant, George Hainsworth, Glenn Hall, Don Head, Sammy Hebert, John Henderson, Gord Henry, Sugar Jim Henry, Hec Highton, Charlie Hodge, Harry (Hap) Holmes, Joe Ironstone, Doug Jackson, Percy Jackson, Ed Johnston, Mike Karakas, Don Keenan, Davie Kerr, Julian Klymkiw, Frenchy Lacroix, Hugh Lehman, Bert Lindsay, Howie Lockhart, Sam LoPresti, Harry Lumley, Cesare Maniago, Jean Marois, Gilles Mayer, Ken McAuley, Jack McCartan, Frank McCool, Tom McGrattan, Gerry McNamara, Gerry McNeil, Al Millar, Ivan Mitchell, Alfie Moore, Jean-Guy Morissette, Johnny Mowers, Dunc Munro, Hal Murphy, Mickey Murray, Jack Norris, Marcel Paille, Marcel Pelletier, Bob Perreault, Jacques Plante, Claude Pronovost, Chuck Rayner, George Redding, Herb Rhéaume, Dennis Riggin, John Ross Roach, Moe Roberts, Earl Robertson, Al Rollins, Wayne Rutledge, Terry Sawchuk, Joe Schaefer, Don Simmons, Al Smith, Gary Smith, Normie Smith, Red Spooner, Phil Stein, Doug Stevenson, Charles (Doc) Stewart, Herb Stuart, Harvey Teno, Tiny Thompson, Joe Turner, Rogatien Vachon, Georges Vézina, Gilles Villemure, Ernie Wakely, Flat Walsh, Carl Wetzel, Ross (Lefty) Wilson, Hal Winkler, Alex Wood, Gump Worsley, and Roy Worters.

Any errors and/or glaring omissions are solely my responsibility.

Sources

Websites

espn.com
goaliesarchive.com
hockeydb.com
hockeygoalies.org
hockey-reference.com
insidehockey.com
newspapers.com
nhl.com
puckstruck.com
sihrhockey.org
theehl.com
thehockeywriters.com
twitter.com
wha-hof.com
youtube.com

Newspapers

Athol Daily News
Atlanta Journal-Constitution (Guy Curtright, Tony Petrella)
Arizona Republic
Baltimore Sun (Ed Atwater, Doug Brown, Albert R. Fischer, Larry Hargrove)
Boston Globe (Bud Collins, Al Filadoro, Ray Fitzgerald, Tom Fitzgerald, Herb Ralby, Jerry Nason, Francis Rosa)
Brantford Expositor
Brattleboro Reformer
Charlotte News

Charlotte Observer (Jack Horan, Dick Pierce)
Chicago Tribune (Charles Bartlett, Ted Damata, Art Dunn, Robert Markus, Rick Talley)
Commercial Appeal
Daily Oklahoman
Dayton Daily News (Ralph Morrow)
Democrat and Chronicle (George Beahon, Hans Tanner)
Deseret News (Brent Checketts)
Des Moines Register (Buck Turnbull)
Des Moines Tribune (Robert Short, Buck Turnbull)
Detroit Free Press (Jack Berry, Jack Carveth, Howard Erickson, Joe Falls, John N. Sabo)
Edmonton Journal (Cam Cole, Dwayne Erickson, Ron Glover, Wayne Overland, Ray Turchansky)
Florida Today
Fort Worth Star-Telegram
Globe and Mail (John Chaput)
Grand Forks Herald
Grand Rapids Press (Michael Zuidema)
Greeley Tribune
Greensboro Daily News (Drexel Hall)
Greensboro News & Record
Hanover Evening Sun
Hartford Courant
Holyoke Transcript-Telegram
Houston Chronicle (John McClain)
Indianapolis News (Dick Denny, Dick Mittman)
Indianapolis Star (Susan Lennis, Dave Overpeck)
Intelligencer Journal
Journal Herald (Bucky Albers)
Journal News
Kenosha News
Kingston Whig-Standard (Ron Brown, Michael J. Rodden, Art Wright)
Lancaster New Era
Lebanon Daily News (Ted Gress)
Lincoln Star (Hal Brown)
Long Beach Independent (Rich Roberts)
Long Beach Press-Telegram (Al Larson)
Los Angeles Times (Chuck Garrity, Dan Hafner, Sam McManis)

Minneapolis Star (Bob Fowler, Chan Keith, Mike Lamey, Max Nichols, Dan Stoneking)
Star Tribune (John Gilbert, Jim Souhan)
Minneapolis Tribune (Dwayne Netland)
Montreal Gazette (Ted Blackman, Dink Carroll, Pat Curran, Red Fisher, Gary McCarthy)
Montreal Herald (Elmer Ferguson, Al Parsley)
Montreal Star (Red Fisher, Charlie Halpin, Richard Low, Baz O'Meara)
Long Island Newsday (Charles Clark)
News-Press
New York Daily News (Red Foley, Jim McCulley, Dana Mozley, Joe Trimble, Hy Turkin)
New York Post (Hugh Delano, Jay Greenberg)
New York Times (Arthur Daley)
Oakland Tribune
Oklahoma City Times
Oshawa This Week
Ottawa Citizen
Ottawa Journal (Gerry Redmond, Bill Westwick)
Owen Sound Sun Times
Paterson Morning Call
Philadelphia Daily News (Bill Fleischman)
Philadelphia Inquirer (Chuck Newman)
Pittsburgh Post-Gazette (Vince Johnson, Jimmy Jordan, Bob Whitley)
Pittsburgh Press (Bill Heufelder, Fred Landucci)
Plain Dealer
Pomona Progress Bulletin
Port Huron Times Herald
Red Deer Advocate (Jon Drummond)
Regina Leader-Post (Bob Hughes, Gregg Drinnan, Tom Melville)
St. Louis Post-Dispatch
Salt Lake Tribune (Steve Rudman)
San Angelo Standard-Times
San Bernardino Sun
San Francisco Examiner (Paul Lippman)
StarPhoenix
Sault Star
Spokane Daily Chronicle (Chuck Stewart)
Sunday News (Herbert B. Krone)

Tampa Bay Times
Toronto Star (Milt Dunnell)
Troy Record
USA Today (Kevin Allen)
Province
Vancouver Sun (Dick Beddoes, Bob Dunn, Roy Jukich)
Wausau Daily Herald
Windsor Star (Marty Gervais, Jim McKay)

Wire Services

Associated Press
Canadian Press
Newspaper Enterprise Association
United Press International

Magazines and Periodicals

The Atlantic (Ken Dryden)
Hockey Blueline
Hockey Digest
The Hockey News
Indianapolis Monthly (Dave Seminara)
Life Magazine
Maclean's
Sport
Sports Illustrated

Books

Adrahtas, Tom. *Glenn Hall: The Man They Call Mr. Goalie*. Greystone Books Ltd., 2002.

Ibid. *The '60s: Goaltending's Greatest Generation*. Self-published, 2018.

Allen, Kevin, and Bob Duff. *Without Fear: The Greatest Goalies of All Time*. Triumph Books, 2002.

Barkley, Harold (photos) and Trent Frayne (text). *Hockey*. Rand McNally & Company, 1969.

Beddoes, Dick. *Dick Beddoes' Greatest Hockey Stories*. Macmillan of Canada, 1990.

Bock, Hal. *Save: Hockey's Brave Goalies*. Avon Books, 1974. McClelland & Stewart Ltd., 2009.

Bower, Johnny, and Bob Duff. *The China Wall: The Timeless Legend of Johnny Bower*. Fenn Publishing Company Ltd., 2008.

Cameron, Steve (editor). *Hockey Hall of Fame Book of Goalies*. Firefly Books, 2014.

Cheevers, Gerry, with Trent Frayne. *Goaltender*. McClelland & Stewart Ltd., 1971.

Cohen, Tom. *Roger Crozier: Daredevil Goalie*. Rutledge Books Inc., 1967.

Denault, Todd. *Jacques Plante: The Man Who Changed the Face of Hockey*. McClelland & Stewart Ltd., 2009.

Druzin, Randi. *Between the Pipes*. Greystone Books Ltd., 2013.

Dryden, Ken. *The Game*. Totem Books, 1984.

Dryden, Murray, with Jim Hunt. *Playing the Shots at Both Ends: The Story of Ken and Dave Dryden*. McGraw-Hill Ryerson Limited, 1972.

Dupuis, David. *Sawchuk: The Troubles and Triumphs of the World's Greatest Goalie*. Stoddart, 1998.

Fischler, Stan. *Behind the Net: 106 Incredible Hockey Stories*. Sports Publishing, 2013.

Ibid. *Bobby Clarke and the Ferocious Flyers*. Warner Paperback Library, 1974.

Ibid. *Goalies: Legends from the NHL's Toughest Job*. Warwick Publishing Inc., 1995.

Ibid. *Hockey Stars of 1972*. Pyramid Books, 1971.

Ibid. *Hockey Stars of 1974*. Pyramid Books, 1973.

Ibid. *Hockey Stars of 1976*. Pyramid Books, 1976.

Ibid. *The Zany World of Hockey*. National Sports Publishing Corp., 1979.

Fisher, Red. *Hockey, Heroes and Me*. McClelland & Stewart Ltd., 1994.

Fitkin, Ed. *Turk Broda of the Leafs*. Baxter Publishing Co., 1950.

Frayne, Trent. *The Mad Men of Hockey*. McClelland & Stewart Ltd., 1974.

Greig, Murray. *Big Bucks & Blue Pucks: From Hull to Gretzky, an Anecdotal History of the Late, Great World Hockey Association*. Macmillan of Canada, 1997.

Grimm, George. *Guardians of the Goal: A Comprehensive Guide to New York Rangers Goaltenders*. Simon & Schuster, 2019.

Hrudey, Kelly, with Kirstie McLellan Day. *Calling the Shots*. HarperCollins Publishers Ltd., 2017.

Hull, Bobby. *Hockey Is My Game*. Longmans Canada Ltd., 1967.

Hull, Bobby, with Bob Verdi. *The Golden Jet*. Triumph Books, 2010.

Hull, Dennis, with Robert Thompson. *The Third Best Hull*. ECW Press, 1998.

Hunt, Jim. *Bobby Hull*. The Ryerson Press, 1966.

Ibid. *The Men in the Nets*. McGraw-Hill Ryerson Limited, 1972.

Hynes, Jim, and Gary Smith. *Saving Face: The Art and History of the Goalie Mask*. Sports Publishing, 2015.

Irvin, Dick Jr. *In the Crease: Goaltenders Look at Life in the NHL*. McClelland & Stewart Ltd., 1995.

Ibid. *The Habs: An Oral History of the Montreal Canadiens, 1940–1980*. McClelland & Stewart Ltd., 1991.

Joyce, Gare. *The Devil and Bobby Hull*. HarperCollins Publishers Ltd., 2011.

Kendall, Brian. *Shutout: The Legend of Terry Sawchuk*. Penguin Books, 1996.

Logothetis, Paul. *Toe Blake: Winning Is Everything*. ECW Press, 2020.

McDougall, Bruce. *The Last Hockey Game*. Goose Lane Editions, 2014.

Oliver, Greg, and Richard Kamchen. *The Goaltenders' Union: Hockey's Greatest Puckstoppers, Acrobats, and Flakes*. ECW Press, 2014.

Orr, Frank. *Great Goalies of Pro Hockey*. Random House, 1973.

Parent, Bernie, and Stan Hochman. *Unmasked: Bernie Parent and the Broad Street Bullies*. Triumph Books, 2012.

Plante, Jacques, and Andy O'Brien. *The Jacques Plante Story*. McGraw-Hill Ryerson Ltd., 1972.

Proudfoot, Jim. *Pro Hockey '72–73*. Simon & Schuster of Canada Ltd., 1972.

Robertson, John G. *Hockey's Wildest Season: The Changing of the Guard in the NHL, 1969–70*. McFarland & Company, Inc., 2021.

Robson, Dan. *Bower: A Legendary Life*. HarperCollins Publishers Ltd., 2019.

Smith, Stephen. *Puckstruck: Distracted, Delighted, and Distressed by Canada's Hockey Obsession*. Greystone Books Ltd., 2014.

Vass, George. *The Chicago Black Hawks Story*. Follett Publishing Company, 1970.

Weekes, Don. *The Biggest Book of Hockey Trivia*. Greystone Books Ltd., 2005.

Whitehead, Eric. *The Patricks: Hockey's Royal Family*. Formac Publishing Co. Ltd., 1983.

Willes, Ed. *The Rebel League: The Short and Unruly Life of the World Hockey Association*. McClelland & Stewart Ltd., 2004.

Worsley, Lorne, with Tim Moriarty. *They Call Me Gump*. Dodd, Mead & Company, 1975.